PLANETARY

HOURS

PLANETARY HOURS

Bob Makransky

The Wessex Astrologer

Published in 2015 by
The Wessex Astrologer Ltd,
4A Woodside Road
Bournemouth
BH5 2AZ
www.wessexastrologer.com

Cover Design by Jonathan Taylor

A catalogue record for this book is available at The British Library

ISBN 9781910531051

Contents

Introduction

The Planetary Hours are an ancient system of assigning planetary rulerships to each hour of the day. The first hour (starting at sunrise) is ruled by the day ruler:

the Sun for Sunday
the Moon for Monday
Mars for Tuesday
Mercury for Wednesday
Jupiter for Thursday
Venus for Friday
Saturn for Saturday

Then, the order of rulerships of subsequent hours follows the Chaldean order of the planets:

Saturn – Jupiter – Mars – Sun – Venus – Mercury – Moon

Note that this is the order of the planets in decreasing speed of revolution around the Sun.

For example, the first hour after dawn on Tuesday is ruled by Mars (the day ruler); the second hour is ruled by the Sun; the third hour is ruled by Venus; and so on. Every 7th hour is ruled by the same planet so for example, if the 3rd hour is ruled by Venus, then the 10th, 17th, and 24th hours will be ruled by Venus as well.

In the *Encyclopedia of Astrology*[*] Nicholas de Vore points out that it is probable that the names of the days of the week derive from the Planetary Hours rulerships, rather than vice versa. In Egypt the first hour of the first day of the week was ruled by Saturn, so the first day became Saturn's day. The 1st, 8th, 15th, and 22nd hours of the first day were therefore ruled by Saturn, making the "25th" hour (i.e. the first hour of the second day) a Sun hour, and the second day thus was the Sun's day. The "25th" hour on the Sun's day was ruled by the Moon, so the third day became the Moon's day; and so on for the rest of the week. When the Hebrews fled from Egypt their hatred for the Egyptians led them to

---

[*] *Encyclopedia of Astrology*, Nicholas de Vore, Littlefield, Adams & Co. NJ 1980.

demote Saturn as ruling the first day, so the Sun's day (the day which began with a Sun hour) became the first day of the week. Beginning the Chaldean order of the planets with the Sun (where logically it should begin with Saturn) may have had symbolical association in the Hebrew mind with idea of Jehovah (the first day being Jehovah's day); and it also makes more sense in terms of the symbolism of the seven chakras to put the Sun first (the crown chakra).

In this system the "hours" are not usually sixty minutes long; rather, a daytime hour is defined to be one twelfth of the time from sunrise to sunset; and a night-time hour is defined to be one twelfth of the time from sunset to sunrise. So obviously daytime hours are longer than nighttime hours in the summer months, and nighttime hours are longer than daytime hours in the winter months. The Planetary Hours are only equal to sixty normal minutes of time at the equinoxes (March 21st and September 22nd). Note that the astrological day begins at dawn, not midnight, therefore the rulers of the hours between midnight and dawn (hours 19 – 24) are those for the *previous* day.

The Planetary Hours have traditionally been used in electing favorable times to initiate activities, and also to time prayers, spells, and magical rituals. The following section shows the sorts of activities traditionally favored by each planet:

Planetary Rulerships

Sun Hours: General success and recognition; spiritual illumination; decisiveness, vitality; activities requiring courage or a mood of self-certainty – making big decisions, scheduling meetings for reaching decisions, giving speeches, launching new projects; seeking favors from father, husband, boss, authorities.

Venus Hours: Love; friendship; artistic and social success; enjoyable, sociable and aesthetic activities such as parties, social gatherings, recitals/performances/exhibitions, weddings, visits, dating and seeking romance; planting ornamentals; buying gifts, clothing, luxuries; beauty treatments; seeking favors from women.

Mercury Hours: Success in studies/writing/signing contracts; making a good impression; routine activities and activities needing clear communications; teaching/learning; important business letters/phone calls; meetings to develop or communicate ideas; buying/selling; routine shopping, errands, travel; job applications/interviews; scheduling activities for children and seeking favors from neighbors, siblings, co-workers.

Moon Hours: Health and healing; home (buying home, moving); journeys/vacationing (time of leaving home or takeoff); activities remote in time or space – meditation, making reservations, finding lost objects or people; planting food crops; hiring employees; seeking favors from mother, wife, employees, the public (advertising, promotion).

Saturn Hours: Discipline and patience; giving up bad habits; overcoming obstacles; success with difficult tasks or difficult people; projects of long duration – breaking ground, laying foundations; planting perennials; treating chronic illness; making repairs; seeking favors from older people (not relatives) or difficult people.

Jupiter Hours: Wisdom, optimism; money (borrowing/lending/investing/earning/winning); activities necessitating enthusiasm; buying lottery tickets; seeking advice/consultation; settling disputes; seeking favors from grandparents, aunts and uncles, advisors (doctors, lawyers, accountants, astrologers).

Mars Hours: Courage, adventure; enforcing your will; success with drastic action (lawsuits, conflicts, going to war, surgery); sports, exercises; risk-taking; making complaints; firing employees; seeking favors of husband or boyfriend.

For example, A man should ask a woman out on a date during a Venus hour; a woman should ask a man out on a date during a Mars hour (gays and lesbians should reverse these significators); one should ask one's boss for a favor during a Sun hour; money should be invested during a Jupiter hour; medical treatments should commence under a Moon hour (except surgery should commence under a Mars hour); and so on.

Magical spells should be cast in the day or two before a favorable transiting aspect (e.g. Venus conjunction Mars for a love spell; Sun conjunct Jupiter for a money spell; Moon conjunct Sun for a healing spell) during an hour ruled by the planet which signifies the object of the spell (a Venus hour for love; a Jupiter hour for money; a Moon hour for health).

The Planetary Hours can also be used as an aid in interpreting natal horoscopes, since both the day ruler and hour ruler contribute a certain flavor to a native's personality.

They can also be used in prediction with an ancient technique known as the *firdaria.* All of these techniques will be explained in detail in the chapters which follow. The last part of this book contains tables and instructions which enable you to calculate Planetary Hours very simply in your head. Or, you can download the free Planetary Hours calculator from my website: http://www.dearbrutus.com/body_planetaryhours.html or from the files of my blog *Magical Almanac*: http://groups.yahoo.com/group/MagicalAlmanac/files/How%20to%20use%20Magical%20Almanac/. This calculator is an Excel worksheet with complete instructions; however when you open it, it will ask if you want to disable the macros. Since it won't work with its macros disabled, click on "Enable Macros" (you may have to have previously reduced the Excel security protocol: Tools => Macro => Security => Low).

The Planetary Hours in Natal Astrology

Monday's child is fair of face
Tuesday's child is full of grace,
Wednesday's child is full of woe,
Thursday's child has far to go,
Friday's child is loving and giving,
Saturday's child works hard for a living,
But the child who is born on the Sabbath Day
Is bonny and blithe and good and gay.

It is said that the Planetary Hours are all that remain of pure astrology, and that they contain everything.

This is a fair statement because Planetary Hours astrology is basically an astrology of luck, whereas conventional astrology of the zodiac and houses is an astrology of social adaptation. Conventional astrology shows how people relate to others, what lessons they are seeking to learn in this lifetime, and how they adjust (or fail to adjust) to the expectations of their parents, spouse, children, co-workers, boss, neighbors, etc.

By contrast, Planetary Hours astrology depicts people as spiritual beings, and shows their relationship to the abstract: their personal (as opposed to social) power and effectiveness, and their ability to make their own decisions and choose their own destinies.

Planetary Hours astrology shows you at your best, at your "you-est." It shows how you tune out static, stress, and external pressure and make contact with your own sense of self at center. It shows how you unhook yourself from society's wheel of rewards and punishments and operate on your own, at your own pace. It shows your most natural and joyous state of being, wherein you need nothing outside of yourself to feel whole, fulfilled, and at peace.

This is why Planetary Hours astrology is an astrology of luck: it points out the moods and mindsets you are in when you are operating at your peak of performance. The following interpretations are not necessarily descriptions of how you act every day, but rather of how you act when your luck is flowing. They describe that side of your personality which you should seek to enlarge until you are able to act with complete effectiveness in your everyday life.

When we look at the day of the week you were born, as opposed to your rising sign in conventional astrology, we are looking at a wholly positive side of your personality and relationship with your environment. Your weekday symbolizes the expression of your highest self, rather than some sort of mask you wear or set of mannerisms designed to elicit some stock response from other people. It symbolizes a more genuine interaction with other people than does your rising sign, and shows you in your most relaxed and natural state of being – the side of you which others find most inviting.

Observe that the astrological day begins at dawn (not midnight). Therefore, if you were born between midnight and dawn (i.e. if your natal Sun falls in the first three houses of a conventional horoscope), then you should read the interpretation for the day of the week before your birthday. For example, if you were born on a Tuesday between midnight and dawn, then you should read the interpretation for Monday. If you don't know what day of the week you were born, the free downloadable Planetary Hours tables calculates the weekday your were born as well as your planetary hour.

Sunday: You are outgoing, self-possessed, poised, and dignified. You have unlimited self-assurance and élan, and unhesitatingly take your rightful place (preferably in the center) of any social group of which you are a part. Because you basically respect yourself as a person, you are able to respect other people as well, and this naturally wins you their respect in turn. You are a natural-born leader, not because you flaunt yourself, but precisely because you are willing to honor other people's viewpoints as being valid from their own side. Although you can have a prissy, prima-donna streak, your lofty noblesse oblige is executed with sufficient good humor so as not to ruffle other people's sensibilities. Indeed, they respect your calm reason and objective judgment. You are practical and down-to-earth, and your unvarnished forthrightness induces other people to look up to you and cede you the lead.

Monday: You are soft, childlike, spontaneous, and possess the eager cheerfulness of a puppy. You are playful and mischievous, and take a positive, constructive view towards life and its problems. You try to avoid conflict, not because you're a shrinking violet, but because you have a genuine love of peace and harmony. You have a strong sense of your own personal space, and a respect for that of others; you are both gentle and firm (on the negative side, unyielding). Because you basically feel good about yourself and truly like yourself, you make it easy for other people to like you as well. You are able to keep cool and collected no matter what is going on around you because you are very attuned to your own inner voice, and you follow your own intuition with little regard for what other people might think of you. Thus you have a somewhat Bohemian or off-beat streak, a determination to just do your own thing in your own time.

Tuesday: You are irrepressible, adventurous, and peppery. You have a shrewd, analytical mind which sees clearly through the ulterior motives of other people, and which instantly grasps the possibilities of profit in any situation. Although not combative *per se* (you don't go looking for trouble), you don't shrink from conflict either. You are fearless in confronting other people directly – eyeball to eyeball, cheek to jowl, and in fact you seem to come alive at any hint of confusion or doubt in an opponent. You are opportunistic without being especially ambitious. You love challenge for its own sake, but have little patience for thinking in terms of long-term goals or empire building. Indeed, you are scornful of what most people consider "security", and prefer living by your own wits to planning for your future. You regard the trappings of comfort – dependence on possessions, other people, and worldly responsibilities – as encumbering baggage to be avoided whenever possible. You prefer keeping loose, agile, and free of commitments so you are always able to land on your feet no matter how hard life buffets you about.

Wednesday: You are unabashed and plain-dealing, and do not hesitate to speak your mind and speak to the point. Your tart, no-nonsense approach to people and your ironic sense of humor cut through pretense and empty gesticulating and go right to the heart of matters. You do nothing for show or effect. Because you feel no need to prove anything to yourself, you feel no need to put on airs, but are able to relax and just be yourself in any company; and your simplicity enables other people to be out-front with you in turn. You tend to rely upon bull-headedness rather than subtlety or guile to get your way; and while your frankness can at times be bruising, your earnestness and sincerity win the admiration of others.

Thursday: You are soft-spoken, polite, and considerate. You possess a detached intellectual curiosity and an open, nonjudgmental attitude towards others. You are forward-looking and hopeful, and are willing to tackle even arduous jobs with a spirit of dedication and enterprise. You are able to carry out any task smoothly and cheerfully because you don't let your personal feelings get in your way. You prefer not to make waves, not because you are shy or feel threatened by people, but rather because you don't need any ego-bolstering from them. You are able to find satisfaction in the punctilious discharge of your responsibilities, and hence you can afford to be generous with others – to live and let live. You are optimistic and always prefer to look at the bright side of things rather than become bogged down in disagreements or bickering.

Friday: You possess a starry-eyed idealism, freshness, and naiveté. Your innocuousness and artlessness disarm other people and put them at ease. You're not afraid to let it all hang out, to express your true feelings openly and make yourself vulnerable to other people, because you feel you have nothing to be ashamed of or to hide. You are thoroughly candid without being brusque; on the contrary, you are soft, open, and approachable. Albeit gregarious, you don't let yourself become too dependent on the approval and validation of other people to buttress your own sense of self-worth. At root you know that your own motives are good, so that you are capable of reaching out to others in a spirit of good will and good faith. Because you basically trust your own motives, you are able to trust in the ultimate good nature of other people as well.

Saturday: You are serious-minded and reserved, and possess a dignified mien and bearing. Your patience and forbearance are the product of a true faith in yourself and the power of the universe to sustain you. You are high-minded and courageous, and are always willing to stand alone on your own two feet. You are hard-working and thorough, without demanding any special recognition for your efforts. You are basically self-starting and self-motivating, and therefore you have little need for or interest in the carrot or stick for encouragement. Although you can be independent to the point of contrariness, and maddeningly aloof and blasé, your self-reliance is a stabilizing influence upon other people.

From both the mathematical and symbolical points of view, the weekday you were born is analogous to your rising sign in conventional astrology, and your Planetary Hour ruler is analogous to your Sun sign. Although it is possible to place all the planets – not just the Sun – in the scheme of 24 Planetary Hours, the calculations for doing this are complex (see Appendix). What standard tables of Planetary Hours show is the Sun's position in the 24 hours.

What your conventional Sun sign shows is a somewhat ostentatious and manipulative side of your personality – the way in which you bid for power and control. By contrast, your planetary hour ruler shows your most decisive and confident mode of action – how you behave when you are free of all doubt, hesitation, or ulterior motive. It shows how you are able to inspire yourself, and by extension, how you are most able to inspire others.

To use the Planetary Hours Tables you must know the latitude and longitude of your birth place as well as your time of birth. You can obtain this information from an atlas or map, or from the internet. Since the Planetary Hours Tables are in Local Mean Time (LMT), you must convert the clock time of birth into LMT: if Daylight Saving Time or Summertime were in effect when you were born,* subtract one hour from the clock time to obtain the Standard Time.

The Standard Time at your location is usually based upon the nearest Standard Time meridian – an even multiple of 15° of longitude measured east and west from Greenwich, England. In America the Standard Time meridians are Eastern Time (75° west); Central Time (90° west); Mountain Time (105° west); and Pacific Time (120° west).

The Local Mean Time varies from the Standard Time by four minutes of time for every degree of longitude your birth place is distant from your Standard Time meridian. To convert Standard Time into Local Mean Time, add four minutes to the Standard Time for every degree of longitude

---

* *The American Atlas* and *The International Atlas* by Thomas Shanks have this information, but you can also download it from the internet.

east of the Standard Time meridian; or subtract four minutes from the Standard Time for every degree of longitude west of the Standard Time meridian. Just remember that east of the meridian the Local Mean Time is later than the Standard Time; and west of the meridian it's earlier. For example, San Francisco is located at 122°25' west longitude, which is 2° 25' west of the 120th Standard Time meridian (Pacific Standard Time). 2.42° x 4 minutes per degree = 9 minutes 40 seconds; so the LMT at San Francisco is about 10 minutes earlier than Pacific Standard Time (subtract 10 minutes from PST to obtain LMT).

Once you know the LMT of birth, go into the Planetary Hours Tables for the week you were born (irrespective of year) and scan down the latitude column (on the left) of either the daylight hours or night hours tables (whichever applies to your birth time) for the value nearest to the latitude of your birth place. For example, San Francisco is located at 37°46' north latitude, so look across the line for 37° latitude until you come to the times before and after your LMT of birth. So if the LMT of birth is 3:00 pm during the week of January 1st to 7th, then your birth occurred during the 10th hour (which began at 2:27 pm and ended at 3:13 pm). If the LMT of birth is 3:00 am during the week of January 1st to 7th, then your birth occurred during the 21st hour of the *previous day* (which began at 2:28 am and ended at 3:39 am); so when you look up your hour ruler in the Table of Planetary Hours Rulers, you should read the hours column for the *previous day*.

Note: if your birth place is located in the southern hemisphere, then reverse the tables: i.e., read the daylight hours tables for night births and the night hours tables for daytime births, reading the hour number from the bottom of the column rather than the top. So in the above example, for birth at 37° south latitude during the week of January 1st to 7th, an LMT of 3 pm falls in the 9th hour (which began at 2:28 pm and ended at 3:39 pm); and an LMT of 3 am falls in the 22nd hour (which began at 2:27 am and ended at 3:13 am of the previous day).

The number at the top of the column for your birth time (or the bottom of the column for southern latitudes) is the hour number, from 1 to 24. Consult the Table of Planetary Hours Rulers for the day of the week on which you were born (the column) and the hour number you were born (the row) to find your Planetary Hour ruler. Once you've done this calculation once or twice, you'll find it's not difficult.

Sun Hour: You are bright, exuberant, positive, and have a winning personality. You take great pride in your personal fitness, and you cultivate at least one interest or area in life in which you are thoroughly competent and expert. You are lordly and gracious without being snobbish or stuffy. Indeed, your personal flair and idiosyncrasies are your most delightful assets; you charge off like Don Quixote with complete assurance and faith in yourself. You have a conspiratorial twinkle in your eye and a sense about you like a little kid up to no good. Your dashing self-confidence and good-natured panache captivate other people and assuage any difficulty

Venus Hour: You are sociable, playful, and devil-may-care. You have an easy manner and a soft, non-assertive approach to other people. You are not so much pliant or indolent as you are blithe and indifferent. You are always able to find some level on which you can enjoy yourself, come what may. You take a creative approach to life, and are able to lavish your complete attention on any relationship or hobby which excites your interest. Although you can have a complacent, self-satisfied streak, your buoyant good humor enlivens any group you are in.

Mercury Hour: You are objective, inquisitive, and have a light touch with others. Albeit sociable, you are emotionally remote. You play the role of detached spectator or impartial arbiter, not because you're afraid to stand up for your beliefs, but because your reach is for understanding rather than proving that you're right. In fact, you have a highly original point of view and a wry sense of humor, together with a fine appreciation of the ironies of existence. Without especially trying to, you make a favorable impression on people because you are fair, high-minded, and more interested in communicating clearly than in imposing your own ideas.

Moon Hour: You are moody, changeable, wistful, and other-worldly. Your gentleness and sense of pathos tend to arouse the protective instincts in others. You like things simple and straightforward, and always need to find a basis of harmony and accord. You are by no means a patsy or pushover, but rather don't feel any overriding need to defend your point of view. You don't so much shun harshness as you willingly bear trials and tribulations without complaint. You maintain a cheerful, philosophical, and consoling attitude which eschews blame or remorse.

Saturn Hour: You are grave, determined, and indomitable. You have a heavy, brooding, grumpy air and a low, daunting growl, which effectively prevents others from trying to cross you. You are hard, tough, and cannot be deflected from the path beneath your feet. You depend upon no one but yourself, and are ready to go to any extreme or take on any burden single-handedly rather than surrender an inch of your independence. You are not so much uncooperative as disinterested; not so much unsympathetic as pitiless. Although you can be cool to the point of rudeness, you nonetheless inspire others with your assiduity and staunch single-mindedness.

Jupiter Hour: You are expansive, outgoing, and optimistic. You throw yourself into your work and relationships with unstinting vigor and joie de vivre. You feel the most alive when you are sharing common goals, interests, and experiences. Although you drive yourself with a high-wire energy, you are patient and accepting in your dealings with others. You are a good teacher and organizer because you are willing to give others the benefit of the doubt. You are conscientious and fair, and are a model to others of unselfishness, keen insight, and whole-hearted enthusiasm.

Mars Hour: You are gutsy, spunky, and never say die. You have a critical, analytical mind and a willingness to roll up your sleeves and get down to work at whatever business is at hand. You are proud of your ability to reason things out, and to take complete responsibility for yourself and the situation in which you find yourself. You are willing (and indeed prefer) to go it alone rather than compromise your own personal vision and designs. Although you can be impatient, argumentative, and authoritarian, your pioneering spirit and utter faith in your own powers makes you a steadying influence on others.

The Planetary Hours in Electional Astrology

Electional astrology involves choosing favorable astrological times to act. It can be considered the inverse of horary astrology (answering a question based upon a horoscope erected for the time the question is put to the astrologer; or the time the astrologer thinks of asking the question; or simply the time some event occurs). Indeed, many of the techniques of traditional electional astrology are basically the same as those of horary astrology: assigning the matter of the election to its proper house (2nd for money, 6th for health, 7th for marriage, etc.) and then finding times when the house ruler is in favorable aspect with the Ascendant ruler (this is the basic approach – horary tradition is filled with a myriad of subsidiary rules).

However, my own channeling and experience – together with the dubiety with which I regard the traditional rules of horary astrology – suggest that employing the Planetary Hours alone (or the Planetary Hours combined with current transits) is sufficient. Using the Planetary Hours to plan your life – or at least the most important affairs, such as asking someone on a date or asking money favors – insures that you are doing all you can to align your desires with the flow of cosmic energy. It is best to act under a propitious Planetary Hour when there is a concurrent favorable aspect to the planet involved (which will be explained in the next chapter on casting spells). See the section on How to Use the Planetary Hours Tables for instructions.

Sun Hours are good for activities requiring confidence, courage, and self-assurance. They favor spiritual endeavors, initiations, and seeking illumination. They are good for making public speeches, defending your reputation and honor, and standing up for yourself generally (but not contending, which is more a Mars thing). They favor decision-making and scheduling meetings in which final decisions are to be taken. They are also favorable for asking favors of influential people, boss, father, and public authorities. However, Sun hours are not especially favorable for dating or marriage since they may result in disagreements. Nor are they good for beginning construction, entering buildings for the first time, or wearing new clothes. It is said to be dangerous to be taken ill during a Sun hour.

Venus Hours are excellent for dating (both asking someone out and meeting up with them) and for marriage (start of wedding ceremony or moment of saying "I do"). They are good for asking favors of women generally (particularly wife or sweetheart, although mother is ruled by the Moon and aunts and grandmothers by Jupiter). Venus hours also favor musical, theatrical, and artistic recitals and performances; parties and social gatherings; and all sorts of pleasurable and enjoyable pastimes such as cooking and dining. They favor shopping – particularly buying gifts, luxuries, and clothing – and also beauty treatments and planting ornamentals. Venus hours are good for beginning journeys (but not voyages, ruled by the Moon). They are not good times for surgery or other drastic action.

Mercury Hours favor mental activities such as commencing studies and taking examinations, writing letters and signing papers, interviewing, making important phone calls and sending important emails, and general buying and selling. These hours are good for teaching and learning, sending children to school,* programming, problem-solving and fixing things generally (including taking medicine). Mercury hours favor all routine, everyday affairs such as errands and shopping; and also activities in which clear communications are needed: scheduling meetings to develop new ideas, settling disputes, and submitting job applications and resumes. These hours are good for dealings with (especially working out problems with) children, neighbors, coworkers, and siblings. Mercury hours are good for beginning journeys but not for returning from a journey since they may cause quarrels. They are not good hours for buying land or houses, hiring employees, or for anything requiring permanence.

---

* It would be an interesting experiment to see whether school performance and faculty satisfaction increases in schools and school districts in which the start of classes each year (and semester) is timed to occur during a Mercury hour.

Moon Hours are favorable for dealings with women, particularly your mother, and for dating and marriage. They also favor activities relating to the general public such as public announcements, advertising, and opening new businesses. These hours are the best for initiating vacations and journeys, particularly voyages (time of leaving home or takeoff); but not good times to return home. They are good for moving and making changes in your home and environment, particularly with a view towards increased comfort and convenience. Moon hours favor all sorts of activities which are remote in space or time, such as meditation, gazing and astral projection, initiating healing procedures, seeking lost objects, and making reservations. Moon hours are good for hiring employees and seeking favors from your mother, from women generally, and from the public. They are good hours for reconciling with enemies and for making new acquaintances. Moon hours are also good for buying pets and planting food crops.

Saturn Hours favor activities requiring discipline and patience, such as forswearing bad habits, tackling difficult tasks and people, breaking off unwanted relationships, overcoming obstacles, making repairs, and starting over after a bad beginning. They are also good for initiating projects of long duration, such as clearing land, breaking ground and laying foundations, treating chronic illnesses (although being taken ill during a Saturn hour is a sign of a lengthy sickness);* also mining and agricultural activities in general, and for buying and selling products of the earth. They also favor geological and archeological digging, antiques, and activities relating to the past. Saturn hours are good for seeking favors from old people and difficult people (excepting relatives), but they are bad for hiring employees. Saturn hours are also considered bad times to borrow money, initiate journeys, cut hair, or wear clothing for the first time.

---

* In a study of times of admission to an intensive care unit in *Considerations* magazine (Volume VI, no. 3, pp. 48-9), Ken Gillman found that there was a significant spike in ICU admissions for Saturn hours on Mars days (i.e. Tuesdays). Totals for ICU admissions during Mars and Saturn hours generally were considerably higher than expectation.

Jupiter Hours are good for practically everything, since they produce optimism, enthusiasm, accord, and harmony. They are good hours for becoming engaged and for weddings. Jupiter hours favor all financial activities including asking money favors, phoning buyers, borrowing and lending, investing, seeking employment, and buying lottery tickets. These hours are also good for settling disputes and for asking favors of influential people, bankers, landlords, merchants, grandparents, uncles and aunts, and clergymen. Jupiter hours favor seeking professional advice from doctors, lawyers, accountant, astrologers and psychics. They are good hours for beginning journeys, especially to foreign countries, but not so good for boarding ships. They are good hours to schedule meetings to reach agreement, for arbitration, and for social functions such as banquets and association meetings. They also favor planting but are not good for purchasing animals. They are not good for surgical operations, but people taken ill during Jupiter hours recover quickly.

Mars Hours favor activities requiring courage, daring, and fortitude. They are good for risk-taking, enforcing your will, making complaints, firing employees, and success with drastic action generally (dental work and surgery, going to war, initiating lawsuits and conflicts).* Mars hours are good for scheduling athletic competitions, sports and exercises, work involving fire and metals, and for seeking favors from your husband, boyfriend, and men in general. However, Mars hours are unfavorable for most other activities, particularly for initiating journeys; and illnesses and disputes which begin during Mars hours can become quite severe.

---

* However, in my book *Topics in Astrology*, where I analyzed the horoscopes of nine wars for which exact times of initial hostilities were known, only the American Civil War and the Russo-Japanese War began during Mars Planetary Hours, and in neither case was there much of a victory for the aggressors (the Confederate States and Japan). Japan "won" but got little for its pains in the end; all that happened was that the Japanese people blamed the United States for the unfavorable peace settlement (since president Theodore Roosevelt had brokered it), which resentment led directly to Japan's involvement in World War II. Vis à vis the Confederate States: they made a good go of it. By all rights, they should have been wiped out in a few months, certainly within a year. But the lucky stroke of the South's acquiring a genius for a military commander, in combination with the military incompetence and blown opportunities of the North, extended that war much, much longer than it should have lasted. Using the Planetary Hours doesn't guarantee success; it just gives you your best shot.

How to Cast Spells

The secret of successfully casting spells is 1) to be aware of what you really want in your heart of hearts; and 2) to choose a propitious astrological time to cast your spell.

Casting spells is basically the same thing as praying. The main difference between casting spells and prayer is that normally prayers are directed to a divinity whereas spells are not (although they can be).

The reason why a magician's spells are usually more effective than most people's prayers is not because magicians have any special innate powers. Rather, it's because their intent is more realistic. Most people pray for their desires to come true, whereas magicians cast spells to be shown how to make their desires come true.

Another reason why most people's spells don't work is because they are too insensitive (i.e., have too much self-pity) to understand that that little "coincidence", or the casual, offhand remark someone made, or the person they happened to bump into in their hurry, or the dream they had that night, or some other little "cubic centimeter of chance" (to use Carlos Castaneda's term) which popped up in the hours or days after casting their spell, was in fact their spell coming true. Very rarely does the Spirit announce its gifts with trumpets blaring. What usually happens is that people cast their spells or make their prayers and the Spirit brings them an opportunity, but the people are too blinded by their preconceived images and expectations, or are in too much of a hurry to see that their spell did in fact come true; it brought them exactly what they were asking for, but they, themselves, rejected it. This is why it is necessary to be aware of what you really want in your heart of hearts when casting spells or praying.

Most people believe that things just happen, or else that an omnipotent God could make things happen if you could somehow fool God. Magicians believe that they must take full responsibility for making their desires come true. That's what intent is – taking full responsibility, leaving nothing whatsoever to chance. Casting spells is not at all like sitting on Santa's knee and dictating a list of what you want. Most people are addicted to some fantasy like winning the lottery, or marrying Mr. or Ms. Right, or meeting a true guru, and then all their problems will be over forevermore. These kinds of fantasies are useful in that they can provide a feeling of hope (false though it may be) to help get through the really hard times. However, addiction to such fantasies tends towards irresponsibility. It dissipates the very intent needed to find true happiness in life. Permanent change requires hard work and infinite patience. The final stroke of success may occur suddenly and even unexpectedly, but the preparation and toil take years and years. That's the difference between the magicians' way and the average person's way. Average people are looking for a quick fix and a free ride, whereas magicians know there ain't no such thing. Casting spells is not done to dictate to the Spirit. It's done for yourself, to strengthen your intent, to commit yourself, *irrevocably*, to the realization of your desires. When a spell is cast, it *always* comes true. The problem is that, if you have been lying to yourself about what you really want in your heart, then you won't see the opportunity when it does pop up.

Most of us have subconscious agendas of unworthiness which contradict what we consciously tell ourselves we want. For example, you may be consciously telling yourself that you want love, or health, or riches, but at any point that your conscious desires seem to be on the brink of being realized, you yourself will do something to blow the opportunity, and then later moan and complain about your bad luck.

Have you ever noticed how often lonely people (who aver that all they want is a relationship) will usually seek love only from people who will reject them, and not from the people who would gladly give it to them (those people they reject themselves)? Or, how often people who cast spells or pray for money ask to win the lottery, rather than be guided on how to start a good business or fulfilling career? Or generally that people irresponsibly ask for miracles, rather than for guidance on how to make their dreams come true? So, the first part of casting effective spells is to know thyself. To change the outward circumstances of your life, you must first change your inner state. You do this by making a definite, unalterable decision. This happens when you get sick to death of your own self-pity and decide to *really* change.

When casting a spell it is also important to address the underlying issue, rather than the presenting problem. For example, once I was casting a spell to bring money (during a Jupiter planetary hour the day before a Sun – Jupiter conjunction). As I was lighting the candle I realized that it wasn't money per se that I wanted, but rather the free time to write what I want to write, instead of having to spend most of my time doing the menial work which I had to do to get by economically. So, on the spot I changed my prepared spiel to a visualization of living in a remote place in nature where I have the freedom to write – write – write to my heart's content without interruption. This often happens to me when casting spells: I'll receive inspiration right then and there (while casting the spell) about how to bring the probable reality of my desire into actuality.

The second point in casting successful spells is to use astrology to time the spell. Why is it necessary to use astrology to choose a time to cast a spell? Well, if you are already lucky – in tune with your innermost desires and capable of reaching out and taking what you want from life with neither shame nor hesitation – then you don't need astrology. Lucky people are using astrology naturally; they have an inner clock which tells them when it's time to act or to refrain from action. However, most of us aren't so attuned to our own inner feelings and the ambient rhythms of the universe. Or rather, we are, but we deliberately (albeit unconsciously) choose unpropitious times to launch new projects, or to cast spells for what we want. Just ask any astrologer how often it's happened that a client has requested a propitious time to, for example, open a new business, or marry, or ask a favor, but when the time came the client wasn't able to use it. This is because the client (subconsciously) wanted to fail. When do you normally cast spells or pray for things? When you're feeling lousy and pitying yourself, right? So at the worst possible (astrological) time. This guarantees that your spells and prayers won't come true.

When casting a spell or praying, it is best to attach your desire to a powerful current of universal energy. It's like the difference between talking normally and talking through a loudspeaker: by attaching your desire to a wave of ambient energy, you magnify its power and increase the likelihood of its realization. This can be done by casting your spell on ephemeral phenomena; by casting your spell at a power place; or by casting your spell at a propitious time or, ideally, by combining these factors.

Ephemeral phenomena such as rainbows, falling stars, dust devils, gusts of wind, etc. are actually the best messengers for taking your spells out into the universe because they spring to life for a moment, and then dissolve back into undifferentiated energy, taking your desire with them. It is also possible to cast a spell on a burning candle, as is done in many churches, or to flags or kites, as is done in the Orient. However, the ephemeral phenomena which you encounter by chance are far more powerful messengers, therefore you should be alert to seize these impromptu opportunities and cast your spell when they occur.

Spell casting at propitious places means using power spots such as shrines, mountaintops, pools and waterfalls, and the abodes of nature spirits. Churches (especially old churches and especially old churches built on sites of previous pagan worship) are often built on power spots. There are also certain trees which facilitate casting spells. To find such a tree, enter a woods (preferably during a lunar planetary hour) and walk in the direction your intuition dictates until you come to a tree which feels "right". Then cast your spell on the spot.

Casting spells at propitious times can be subsumed under the topic *electional* astrology. Like everything else in astrology, there are lots of ways of doing this. What follows is how I've channeled to do it, and this system works well for me. There are basically three steps to choosing a propitious time to cast a spell or launch any enterprise: finding a proper day, finding a proper hour, and finding a proper moment. Of these, the proper hour is far and away the most important, so if you're pressed for time and need to cast a spell in a hurry, or if you have no knowledge of astrology, you can skip steps 1 and 3 below and just cast your spell during a propitious hour. There are propitious hours for every activity several times each day.

The reason why astrology (and magic generally) doesn't "work" as well nowadays as it did in the past is because it is peripheral to the central concerns of our society: very little energy is presently being focused in that direction. Warlike societies tend to be successful at war; commercial societies like ours tend to be successful at commerce; spiritual societies tend to be successful at spiritual endeavors; and magical societies (such as Guatemala, which is the witchcraft capital of the world) tend to get magic to work quite well. Whatever a society (or an individual) has faith in is what it tends to manifest.*

---

* This is a common mistake astrologers make: assuming that technique qua technique has anything to do with anything; e.g., that Vedic technique is more

Most of us have rationalist-materialistic or spiritual-materialistic backgrounds, and hence have little native faith in magic or astrology. Faith, like knowledge, is handed down from generation to generation, and our New Age generation is the first of the new magicians. It is necessary for us to plug away at magic on blind faith for a while until we eventually start seeing positive results, which is what builds real faith. However, we can take a faith short-cut by tuning in to existing wavelengths of knowledge; by using the Planetary Hours we are forging a link with the ancient magician-astrologers and the spirits who guided them.
Let's look at the procedure step-by-step:

1) Choosing a Propitious Day: First identify what it is you are casting a spell for with the relevant planet (see the Table of Planetary Rulerships in the introduction). For example, if what you want is money, then you must look to the planet Jupiter. In an astrological ephemeris scan ahead for a day when there is a good transiting aspect to Jupiter – either to transiting Jupiter, or to Jupiter in your natal chart (if it is not afflicted), and note the time when this aspect is exact.

Optimally, the other planet involved in the aspect should also be relevant to what you want: if you want a steady income and a sense

---

effective than Occidental technique; or that Renaissance practitioners got more effective results than modern astrologers do (ergo we should ape their techniques).

In the first place, IF (big "If") Hindu astrologers are more accurate than us westerners; or IF Renaissance astrologers were more accurate than us moderns (which – judging from Kepler's predictions for Albrecht von Wallenstein's horoscope in Ken Negus' article in *Considerations* XV: 4, or Regiomontanus' predictions for the Holy Roman Emperor Maximilian I in Rumen Kolev's translation of *Codex Vindobonensis Palatinus 5179* – is a dubious proposition, to say the least), then it is most likely the case that Vedic or Renaissance astrologers obtained better results than we do because they operated in an ambience which was conducive to astrology. For one thing, when the study of astrology is respected by a society (rather than being considered an object of opprobrium), many fine minds are attracted to the subject (which is very rare indeed in the contemporary Occident). But the real reason we modern western astrologers are in such bad shape is because we have lost touch with the source: the spiritual guardians of astrological knowledge who gave this science to the human race in the first place, and who traditionally guided and informed practitioners in making accurate predictions.

of security, then try to find a good aspect between Jupiter and Saturn (permanence); if what you want is money so you can afford some luxuries and enjoyment, then try to find a good aspect between Jupiter and Venus; if you want money so you can get ahead in life, then try to find an aspect between Jupiter and the Sun. Most of the time, unless you're willing to wait for some months, you will be circumscribed in what choices are available, so at a pinch you can always go with aspects to the Moon, which forms every possible aspect with every planet every month. Only favorable aspects should be used (conjunctions, sextiles, and trines); ignore unfavorable and minor aspects, and parallels of declination.

2) Choosing a Propitious Hour: Once you have located a propitious day, locate an hour ruled by the planet in question (Jupiter in our example) on that day. If you're not paying attention to the transits, then just choose one of the three or four Jupiter hours which occur that day which is convenient for you.

If you are looking at the transits check the following: if the transiting aspect does not involve the Moon, then you can use any of the Jupiter hours which fall within twenty-four hours before the exact time of the aspect; and if the transiting aspect does involve the Moon then you must use that one Jupiter hour which falls just before the exact time of the transit. If the aspect becomes exact during a Jupiter hour, then use the space in time between the beginning of the Jupiter hour and the exact time of the transit (this is actually the ideal situation).

3) Choosing a Propitious Moment: You can just go with the transiting aspect and planetary hour, but if you like doing calculations you can refine the technique further by using a table of houses to see whether a natal or transiting planet (preferably the one which rules whatever it is you are casting your spell for) crosses any of the four angles during the planetary hour in question. However, this isn't all that important, so if you don't know how to do these calculations, don't worry about it.

Now that you have found a propitious time to cast your spell, you must consider the form it will take. Write down ahead of time exactly what you want, so that you don't forget anything when the time comes. However, it's best not to be too specific in what you're asking for, such as to win the lottery, or to have such-and-such a person fall in love with you. It's best just to ask for wealth, or love from some unnamed person. Let the Spirit handle the details – it knows what it's doing. For suggestions, see the Book of Shadows at the end of this chapter; but this is merely to give you the idea – you don't have to slavishly copy these spells exactly.

If you have an accustomed mode of prayer, then just pray the way you usually do. If not, then you can adapt this formula to suit your own taste and needs: "Spirit – please bring me (whatever you are asking for), and please bring it to me really soon! Thank you!" It's important that you say "really soon", or any contradictory subconscious agendas you may have will use this loophole to defeat the spell. It's also important to say "thank you" at the end, as a reminder that the Spirit doesn't owe you (or anybody) anything. After all, the Spirit has given you life; after that anything else is gravy. When the time draws near, prepare a little altar with something that symbolizes the Spirit above it (this can be a picture of Jesus if you're a Christian, or just a cut-out picture of an eye, or whatever symbolizes the Spirit for you). Also put on the altar objects which symbolize what you want (money if you want money; cut-out pictures of lovers if you want love; pictures of healthy, active people if you want health, etc.). Then put a stick of sweet-smelling incense on the altar, and a candle whose color symbolizes what you're asking for (green for money, pink for love, white for health or spiritual illumination, etc.). The traditional colors associated with the planets are:

Sun = gold yellow
Venus = white or pink
Mercury = blue
Moon = silvery white
Saturn = black
Jupiter = red-brown or purple
Mars = red

Just prior to the chosen time light the incense. Then, at the precise moment chosen for the spell, light the candle. Call upon the Spirit to grant your wish. It's okay to read it, but you should do this with feeling – true longing for whatever it is that you want. Picture in your mind's eye your desire coming true as you call for it, and let yourself feel all the joy you would feel if your desire did come true. That's the important part: giving yourself permission (space in the midst of your self-pity) to feel happy. Imagine as though your desire is already true, and you're just hanging around in the waiting room for a bit till the Spirit finds it and hands it to you. Don't worry about whether you are doing it right. If you're doing it in good faith with true longing, then you're doing it right.

After lighting your candle and reciting your spiel (mentally or out loud – out loud is best if there aren't other people around), watch the candle closely for an omen of how your spell will turn out. If it is difficult to set up or to light the candle, then it will be difficult for your desire to be realized (there will be difficulties; it will require much work or delay). If the flame wavers or smokes, then this is not a good omen. If the flame is straight and true, then the wish will be granted. If the flame dies or the candle goes out, then the desire will not be realized or there will be major disappointment in its realization. Wax dripping down the candle can indicate preoccupations, or the demands of other people (that impede). If the candle burns all the way down to nothing, that's a good sign.

Flames have auras just as people do; and if you can see auras you can read a lot from them. Cardinal directions can be read from the aura (as well as from the direction the flame leans). If a candle is lit for a person (to ask something for someone) then the aura can be read as if it were that person's aura (for health or emotional information about that person).

If there are dark spots in the flame or in its aura, then there will be troubles (or enemies). If the wish is for health, then the part of the flame (left, right, center, up, down) in which the spots appear indicate trouble areas in the body. If the wish is for money, then, for example, a large flame with a dark spot within it means that the wish will be granted, but the money will be disappointing or soon be lost. Two or more dark spots in the flame indicate two or more (difficulties, people involved, whatever).

If asking for money for a specific purpose (which is better than asking for money for the sake of money), reach into the flame (quickly) with first one hand then the other as if grasping money from it in handfuls (of $10s, $100s, $1000s or whatever denomination of money you are asking for). When you feel a block or your hand gets heavy (after X handfuls), then that's how much money you can expect to get.

Be alert to any serendipitous events that occur while or shortly after you cast your spell, such as shafts of sunlight suddenly appearing through the clouds, or the sudden appearance of singing birds (if you are outside), or a phone call or unexpected visit. These are good omens for your spell coming true. Similarly, when performing a Scat ritual to get rid of some unwanted person from your life or to cast out demons, if you are attacked by a horde of insects, or stumble and fall and hurt yourself shortly after casting your spell, then these are also good omens (the meaning is that the person's demons are striking back at you, therefore your spell worked. Note that this is true only of Scat-type rituals; in most other circumstances such happenings are decidedly evil portents).

And pay very, very close attention to the people you "happen" to run into, the things they say, and all unusual occurrences and dreams in the hours and days after casting your spell. These sorts of omens are a font of information and inspiration on how to make your spell come true. Oftentimes people think that their spells didn't work, but all that happened was that they ignored the answer when it popped up in front of them.

If you don't feel comfortable with all the ritual, you can dispense with it. The ritual is just for your own sake, to lend a sense of importance and ceremony to the occasion – not to impress the Spirit. The only things of importance are to cast your spell with true longing, at a propitious time.

When you finish your spell, leave the area and let the incense and candle burn down, and then dismantle the altar and dispose of what's left of the candle and incense by burying them. Once a spell has been cast there's no need to repeat it unless you feel your own resolve weakening and want to strengthen it.

Sometimes astrologically guided spells work so fast that the results are startling. At other times, when there are powerful contradictory subconscious agendas in place, it takes a while for your spell to come true, but nonetheless you ought to be able to feel your spell working right away in the sense of feeling your inner obstructions dissolving and your inner attitude changing. Be assured that spell casting carried out in good faith always works, so don't waste spells on anything frivolous, since then you're committed to them. Be sure you really want what you're casting a spell for.

Book of Shadows

A Book of Shadows is merely a collection of spells and rituals. All thought forms of desire can be considered to be commands to the Spirit; what makes spells special is the attention paid to them and the importance placed on them. This is why we must not dissipate our intent in casting thoughtless desires out willy-nilly, such as by casual window-shopping or coveting what we see on the television or the internet, or being jealous of other people. We must focus all our desire on one particular object. It is precisely by inflaming our desires for a myriad of objects which we don't even want that our decadent society saps our wills and keeps us in bondage. Casting spells won't work if you scatter your intent in every direction at once. The author of *Picatrix* avers the importance of clear, one-pointed intent in making talismanic magic effective: "The maker of a talisman must be knowledgeable of the astrological ratios and formulas, confident of what he is doing and clear of any doubt or uncertainty in what he is doing in order to enforce the function of the speaking soul whereby the will, from the same causes reaches its (the talisman's) maker to obtain the sought result."*

The difference between spells and rituals is that rituals are done to invoke spirits (i.e. are performed basically to propitiate the spirits – to keep them happy and pliant), whereas spells are cast for particular purposes such as wealth, healing, love, etc. Spells can be considered the same thing as prayers, although prayers normally are directed towards a deity, whereas spells may or may not appeal for the intercession of spirits or a deity.

Both spells and prayers, as well as positive thinking, can be subsumed under the rubric Creative Visualization (C.V.), which is the name for the basic technique involved. There is nothing "magical" about spells; the words employed don't matter as much as the intent behind the words. It is much better if you create your own spells, in your own words, rather than borrow spells from some other source. However, if you are invoking spirits then you must be scrupulous in following the wording of the invocation precisely, as well as observing the correct day / time / astrological aspect required, if there is one, and copying the sigil correctly.

---

* *Picatrix*, trans. by Hashem Atallah, Ouroboros Press, Seattle 2002, p. 19.

This is because some spirits – though not all – are rather exigent in their requirements and demand full attention to what you are doing.*

After the spell is cast it is best to forget about it (insofar as you are capable of doing this) rather than to keep ruminating or fantasizing about it (which tends to dissipate the power of the spell). Once the intent has been set up by the C.V., the only way to make it happen, to let the Spirit be free to do your bidding, is to drop the concern completely. What locks the Spirit up and prevents it from helping us is our inability to just let go and abandon ourselves to it; to just trust it to come through for us.

Master magicians are able to just drop an obsessive concern because they have their true feelings so finely tuned that they can switch them off and on at will. They are not as wrapped up in their desires and feelings as are average people. They don't have such an ego stake (success/glory versus failure/shame) in the outcome of anything, so they can throw their attention completely behind a desire, and just as completely release it. Average people can't do this – they cling, and cling, and cling to their desires and thought forms; they don't know how to let go and they don't have the discipline to be able to just drop something without looking back. So what average people have to do is to trick themselves: after setting up an intent through obsessive concern, they should then arbitrarily choose some other area of their lives to become obsessively concerned about, and shift all their intense, obsessive desire to this other area.

What follows are merely suggestions and examples. You must adapt the model to your own taste, to create spells that are meaningful to you, personally. The important thing is to imagine your desire coming true in the now moment. This means imagining yourself to be in the midst of your desire coming true, rather than being a detached observer (as you do in normal fantasizing and daydreaming). For example, in casting a love spell you must imagine yourself to be looking the other person directly in the eye and talking sincerely to them, and listening to what they have to say, rather than viewing them from a distance (as you do in romantic or sexual fantasies).

---

* See Franz Bardon's *The Practice of Magical Evocation* (Dieter Rüggeberg, Wuppertal, 1970) for examples. The Mayan spirits I invoke are more laid-back.

As you cast the spell, imagine in your mind's eye your desire coming true right *now*, and let yourself feel all the joy you would feel if that were indeed the case. In other words, Creative Visualization is a matter of hypnotizing oneself (if only momentarily) into believing that your desires are already true. This is how we reach out to the probable realities in which we realize our desires: by breaking the hypnotic spell of our obsessive moods of unhappiness, by giving hope a little elbow room in there, so it can nudge its way through the gloom of our customary self-pity. Hope is the fuel that propels desire lines forward. This means faith not in ultimate success, but in ultimate self-worth. In the end you have to abide by the dictates of power. You win a few, you lose a few; that's the way it goes.

Asking favors: Use a relevant hour (Sun for father/boss; Moon for mother /employee; Mercury for children/neighbor/coworker; Venus for female friend or lover; Mars for male friend or lover; Jupiter for advisor; Saturn for old or difficult people). Light a candle whose color corresponds to the planetary hour ruler, and while doing so vividly imagine that you are looking the person directly in the eye. Calmly and confidently explain why you need this favor from the person. Give your reasoning and (if possible) explain how doing you this favor will be beneficial to them also. Imagine them granting your desire with cordiality and generosity; smile at them and shake their hand, then walk away and *forget about it.* In the absence of time constraints, after doing the C.V. don't bring the favor up yourself, of your own accord; wait until the proper moment to approach the person arrives on its own momentum.

Love Spell: Use a Venus hour (straight women or gay men can use a Mars hour instead – particularly if sex is more important than companionship). At this moment light a pink candle and imagine that you are right there in front of your beloved (or if you don't have a beloved, a beautiful stranger). Look him or her directly in the eyes; take his or her hands in yours, and say everything that is in your heart. Then listen to what he or she has to say and let the thing flow as it will. Then embrace and kiss as if it were really happening right now, and feel yourself filled with joy and happiness! Then with a sigh, squeeze their hands, wish them well, and let them go.

Both the Asking favors (above) and Love spells are essentially the same thing as bewitching the person, except casting spells is usually only done once, at a favorable astrological time; bewitching is carried out on a daily (or even moment-to-moment) basis for a while to build up pressure, before dropping the procedure and turning one's mind to other things.

Money Spell: Use a Jupiter hour (or hour ruled by a strong, well-aspected planet in your natal 2nd house). At the chosen time light a green candle, take a deep breath, and vigorously shake your body to shake off all your money worries. Imagine that you have plenty of money for all your needs and never need to worry about money ever again! It's better not to focus on money in itself, but rather on what you need the money for; that these needs are being abundantly met, and you are joyous and positive about your future! Feel how happy and satisfying it makes you that you have such abundance that you can be philanthropic and give money to others who need it and to help save the earth. It's important that you see yourself as being wealthy enough to give money away, rather than imagining yourself pigging out; that you are a conduit for money, rather than it all stops with you. Appreciate how great it feels to be free of money worries forever!

Enlightenment/wisdom/knowledge Spell: Use a Sun hour. At this moment light a white candle; take a deep breath, and imagine that all barriers separating you from other people and the world around you have dissolved, and you feel a white light enveloping you with joy! Then:

Feel that you are truly connected to the universe
That you have been chosen to save the world
That you have been chosen to reach out to every being that comes in contact with you
That your love knows no bounds and gives you joy such as you never thought was possible

Health Spell: Use a Moon hour (you can use a Mars hour for surgery or Saturn hour to begin treatment for chronic illness, but then the Moon should be applying to a favorable aspect with Mars or Saturn, respectively). At this time light a white candle and imagine yourself (or the person you are praying for) to be healthy, happy, and full of zip! Whatever activities may have been curtailed by your illness, imagine yourself renewing them with increased verve and enthusiasm! Feel yourself brimming with vigor and energy, do a little dance of joy and thanksgiving for your healing!

Success in Studies: Use a Mercury hour. Light a blue candle at this moment, take a deep breath, and imagine that you are in school and are feeling confident and pleased with your understanding and progress! See yourself reciting in class and feel that you are making a good contribution to the class and have the esteem of your teachers and classmates! You are so happy to be in school because you are learning so much and are having lots of fun!

Going to War: Use a Mars hour. At this time you should light a red candle, visualize the person you are praying for as if he or she was standing right in front of you looking you in the eye. If you are doing this for yourself, visualize yourself in the midst of war with a feeling of calmness, courage, and confidence in your own abilities. Take a deep breath and blow all your worries and doubts away and leap forward with abandon! Spread your arms wide and cast a white light of protection around the person (or imagine that white light is descending from above to surround and protect yourself). Imagine that the person is standing calm and self-assured inside this white light of protection. Then wish the person well and bid them well on their way into the light.

Conflicts/firing employees, etc: Use a Mars hour. Light a red candle for courage. If it's a matter of standing up to someone and telling them off, imagine them standing right there in front of you and speak exactly what's on your mind calmly and assuredly, with no gloating, anger, or personal feeling at all. Imagine yourself tearing off the ties which bind you; jump forward out of the situation which is holding you back and spring into the light of freedom!

Scat Spell: (to cast out demons, banish negative thought forms, and get rid of bothersome people): Use a Saturn hour. Light a black candle, take a deep breath, and imagine yourself confronting the oppressive person or situation with cold detachment and indifference. It's important that you have no sense of gloating, or a desire for vengeance, or for anything more from this person. Then throw your arms outward forcefully and decisively as if to cast off the oppressive person or situation. You can also jump up and down and shake your body vigorously to shake the person's bad vibes off. I do a Greek brigand's folk dance (*Vari Khasapiko*) to banish people from my life. You don't visualize something bad happening to the person, but rather feel how happy and light you are now that person is gone or that situation is behind you!

Example: to get rid of a lover who has outlived his/her usefulness, at the correct moment light a black candle and imagine your ex is standing right in front of you and telling you that they've decided that they've had enough of you. Don't feel rancor; feel relief. It's important that you don't do this C.V. in a mood of anger, particularly if your ex is a vampire who is sucking your energy by provoking your anger. You have to call it quits in the C.V. – not take pleasure when they get their comeuppance (as you do in normal daydreaming). Take deep breaths, or jump up and down and shake your body, until you are calm and in command of yourself. Then imagine taking your erstwhile lover's hands in both of your own; look him or her squarely in the eye, and say in your own words and using your own sentiments, "It's had its good times, hasn't it? But now it's time we each went our own way." It's important that you emotionally connect to (remember) the good times if you really want to get past this person. Then wishing him or her the best of luck in their future journey, turn around, wipe your hands of it, walk away and don't look back.

The Firdaria

The firdaria is an ancient prediction technique which divides a person's life into periods (and subperiods) of time ruled in turn by each of the planets in Chaldean order. Daytime births begin with a Sun period and night births begin with a Moon period; and from then on the planetary rulerships follow the Chaldean order for a specified number of years proper to each planet (and the Moon's nodes)*:

Daytime births	**Night births**
Sun's firdaria = 10 years	Moon's firdaria = 9 years
Venus' firdaria = 8 years	Saturn's firdaria = 11 years
Mercury's firdaria = 13 years	Jupiter's firdaria = 12 years
Moon's firdaria = 9 years	Mars' firdaria = 7 years
Saturn's firdaria = 11 years	Sun's firdaria = 10 years
Jupiter's firdaria = 12 years	Venus' firdaria = 8 years
Mars' firdaria = 7 years	Mercury's firdaria = 13 years
North Node's firdaria = 3 years	North Node's firdaria = 3 years
South Node's firdaria = 2 years	South Node's firdaria = 2 years
Total = 75 years	Total = 75 years

If the person lives longer than 75 years, then the cycle starts over again at the beginning (either with a Sun firdaria if a daytime birth or a Moon firdaria if a night birth). Each of these firdaria is further divided into seven equal subperiods – also ruled by the planets in Chaldean order – starting with the firdaria ruler.

For example, the first subperiod for a person born at night is a Moon/Moon subperiod which runs from birth till age 1.29 years (= 9/7). The second subperiod is a Moon/Saturn subperiod which runs until age 2.57 years (= 2 x 9/7). The third subperiod is a Moon/Jupiter subperiod which runs until age 3.86 years (= 3 x 9/7). And so on: the final subperiod in

* Note that there is a variant of the firdaria scheme in which, for night births, the two nodes' firdaria are inserted in the middle (between Mars' firdaria and the Sun's firdaria) instead of at the end.

the Moon's firdaria is a Moon/Mercury period which begins at age 7.71 years (= 6 x 9/7) and ends on the 9th birthday, at which time the Saturn firdaria commences. The Saturn firdaria runs for the next 11 years: the first subperiod is a Saturn/Saturn period which runs till age 10.57 years (= 9 + 11/7); the second subperiod is a Saturn/Jupiter period which runs until age 12.14 years (= 9 + 2 x 11/7); and so forth.

In contrast to the progressions, directions, and transits which point to specific events in time, the firdaria indicate a tone or flavor, or perhaps a new direction or point of departure, in the life. Occasionally firdaria do indicate specific events: for example, my Saturn firdaria began on my 40th birthday (like everyone who is born during the daytime), and my grandmother – the only person in my dysfunctional family who loved me – died the very next day. But in general the firdaria indicate emotional trends or undercurrents, rather than concrete events.

Calculating the firdaria is rather straightforward (and there are websites, such as firdaria.com, which perform these calculations for free). Using the Table of Day Fractions, express the birth date as a year and decimal fraction; for example, a birthday on October 27, 1858 is expressed as 1858.822. Then to find when a firdaria or firdaria subperiod begins just add the number of years (and decimal fraction) listed in the Tables of Firdaria Starting Dates for that subperiod to the birth year and fraction; and then go back into the Table of Day Fractions to see what day of the year that corresponds to. For example, for a night birth on October 27, 1858, the Venus/Saturn subperiod began at age 52.429 + 1858.822 = 1911.251, which going back into the Table of Day Fractions yields a date of April 1, 1911.

Table of Day Fractions

	Jan	Feb	Mar	Apr	May	Jun	Jul	Aug	Sep	Oct	Nov	Dec
1	0	.085	.164	.249	.332	.416	.499	.584	.668	.751	.836	.918
2	.003	.088	.167	.252	.334	.419	.501	.586	.671	.753	.838	.921
3	.005	.090	.170	.255	.337	.422	.504	.589	.674	.756	.841	.924
4	.008	.093	.173	.258	.340	.425	.507	.592	.677	.759	.844	.926
5	.011	.096	.175	.260	.342	.427	.510	.595	.679	.762	.847	.929
6	.014	.099	.178	.263	.345	.430	.512	.597	.682	.764	.849	.932
7	.016	.101	.181	.266	.348	.433	.515	.600	.685	.767	.852	.934
8	.019	.104	.184	.268	.351	.436	.518	.603	.688	.770	.855	.937
9	.022	.107	.186	.271	.353	.438	.521	.605	.690	.773	.858	.940
10	.025	.110	.189	.274	.356	.441	.523	.608	.693	.775	.860	.942
11	.027	.112	.192	.277	.359	.444	.526	.611	.696	.778	.863	.945
12	.030	.115	.195	.279	.362	.447	.529	.614	.699	.781	.866	.948
13	.033	.118	.197	.282	.364	.449	.532	.616	.701	.784	.868	.951
14	.036	.121	.200	.285	.367	.452	.534	.619	.704	.786	.871	.953
15	.038	.123	.203	.288	.370	.455	.537	.622	.707	.789	.874	.956
16	.041	.126	.205	.290	.373	.457	.540	.625	.710	.792	.877	.959
17	.044	.129	.208	.293	.375	.460	.542	.627	.712	.795	.879	.962
18	.047	.132	.211	.296	.378	.463	.545	.630	.715	.797	.882	.964
19	.049	.134	.214	.299	.381	.466	.548	.633	.718	.800	.885	.967
20	.052	.137	.216	.301	.384	.468	.551	.636	.721	.803	.888	.970
21	.055	.140	.219	.304	.386	.471	.553	.638	.723	.805	.890	.973
22	.058	.142	.222	.307	.389	.474	.556	.641	.726	.808	.893	.975
23	.060	.145	.225	.310	.392	.477	.559	.644	.729	.811	.896	.978
24	.063	.148	.227	.312	.395	.479	.562	.647	.732	.814	.899	.981
25	.066	.151	.230	.315	.397	.482	.564	.649	.734	.816	.901	.984
26	.068	.153	.233	.318	.400	.485	.567	.652	.737	.819	.904	.986
27	.071	.156	.236	.321	.403	.488	.570	.655	.740	.822	.907	.989
28	.074	.159	.238	.323	.405	.490	.573	.658	.742	.825	.910	.992
29	.077	.162	.241	.326	.408	.493	.575	.660	.745	.827	.912	.995
30	.079	*	.244	.329	.411	.496	.578	.663	.748	.830	.915	.997
31	.082		.247		.414		.581	.666		.833		1.00

* in leap years you can add .003 to the fraction for days after February 28th; or, you can just ignore it since a day more or less doesn't matter much in the firdaria.

Table of Firdaria Starting Dates – Daytime Births

SU/SU	0.000	ME/SA	21.714	SA/VE	46.286	MA/JU	69.000
SU/VE	1.429	ME/JU	23.571	SA/ME	47.857	N.NODE	70.000
SU/ME	2.857	ME/MA	25.429	SA/MO	49.429	S.NODE	73.000
SU/MO	4.286	ME/SU	27.286	JU/JU	51.000	SU/SU	75.000
SU/SA	5.714	ME/VE	29.143	JU/MA	52.714	SU/VE	76.429
SU/JU	7.143	MO/MO	31.000	JU/SU	54.423	SU/ME	77.857
SU/MA	8.571	MO/SA	32.286	JU/VE	56.143	SU/MO	79.286
VE/VE	10.000	MO/JU	33.571	JU/ME	57.857	SU/SA	80.714
VE/ME	11.143	MO/MA	34.857	JU/MO	59.571	SU/JU	82.143
VE/MO	12.286	MO/SU	36.143	JU/SA	61.286	SU/MA	83.571
VE/SA	13.429	MO/VE	37.423	MA/MA	63.000	VE/VE	85.000
VE/JU	14.571	MO/ME	38.714	MA/SU	64.000	VE/ME	86.143
VE/MA	15.714	SA/SA	40.000	MA/VE	65.000	VE/MO	87.286
VE/SU	16.857	SA/JU	41.571	MA/ME	66.000	VE/SA	88.423
ME/ME	18.000	SA/MA	43.143	MA/MO	67.000	VE/JU	89.571
ME/MO	19.857	SA/SU	44.714	MA/SA	68.000	VE/MA	90.714

Table of Firdaria Starting Dates – Night Births

MO/MO	0.000	JU/SU	23.423	SU/SA	44.714	ME/VE	68.143
MO/SA	1.286	JU/VE	25.143	SU/JU	46.143	N.NODE	70.000
MO/JU	2.571	JU/ME	26.857	SU/MA	47.571	S.NODE	73.000
MO/MA	3.857	JU/MO	28.571	VE/VE	49.000	MO/MO	75.000
MO/SU	5.143	JU/SA	30.286	VE/ME	50.143	MO/SA	76.286
MO/VE	6.429	MA/MA	32.000	VE/MO	51.286	MO/JU	77.571
MO/ME	7.714	MA/SU	33.000	VE/SA	52.429	MO/MA	78.857
SA/SA	9.000	MA/VE	34.000	VE/JU	53.571	MO/SU	80.143
SA/JU	10.571	MA/ME	35.000	VE/MA	54.714	MO/VE	81.429
SA/MA	12.143	MA/MO	36.000	VE/SU	55.857	MO/ME	82.714
SA/SU	13.714	MA/SA	37.000	ME/ME	57.000	SA/SA	84.000
SA/VE	15.286	MA/JU	38.000	ME/MO	58.857	SA/JU	85.571
SA/ME	16.857	SU/SU	39.000	ME/SA	60.714	SA/MA	87.143
SA/MO	18.429	SU/VE	40.429	ME/JU	62.571	SA/SU	88.714
JU/JU	20.000	SU/ME	41.857	ME/MA	64.429	SA/VE	90.286
JU/MA	21.714	SU/MO	43.286	ME/SU	66.286	SA/ME	91.857

Theodore Roosevelt's Firdaria

The easiest way to see the firdaria in action is with an example. Here we will take a look at Theodore Roosevelt's firdaria, with the most important events which occurred during each period. Although – as with every astrological technique – there are things which don't fit the symbolism or make sense, on the whole, TR's firdaria do work well enough to reveal how the system can be interpreted. Of course, a person's public life and record don't show everything that was going on in his personal life – his relationships, hopes and dreams, private pursuits. However, TR's life is well-documented (by himself and others).

The firdaria are interpreted principally in terms of the symbolism of the firdaria and subperiod rulers involved. For example, during most of TR's Sun subperiods he gained greater self-confidence, recognition, and preferment. During his Mercury subperiods he usually initiated new studies or major writing projects. Moon subperiods often brought family matters to the fore, or were periods of recuperation. Mars subperiods tended to be especially conflictive, and Saturn subperiods disappointing. Also, the natal horoscope must be examined to determine the conditions of the firdaria and subperiod rulers by sign (essential dignity) and angularity, as well as whether there is an aspect, parallel, or reception between them in the natal chart. If the firdaria and subperiod rulers are in bad aspect in the birth horoscope then their firdaria will be unfortunate, even if the planets are benefic (e.g., TR's Venus/Jupiter and Jupiter/Venus periods were unfortunate since these planets are in opposition across the angles in the natal horoscope; and Jupiter is weak by sign). Similarly, although natal Moon and Mars are strong by sign, their opposition means that the Mars/Moon period will be rife with conflict and disappointment.

In the absence of a special relationship (aspect or reception) between the two rulers in the natal horoscope, it can be useful to look at the inherent harmony or disharmony between these two planets to determine whether a subperiod will be forward-going or difficult. Two such schemes are listed in the following tables (my scheme is based upon whether the conjunction can be said to be favorable or unfavorable):

Table of Favorable and Unfavorable Planetary Combinations

	(per Morinus)							(per Makransky)					
	SU	VE	ME	MO	SA	JU		SU	VE	ME	MO	SA	JU
VE	+							–					
ME	+	+						–	–				
MO	+	+	+					+	+	+			
SA	–	–	+	–				–	–	+	–		
JU	+	+	+	+	+			+	+	–	+	+	
MA	+	–	–	–	–	–		+	+	+	–	–	+

The following natal horoscope is calculated for the Sunshine House System – see my book *Topics in Astrology* for an explanation.

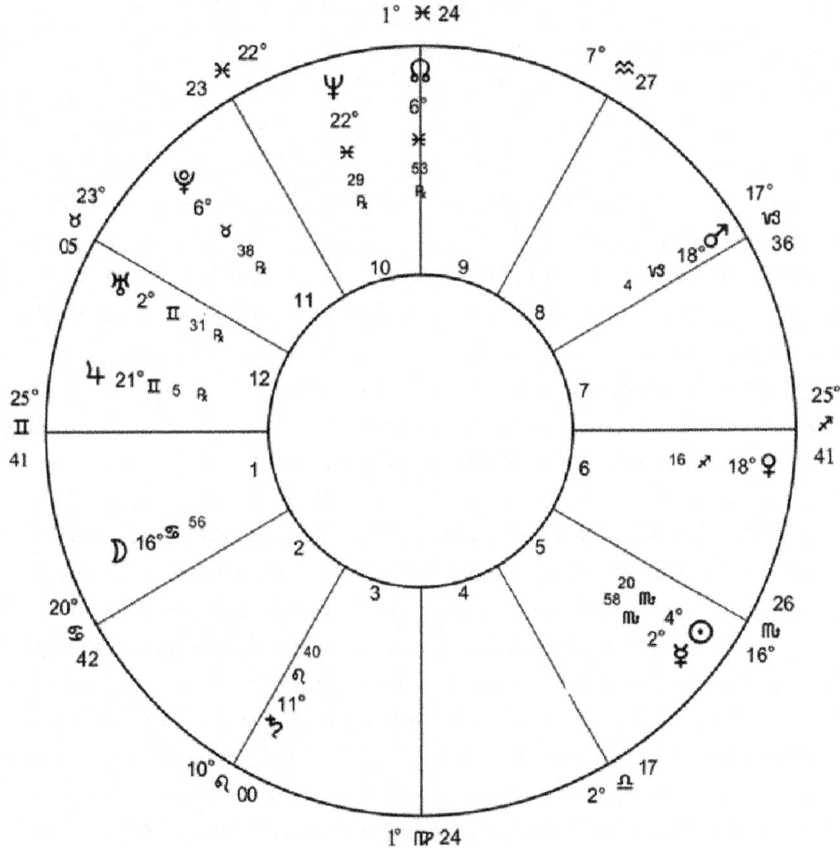

Theodore Roosevelt
October 27, 1858, 07:49 PM (–5 hours), New York 74W0 40N43

To avoid footnotes, references are embedded in the main text. The numbers in <brackets> are page numbers from:

from 27 October1858 to 13 September 1901
The Rise of Theodore Roosevelt by Edmund Morris, Ballantine Books NYC 1979.

from 14 September 1901 to 4 April 1909
Theodore Rex by Edmund Morris, Random House NYC 2001.

from 9 March 1909 to 18 January 1919
T.R – The Last Romantic by H.W. Brands, Basic Books NYC 1997.

(*Autobio*) = *Autobiography*, 1913, Project Gutenberg ebook 2002.

MOON/MOON FIRDARIA BEGAN – October 27, 1858
Moon/Saturn – February 8, 1860 = unknown
Moon/Jupiter – May 23, 1861 = fall 1861. TR's father left home (to go to war); sadness and lots of illness (TR had been in ill health from asthma from the beginning). This scarcely fits the Moon/Jupiter symbolism; but in the summer of 1862 his father visited, which made TR very happy. <41>
Moon/Mars – September 4, 1862 = spring 1863. TR's family moved into a summer home (Luantaka); he loved it, <45> the family returned for the next 4 years.
Moon/Sun – December 18, 1863 = unknown
Moon/Venus – April 1, 1865 = unknown
Moon/Mercury – July 14, 1866 = unknown

SATURN/SATURN FIRDARIA BEGAN – October 27, 1867 = summer 1868. The family was at a new summer place where TR began keeping a diary, <49> health not good. But what the Saturn symbolism probably refers to is that TR's mother was losing her mind, entering a life-long depression. <49> She had been despondent since the end of the Civil War, since she was a Southerner, but it got noticeably worse now – perhaps what the natal Moon-Mars opposition is all about. On 12 May 1869 TR embarked on a trip to Europe of over a year's duration, <49-50> but he disliked it: "I do not think I gained anything from this particular trip abroad. I cordially hated it, as did my younger brother and sister." (*Autobio* 20)

Saturn/Jupiter – May 22, 1869 = TR arrived in England 5/21/69; sick the whole trip, <51> the only thing he enjoyed was mountain climbing. He returned to NYC in September 1870.

Saturn/Mars – December 17, 1870 = about this time – in a promise to his father – TR began working out to build his body and health. <60> Usually, Saturn/Mars and Mars/Saturn periods are very difficult, but here TR manifested the Saturn/Mars symbolism in a positive way, using sheer willpower to oppose an intractable health problem (Mars and Saturn have no natal aspect, but exalted Mars is disposed of by Saturn). By the summer of 1871 he was no longer ill. <61> In winter-spring 1871-72 TR took up taxidermy, <61> (*Autobio* 24) and the summer of 1872 he received his first gun (a present from his father), which was the beginning of a life-long interest in hunting (which fits the Mars symbolism).

Saturn/Sun – July 13, 1872 = in late summer 1872 humiliation by bullies made him take up boxing, <63> (*Autobio* 31) and in late fall 1872 he received his first set of eyeglasses, which completely changed his perspective on himself: "My first pair of spectacles ... literally opened an entirely new world to me. I had no idea how beautiful the world was until I got those spectacles. I had been a clumsy and awkward little boy, and while much of my clumsiness and awkwardness was doubtless due to general characteristics, a good deal of it was due to the fact that I could not see and yet was wholly ignorant that I was not seeing." <62> (*Autobio* 24) The boost in self-confidence during this period is typical of TR's Sun subperiods (even though the two planets are square in the natal horoscope – Sun disposes of the weak Saturn). Fall 1872 TR left for a second trip to Europe which he thoroughly enjoyed (his interest in natural history peaked), and he spent the summer of 1873 in the home of a German family, enjoying their Gemütlichkeit. (*Autobio* 26)

Saturn/Venus – February 7, 1874 = TR returned from Europe three months previously to a new tutor, new studies, <75> and a new house. (*Autobio* 26-7) In the spring of 1874 his family moved into a new, permanent country home <75> and TR spent that summer birding in Adirondacks. <90> It was a joyous Venus subperiod (Venus and Saturn are natally trine). In July 1875 TR took the Harvard entrance exams and did excellently; <76> it was during this Venus subperiod that he became involved with Edith Carow (his first love and second wife). <76>

Saturn/Mercury – September 4, 1875 = summer 1876 deepened TR's intimacy with Edith; <78> and they had reached an "understanding." <79> The Mercury symbolism is reflected in the fact that in September 1876 TR entered Harvard. Moreover, the following month he was insulted at a political rally, <82> which sparked his first involvement in politics.

Saturn/Moon – March 31, 1877 = freshman year, after a talk with his father, TR decided to become a scientist (*Autobio* 29) – a decision he later rescinded. The Saturn/Moon symbolism probably refers to the death of TR's father in February 1878, which threw TR into a depression for months. In the summer of 1878 he fought with and broke up with Edith. <98> In October 1878 he met Alice Lee, who later became his first wife. <102-4>

JUPITER/JUPITER FIRDARIA BEGAN – October 27, 1878 = Fall 1878 TR got into his preferred Harvard social club and began courting Alice seriously. Also, under her influence, TR was getting more seriously into politics <110> until by summer 1879 he finally gave up the idea of a science career in favor of politics. <116> Spring 1879 he made a trip to the backwoods of Maine where he found he could hold his own with "real woodsmen" and he made some life-long friends. <110> Winter 1879 he began writing his first major literary work on the Naval War of 1812. <122> In short, during this Jupiter/Jupiter firdaria TR embarked upon all three of his subsequent careers: politician, outdoorsman (rancher), and writer; and in January 1880 Alice consented to marry him. At the end of this Jupiter firdaria in June 1880 TR graduated Harvard magna cum laude. <128>

Jupiter/Mars – July 14, 1880 = TR was married in October 1880 <133-35> and entered Columbia Law School the next month. <137> What the Jupiter/Mars symbolizes, however, is probably that in the winter of 1880-81 he began hanging out at a local Republican Club: <142> "The men I knew best were the men in the clubs of social pretension and the men of cultivated taste and easy life. When I began to make inquiries as to the whereabouts of the local Republican Association and the means of joining it, these men – and the big business men and lawyers also – laughed at me, and told me that politics were 'low'; that the organizations were not controlled by 'gentlemen'; and ... that the men I met would be rough and brutal and unpleasant to deal with. I answered that if this were so it merely meant that the people I knew did not belong to the governing class, and that the other people did – and that I intended to be one of the governing class." (*Autobio* 55) He threw himself into the rough-and-tumble of local politics, and in November 1881 he won election to the state assembly. <153> By the end of this Jupiter/Mars subperiod he had proven himself a scrapper who wasn't afraid to take on political Goliaths. (*Autobio* 67,71-2)

Jupiter/Sun – April 1, 1882 = during this Jupiter/Sun period TR's work in the assembly brought him considerable renown: he was re-elected to the assembly by a record 2–to–1 majority in November 1882 and was nominated by acclamation the Republican candidate for speaker of the assembly in January 1883 (although he lost to a Democrat). Governor (later president) Cleveland called upon him to push Civil Service Reform; <188> and by the end of the assembly session he was considerably more self-assured (Jupiter/Sun). <197> Also during this period TR made his first trip out west and loved it – going berserk when he killed his first buffalo. <224> Fall 1883 he returned east and handily won re-election to state assembly. <228>

Jupiter/Venus – December 18, 1883 = this is a bit of a puzzle, since Jupiter/Venus normally indicates happiness, although in TR's natal chart these planets are in opposition across the Ascendant/ Descendant axis and form a T-Square with Neptune. Also, the firdaria are not the only game in town: Mars by primary direction conjoined TR's Descendant now too. On Valentine's day 1884 both TR's mother and wife died (the latter giving birth). TR was stunned, dazed, and he blotted Alice (and his newborn daughter) out of his mind. He sold his new mansion and threw himself into work in order to forget. At the Republican state convention in April 1884 TR was in the saddle and triumphant, but he broke relationships with several old friends and allies (he had outgrown them). <255> That June he returned to the west where he found and purchased a perfect spot for a ranch house. <278> He wrote and published *Hunting Trips of a Ranchman* and spent the summer of 1885 cowboying on a 5-week roundup – an experience which changed and matured him and made him physically powerful. <303>

Jupiter/Mercury – September 4, 1885 = in early October 1885 TR fell in love with Edith Carow (his childhood sweetheart) and proposed marriage to her the following month. <313> Also during this period he had some thrilling adventures out west. He ran for mayor of NYC, but lost the election in November 1886, and he married Edith the following month. However, the main thing which occurred during this period was that his ranching business out west was completely destroyed by a terrible winter; he visited Dakota in the spring of 1887 and was devastated by his losses – he was now facing poverty. Since the political outlook was bleak he realized that he would have to support himself by writing (which fits the Mercury symbolism). <373-4>

Jupiter/Moon – May 23, 1887 = in June 1887 TR began writing his 4th book, *Gouverneur Morris*, <378> finished in early September. Also, his first son, Ted, was born this month. He made a hunting trip to Dakota at the end of the year, and it was at this time he became a conservationist (founding the Boone & Crocket Club in December). <384> In January 1888 he began writing his magnum opus *Winning the West*, <387> which took seven years to complete; the first volume was finished in December 1888. Perhaps Jupiter/Moon refers to this being a period of recuperation and settling down into "normalcy" after the tumultuous events of the previous few years.

Jupiter/Saturn – February 7, 1889 = during this period TR re-entered politics after a five-year hiatus through an appointment (arranged by a good friend) as Civil Service Commissioner, <392> and, congruent with the Saturn symbolism, he immediately got himself involved in fierce battles with special interests: "The first effort of myself and my colleagues was to secure the genuine enforcement of the law. In this we succeeded after a number of lively fights. But of course in these fights we were obliged to strike a large number of influential politicians … Accordingly we soon found ourselves engaged in a series of contests with prominent Senators and Congressmen." (*Autobio* 116) His crusading made him powerful enemies, including President Harrison. <408> At the beginning of 1890 Congress appointed a committee of his enemies to investigate him <418> and he was vilified in the press, <419> but he was completely exonerated in the spring of that year. Vis a vis Jupiter/Saturn, it was around this time that TR began to covet the presidency. <422> Also during this period the first volume of *Winning the West* was published to very favorable reviews, <404> and his second son, Kermit, was born. <412>

MARS/MARS FIRDARIA BEGAN – October 27, 1890 = the Mars symbolism refers to the fact that in January 1891 TR's brother Elliott, who had been drinking himself to death for some time, now was about to have bastard son. <430> This really angered TR; <431> also now there were lots of attacks against him in Congress. <432> In March 1891 TR began investigating President Harrison's supporters in Maryland, <433> and his final report was severely attacked within his own party <435> and turned President Harrison against him. Between the scandalous news about his brother (which broke in the newspapers in August 1891) <442> and his political battles with the president and administration <443> this was generally a very angry period. <445>

Mars/Sun – October 27, 1891 = on a trip to Europe in January 1892 TR patched things up (temporarily) with his wayward brother, which fits the Mars/Sun "male relationships" symbolism. <445> More importantly for his self-confidence and public repute (Sun), he spearheaded a Civil Service reform investigation through the House of Representatives which led to savage attacks from his enemies, but in the end TR was completely vindicated. <452> This was a major political triumph for TR and an embarrassment to the Harrison administration, and in fact it was the main reason that Harrison lost the 1892 presidential election to Cleveland. <452>

Mars/Venus – October 27, 1892 = the Democratic win in November 1892 meant that TR, a Republican, was politically out of it for four years. The only major event during this period was the Panic of 1893, which hurt TR financially (Venus subperiods don't seem to have been very happy for him), <471> although he published *Wilderness Hunter*, which many consider to be his best book. <471>

Mars/Mercury – October 27, 1893 = winter-spring 1894 TR wrote volumes 3 and 4 of *Winning the West*, <471> and a son was born that April. Mars/Mercury probably refers to his brother's death in August 1894, which really broke TR up; they had been close in youth, now he cried like a child. <474> He was depressed that fall: he refused an offer to run for mayor of New York City (at his wife's urging – a decision he later regretted), <475> and he returned to work at the Civil Service Commission thoroughly demoralized.

Mars/Moon – October 27, 1894 = a conflictive time, since Moon and Mars are in opposition in the natal horoscope. In spring 1895 TR was appointed NYC Police Commissioner and – as was his wont – immediately began to shake things up <488,491> and make lots of enemies, including the Chief of Police. <491> He began to prowl the city at night incognito to spy on the police force, <505> and he engendered lots of antagonism including a letter bomb which he received in August. <506> His stand lost a lot of New York City votes in the November 1895 election, so the Republican Party distanced itself from TR, and he was abandoned by everyone.

Mars/Saturn – October 27, 1895 = the landslide Democratic victory in New York in November 1895 angered him, and he found himself in opposition to the NYC machine boss and his fellow Police Commissioners. The machinations, treachery, and stress of this period culminated in TR's receiving more letter bombs, and him challenging his chief opponent to a duel in May 1896. <531> All that summer he was unsuccessfully fishing for a presidential appointment to Secretary of the Navy, but President McKinley and Mark Hanna (McKinley's handler) opposed him. <545>

Mars/Jupiter – October 27, 1896 = McKinley's victory in November 1896 boosted TR's hopes of a Naval appointment; but the expected appointment was not forthcoming, <556> and his work in the Police Commission bogged him down. <558-9> Finally, in April 1897 he became Assistant Secretary of the Navy <565> and immediately became leader of "Manifest Destiny" warhawks. <568> His outspoken call to arms <570> caused a nationwide sensation <571-2> and outraged his boss. <579> He would exceed his authority when his boss was away, and reveled in real power for the first time in his life, congruent with the Mars/Jupiter symbolism. <580-1> He also wangled from President McKinley the promise of a special army commission in the event of war. <586>

SUN/SUN FIRDARIA BEGAN – October 27, 1897 – this period was most definitely TR's apotheosis. It opened with the birth of his 6th child, Quentin, in November. In February 1898 the explosion of the *Maine* in Havana harbor <598> and the declaration of war on Spain was just the opportunity TR had been hoping for. In April TR was named Colonel of a special regiment, the Rough Riders, which he recruited from cowboys and frontiersmen he had known, <615>(*Autobio* 187ff) and in June he landed in Cuba. TR called the Battle of San Juan Hill on July 1st "the great day of my life." <650>(*Autobio* 212) He returned to the U.S. in August "the most famous man in America", <665> and that November he handily won the New York gubernatorial election. <686> By spring 1899 TR found himself once more in combat with the same machine boss who had made his life miserable when he was Police Commissioner.

Sun/Venus – April 1, 1899 = most of this period TR was wrestling with his old political enemy, but he was angling for the 1900 Republican Vice Presidential nomination. <705> He was nominated in June 1900 with the enthusiastic support of his boss and enemy, who wanted to get TR out of New York politics by kicking him upstairs. <729>(*Autobio* 250)

Sun/Mercury – September 4, 1900 = McKinley and TR won in a landslide in November 1900. <732> In September 1901 McKinley was assassinated and TR was sworn in as President. <15> Within two months he had started his trust-busting crusade with an action against a railroad trust (Mercury rules legal matters and contracts), <62>(*Autobio* 339 ff) and he also pushed through a treaty for the United States to build a canal across Central America (one of his dreams). <67>

Sun/Moon – February 8, 1902 = was a period of many triumphs in which he realized many of his heart's desires (Sun/Moon) and made his re-election in 1904 a certainty. <170> Among his successes: he launched his trust-busting with a suit against a railroad combination, <89, 219> got a Panama Canal bill introduced to congress, (*Autobio* 404) pushed through conservation and land reclamation legislation, (*Autobio* 317) settled a nasty strike in the coal fields, <134>(*Autobio* 368, 374) and settled an international incident over Venezuela. <177-180> On the other hand, he was involved in a bad accident in

September 1902 (Moon does oppose Mars in the natal chart) which killed his beloved bodyguard and required several surgical operations, and caused him tremendous pain for months afterwards. <141-2> By the end of this subperiod, however, he was feeling better and walking normally; he even went bear hunting (which resulted in the invention of the Teddy Bear). <174>

Sun/Saturn – July 15, 1903 = a week after this Saturn subperiod began Wall Street collapsed, causing a financial panic <260-1>. The beginning of September 1903 an assassination attempt shook him deeply, since – while he had made many enemies among the wealthy and powerful – he hadn't realized that the labor force was against him too. <266> On the positive side he continued his conservation program with a Public Lands commission, (*Autobio* 327) and the Panamanian "revolution" paved the way for his canal project. <289> (*Autobio* 407) He received much money now, <305-6> and also handily won the Republican nomination for president; <328> (*Autobio* 308-9) he won the November 1904 election in a landslide. <363-4>

Sun/Jupiter – December 17, 1904 = his second inaugural. Around this time TR began losing sight in left eye due to a boxing injury (Venus and Jupiter subperiods are not particularly favorable for him). <376> (*Autobio* 42) He successfully mediated the settlement of the Russo-Japanese war, <414-15> which was a great triumph, and he continued his reform program with the formation of an Interstate Commerce Commission, <423> and by pushing his Pure Food and Meat Packing and railroad reform bills through congress. <447> His daughter Alice was married during this Jupiter subperiod as well. <437>

Sun/Mars – May 23, 1906 = as is usual of Mars subperiods, this one brought TR lots of conflict after the triumphs of his earlier presidency. Although June 1906 saw the passage of legislation protecting national monuments and the Pure Food and Drug Act, <448> TR's handling of a racial incident involving Negro soldiers in Texas that summer angered American Negroes greatly. This Brownsville Incident has been called the "major mistake of his presidency", <535> and led to his congressional enemies pressing for an investigation. <477> TR's vitriolic rebuttal and attack on his enemies in the Senate caused a big scandal. <480> A war scare with Japan necessitated TR's sending the fleet to demonstrate. <485, 494> (*Autobio* 302) More importantly, the stock market crashes and Panic of 1907 engendered virulent criticism of TR's targeting big business with his reforms. <495> Also during this period TR's son Archie was very ill and almost died. <489>

VENUS/VENUS FIRDARIA BEGAN – October 27, 1907 = TR approved a trust deal to save the economy <499>(*Autobio* 347-8) in November 1907; and he had many triumphs with congress over inheritance and income tax, national incorporation of interstate business, government control of railroad rates, eight-hour day, and more battleships. He created a National Conservation Commission, <519> and about now conceived the idea of going on an African safari. Politically, he was becoming disaffected with his chosen successor Taft.

Venus/Mercury – December 17, 1908 = in February 1909 the Great White Fleet – TR's special pride and joy – returned from around the world cruise: <549> the "apotheosis of Roosevelt." <TR - 642> He retired from office in March 1909 and left immediately on a one-year African safari about which he published lively journalistic travel reports, <642> (*Autobio* 37) which fits the Mercury (travel, journalism) symbolism.

Venus/Moon – February 7, 1910 = tail end of the Africa trip; after safari TR traveled through Egypt and to Europe where he met Kaiser Wilhelm and <661> he returned to the U.S. in June 1910 "a changed man." <670> The main event of this subperiod is that he became a grandfather (he adored children) and he traveled to California in spring 1911 to visit his new grandson (which fits the lunar symbolism). <685>

Venus/Saturn – April 1, 1911 = his wife was gravely injured in a riding accident and required two months' recuperation. <693> The main event of this subperiod was TR's decision to run for the Republican nomination in 1912 (against his former protégé, now enemy, Taft). <703>

Venus/Jupiter – May 22, 1912 = in June 1912 he lost the Republican nomination ("We stand at Armageddon and we battle for the Lord"). <716-18> In August he was nominated by the Progressive Party and began a barnstorming campaign across the U.S. <720> In October he was shot; <720> and in November he lost the election to Wilson (but at least he beat Taft, which was perhaps his main object). <724> Venus and Jupiter subperiods were not as favorable for TR as they are for most people. Also during this period he began writing his autobiography, and his daughter Ethel was married. <729>

Venus/Mars – July 14, 1913 = This period was not so much one of conflict (as were most of TR's Mars subperiods) as of tremendous daring and danger. In February 1914 TR embarked on a great adventure in the Amazon <740ff> which turned into a disaster. His team ran out of supplies and TR was sickly with jungle fever; <742> he lost the sight in one eye, <754> and he and his crew were in pretty bad shape, facing death for months. Finally in mid-April they arrived at a trapper's home and knew they would be okay. <743> TR returned to NYC in May, <743> and World War I broke out three months later.

Venus/Sun – September 4, 1914 = unlike most of his Sun subperiods, this one was not good for TR's prestige and reputation. In November 1914 the Progressive Party was defeated everywhere but California, which was a major setback <747> and the end of the party; and made TR consider leaving politics for good. In spring 1915 a libel suit was brought against him which in the end improved his popular image. <760>

MERCURY/MERCURY FIRDARIA BEGAN – October 27, 1915 = since TR was born during a Mercury hour on Mercury's day, one might expect some sort of important events now – but not so. In 1916 TR attacked Wilson's war policies; <760ff> and although he intensely disliked Wilson he only grudgingly campaigned for the Republican nominee Hughes. <774> In April 1917 he had a good visit with Wilson and asked the president to let him lead a division, <781> but nothing came of it. The only Mercury event now was that he took the job of editorial writer for the Kansas City Star. <787>

Mercury/Moon – September 4, 1917 = TR entered a hospital for surgery in February 1918. <794>

Mercury/Saturn – July 14, 1918 = in July 1918 came the news of his beloved son Quentin's death in battle; <797> it left him distraught, he never got over it. <802-3> After the fall elections he got sicker and sicker <810> and returned to the hospital for most of November-December. <810> In early January 1919 he again fell ill, <811> and he died of a coronary embolism on January 6th (which fits the Saturn symbolism).

Appendix: The Generalized Planetary Hours

The Generalized Planetary Hours is a system for placing all of the planets – not just the Sun – within a scheme of twenty-four half-houses each ruled by one of the Chaldean planets in turn. Thus, for example, a Moon election (healing, moving, traveling) should be done when the Moon is in a Moon-ruled hour – rather than when the Sun is in a Moon-ruled hour, as is done in the simple Planetary Hours. A Venus election (asking someone for a date, or scheduling a party or recital) should be done when Venus is in a Venus hour; and a Jupiter election (buying a lottery ticket or asking a financial favor) should be done when Jupiter is in a Jupiter hour (rather than the Sun being in these hours, as is done conventionally). It also may occur that Venus will be in a Venus hour at the same time that Jupiter is in a Jupiter hour, at a time when Venus and Jupiter are simultaneously applying to favorable transiting aspect. These are just some of the possibilities of using the Generalized Planetary Hours in making elections. Generalized Planetary Hours horoscopes and calculations are available from AstroApp.com.

As in the simple Planetary Hours, the first hour is the lower half of the usual 12th house in a conventional horoscope, and it is ruled by whichever planet rules that day: Sun if Sunday, Moon if Monday, Mars if Tuesday, Mercury if Wednesday, Jupiter if Thursday, Venus if Friday, and Saturn if Saturday. Then each succeeding hour (moving clockwise) is ruled by the corresponding Chaldean planet in order: Sun – Venus – Mercury – Moon – Saturn – Jupiter – Mars. Thus hours spaced 7 apart (e.g. the 1st, 8th, 15th, and 22nd) are always ruled by the same planet.

In addition to its utility in making elections, the Generalized Planetary Hours can be used as a new kind of natal horoscope. The zodiac of signs is jettisoned altogether: planetary positions are stated in terms of hour and decimal fraction (how far into that hour the planet has progressed) or hours and minutes (the decimal fraction multiplied by 60); but in practice the decimal fraction is ignored (except in primary directions, as described further on).

Aspects are taken from hour to hour rather than with orbs in longitude; thus, for example, two planets are considered to be in a sextile aspect if they lie in hours which are spaced 4 apart; in square aspect if they lie in hours which are spaced 6 apart; in trine aspect if they lie in hours which are spaced 8 apart; and in opposition aspect if they lie in hours which are spaced 12 apart. One important facet of interpretation is consideration of the aspect (if any) between a planet and its hour ruler as indicating how easily or difficult affairs symbolized by that planet and hour will go.

My informants recommend that we astrologers use this new method of calculating horoscopes and making predictions, because the old way has been too "trampled upon" and misused by generations of inept astrologers. The zodiac is like a tool which has been banged about by incompetent craftsman and so has lost its sharp edge. In any case, the spiritual guardians of astrological knowledge find it more difficult to connect to and inspire modern astrologers (as they did our predecessors) because the methods we are using have been rendered profane.

We occidental astrologers – like the rationalistic-materialists who control academia – like things to be "reasonable", that is, to be in line with our preconceived concepts. We like things to change smoothly and steadily, so that's the only part of nature we study. But the universe is actually infinitely complex and utterly chaotic, thus only a model which is complex and chaotic is going to be a good reflection of it. Hence the Generalized Planetary Hours uses "hard cusps": aspects are not measured over the line of the cusp no matter how close they are in space (all aspects are taken from hour to hour). In the predictive techniques listed in the following pages, rulerships change suddenly and drastically at dawn. This is why G.P.H. astrology is complex and discontinuous, to better reflect the reality of the universe. When aspects are measured from hour to hour (instead of with orbs in longitude), one begins to see aspects taking on wholly new meanings, and you can tune in to a whole new dimension of what aspects are really all about.

However, the principal analysis in Generalized Planetary Hours astrology is based more upon the hour rulerships than upon the aspects. As Dr. Marc Edmund Jones pointed out, the more abstract the symbolism, the more powerful it is. G.P.H. horoscopy is an astrology of luck, in contradistinction to conventional horoscopy, which is an astrology of social adaptation. Where conventional horoscopes reveal the natives' response to cultural and group conditioning, G.P.H. charts are soul horoscopes, showing luck (fate) rather than psychology. In theory these charts should be able to distinguish between, for example, residents of Beverly Hills and residents of the slums of Mumbai. Powerful G.P.H. charts (those with many planets in their ruling hours or in hours ruled by friendly planets) are not unlike conventional charts with lots of angular planets; but these operate on a deeper, more subconscious level. Conventional charts with lots of angular planets are shrewd, cunning, and manipulative, whereas G.P.H. charts with lots of planets in their own hours show adaptability and fluidity, a facility for seizing opportunities and avoiding pitfalls:

The Sun in its own hour makes the native brassy, self-assured (pushy), unapologetic, sardonic, demonstrative.
The Moon in its own hour gives the native a puppy-like innocence and naïveté – sensitive, fresh, and unaffected.
Mercury in its own hour makes the native thoughtful, sincere, convincing, contemplative, noncommittal (vacillating).
Venus in its own hour is childlike, unassuming, unvarnished, enthusiastic.
Mars in its own hour demands respect.
Jupiter is good with people and the public.
Saturn is determined, inflexible, (cold and ruthless).
The node in a Moon hour is soft, vulnerable, intimate (easily hurt).

To read the hours is like reading the houses in a conventional horoscope, except that in spirit, desires are viewed as a weakness (unlike the material plane, where desires are a good thing). Each hour of the chart has a specific meaning (health, love, money, etc.) derived from/related to the meanings of the 12-fold house it occupies (i.e. each half-house takes on some of the meanings of the whole house). In a general kind of way, planets posited in odd hours have successfully completed their spiritual work, whereas planets posited in even hours still have something to accomplish in this area – some lesson still to be learnt, or fear to be overcome. Planets in odd hours have learned their lessons about their desires – they have a purer approach to that planet's energy than even houses, in which the planets are still caught up in desire – running around in little circles somehow. Moreover, the "angular" hours are taken to be 1 – 7 – 13 – 19 (rather than 6 – 12 – 18 – 24 as in conventional astrology); i.e. a planet is powerful as it leaves conjunction with an angle, not as it applies to it.

Interpretation proceeds from the meaning of an hour (health etc.) and the relationships between planets occupying that hour and the ruler of that hour. If Saturn occupies an hour ruled by the Moon, that is not a good combination, although it can be ameliorated to some degree if the two bodies are also in favorable aspect (or exacerbated by unfavorable aspect).

One approach to interpreting these charts is by looking at the native's "Tree" – the list of planets according to their hour rulers. For example, Prince Charles' Tree looks like this:

Ruler	**Chakra**	**Prince Charles' planets**
Sun	Crown	MA, JU
Venus	Brow	UR, PL
Mercury	Throat	SU, ME
Moon	Heart	VE, NE
Saturn	Solar Plexus	MO, NO
Jupiter	Sacral	(none)
Mars	Root	SA

All planets on a given level (having the same hour ruler) are related as if by aspect. Empty levels (such as Jupiter in the example) are significant by that fact alone, as are heavily weighted levels. The tree can be viewed as the person's body, indicating where the person puts his or her energy and what levels are being ignored. It is possible for pairs of planets to be in mutual reception (each posited in an hour ruled by the other), and, as in Prince Charles' case, there can be sole dispositors: here Mercury is sole dispositor since it is in its own hour and disposes of the Sun; the Sun in turn disposes of Mars and Jupiter; Mars disposes of Saturn which disposes of the Moon which disposes of Venus (and Neptune), and Venus disposes of Uranus and Pluto. Mercury as a sole dispositor indicates natives who are thoughtful, contemplative, sincere, and convincing. So Mercury is very powerful in the Prince Charles' G.P.H. horoscope (a sharp, acute mentality), and Jupiter, by contrast, is quite weak (showing hesitancy, lack of true faith). The north node is considered to be in its own ruler when it is in a Moon hour.

When there are three or more planets in their own hours, what is shown is great freedom to choose one's own path in life, for good or ill; independence, leisure, ease, comfort. These natives either enjoy fortunate circumstances from birth, or else (if poor in youth) they have a knack for making their way in the world because people tend to give way to them. A preponderance of planets in their ruling hours is the mark of very lucky natives who find it easy to bend the rules to their own liking and win ready acceptance for their own desires. For example, in dealing with rigid institutions, these are the people who can always get special exceptions made in their case. They keep loose, don't permit themselves to be tied down or inhibited by the caution and uncertainty which daunt most people. Like cats, they always land on their feet.

The problem is that a preponderance of planets in their own hours inclines towards laziness and self-satisfaction, which tends to increase after middle age. Most preponderance natives have little of the "there but for the grace of God go I" attitude. They tend to forget that they are lucky because they were born with luck – they easily come to believe that they *deserve* their good fortune. This is why it's best for a horoscope with a preponderance of planets in their ruling hours to also be severely afflicted vis a vis the aspects, since in this case the natives have a natural brake or reality check on their rapacity in the form of constant rejection by, and conflicts with, other people (even though they always win out in the end). This is more conducive to self-examination than when the natives are not only indulgent, but also receive approbation for their indulgence. On the other hand, when there is a preponderance of planets in hours ruled by enemies, then there will be bad luck, dashed hopes, and continual crises and dissatisfaction throughout the life.

In looking at a person's tree, particular attention must be paid to the harmony/disharmony of the planet and level. For example, the Saturn level (Grounding) is ideal when planets that operate harmoniously with Saturn (namely ME, JU, SA, & UR) are placed there. Planets placed there which interact inharmoniously with Saturn (SU, MO, VE, MA, NE, PL) show some kind of incongruity – a "round peg in a square hole". Too heavy a weighting on the Saturn level shows too grounded a person – i.e. a need to lighten up, not be so heavy and arrogant, to distribute some of that spiritual energy to other levels. And similarly for the other planets.

To go from this generalized type of chakric/energy analysis to true diagnosis of physical ailments and treatments, it is necessary to use intuition (exactly as in natal interpretation). So a Saturn-level imbalance could in a given case cause an ailment of the head or back as well as the feet/legs; that specific sort of information has to be obtained psychically (channeled) once the chakric/energy analysis has been done by looking at the tree.

Synastry is carried out not hour-to-hour, but rather by comparing the two people's trees to see what planets appear on what levels – so if John's Sun and Mary's Moon are both in hours (in their respective natal G.P.H. horoscopes) ruled by Mars, then this is like a "conjunction" (for better or worse, and better for John and worse for Mary, since the Sun likes Mars but the Moon doesn't).

The Generalized Planetary Hours charts can also be used in horary astrology. Select a planet to rule the question, for example Jupiter if about money, Venus if a male seeking love, Mars if a female seeking love, etc. and then calculate the hour in which that planet lies, and its ruler. If the significator of the question lies in its own hour, the answer is very favorable indeed. If it lies in an hour ruled by a friendly planet, or it favorably aspects its ruler, then the answer is favorable. If it lies in an hour ruled by an enemy planet, or if it afflicts its ruler; then the answer is unfavorable.

Prediction in the Generalized Planetary Hours is by secondary progression, which results in a firdaria kind of scheme which changes suddenly at dawn each succeeding day (i.e. at roughly the same time every year). In other words, when the Sun by quotidian progression arrives at the progressed Ascendant each year, all the hour rulerships change. So if Saturn was in an hour ruled by Venus, it then moves into an hour ruled by itself – implying that this year will be a better year for Saturn kinds of things (whatever Saturn meant in the natal horoscope). In other words, if you want to see what the 30th year of life looks like, set up a chart for 30 days after birth. The planets move through the whole 24 hours in the course of a year. So for example, if Saturn was in the first hour in January 2014, it will also be in the first hour in January 2015, but now its ruler is different.

If you want to see what October 2015 will be like, which is (let us say) 30 years and x months after birth, you cast a chart for 30 days and y hours after birth. You notice that at this time the Sun is in an hour friendly to it, and so is Venus, but Jupiter and Saturn are in hours unfavorable to them (ruled by enemies). Then you will know that this period is good for matters ruled by the Sun and Venus in the radix – so for matters ruled by the hours in which they were posited natally, and which they rule natally, as well as for dealings with authorities, women, etc. Whereas matters related to hours ruled by Jupiter and Saturn in the radix will not go well this month.

Each planet goes through an hour in a little over two weeks (roughly), and since there are ten planets there will be an average of at least one change in favorable/unfavorable matters every day or two. So this is a day-to-day system of prediction, which will come up with the tone of each day, week, and month (rather than predicting outstanding events). It will help in making plans and decisions – the usual stuff of life.

What we're keeping track of here are periods when Jupiter (say) is in a Jupiter hour at the same time that Mars is in a Mars hour (for elections). It is also possible to track bad periods, when lots of planets are in hours with whose rulers they conflict.

What makes this system interesting is that the hour rulerships change ever year (at progressed dawn), so that while it's true that Saturn (say) passes into and out of the 6th hour on about the same date every year, the ruler of the 6th hour will be different every year. Malefics passing through hours ruled by enemies signify a bad fortnight for the affairs ruled by that hour (especially the dates when they enter or leave that hour).

If you make a list of the outstanding days of your life; and you take a look at the hour rulerships those days, sorted as to, for example, all the days when the Sun was in an hour friendly to itself compared to when it was in an enemy's hour, and so forth with the other planets, you will soon get a feel for what it means to have a day when your Sun is in its own ruler (or in an enemy ruler).

In Generalized Planetary Hours primary directions, the Midheaven is moved forward at the rate of the Placidian True Solar Arc in Right Ascension: the MC moves in R.A. at the same speed that the secondary progressed Sun is moving in R.A. The Ascendant is dragged along at the same rate in Oblique Ascension. The Right Ascensions and declinations of natal planets are used to compute January 1st positions (in hours) each year. Every planet is in each hour for roughly 15 years. The hours are divided up into 60 "minutes", each about three months long in real time. The cusps (dates when planets change minutes and – especially – when they change hours) are important; however, the thing is read like the firdaria, i.e., in terms of planetary periods: times when Venus is in her own hours are favorable for Venusy things, and Venus in Saturn hours are disappointing for Venusy things. (Note that in the primary directions the hour rulers remain the same as in the natal horoscope until the Sun crosses the Ascendant).

Just as the planetary periods in the firdaria are subdivided into subperiods, rulerships of the sixty minutes of each hour start with the hour ruler. When a planet enters a new hour or minute it comes under the influence of that hour's ruler, that minute's ruler, and also any planets posited in that hour in the natal horoscope. Aspects are taken between directed planets and natal planets from hour to hour: so if natal Mars is located at 15.65 hours = 15 hours 39 minutes, then opposition Mars falls at 3 hours 39 minutes, and trine Mars falls at 7 hours 39 minutes etc.

Most people are not attentive enough to their own mental patterns and mood swings to understand or feel how dependent they are on underlying cosmic rhythms. By keeping track of favorable/unfavorable Generalized Planetary Hours periods you'll find it easier to ride them, bend with them, and be attentive to your own inner moods and necessities instead of going against the spirit of the time.

Defining the Generalized Planetary Hours

NOTE: A person born between midnight and dawn is considered to be born on the previous day (since the G.P.H. day runs from dawn to dawn rather than midnight to midnight).

In the simple Planetary Hours, the Sun's diurnal (declination) circle is divided into twelve equal arcs above the horizon and twelve equal arcs beneath the horizon. Since the Sun, by definition, lies upon its own diurnal circle, this is all the information which is needed to place it in its correct Planetary Hour. However, if the other planets are to be included in this scheme as well as the Sun, there must be some way of projecting their positions onto the Sun's diurnal circle; there is no self-evident way of doing this.

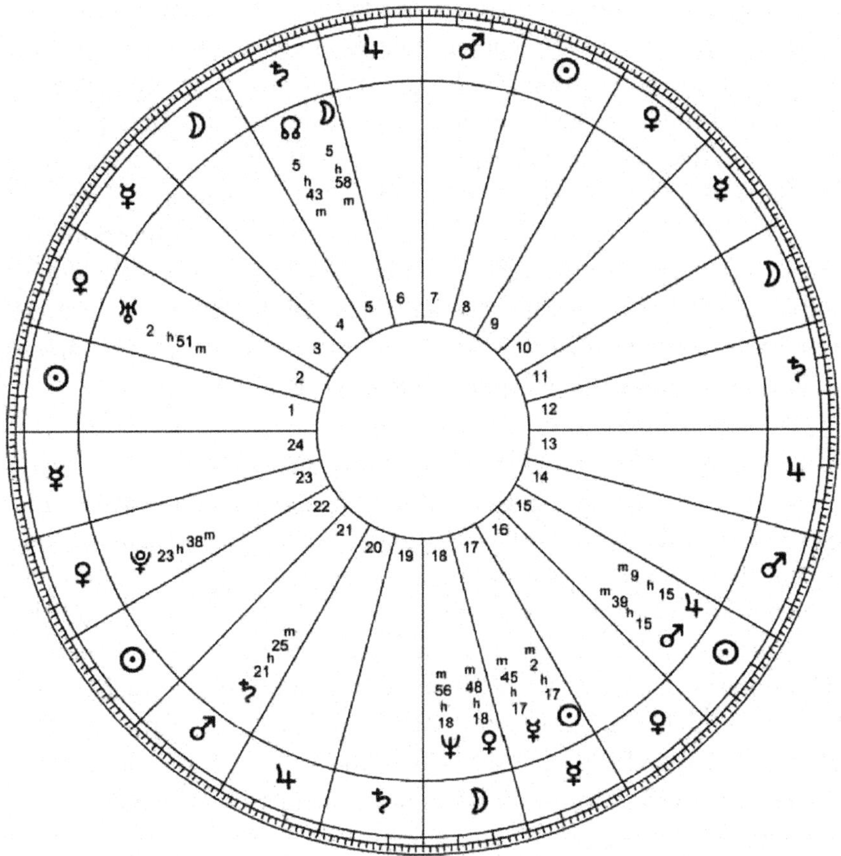

Prince Charles
November 14, 1948, 09:14 PM, London, England 0W10 51N30

Actually, however, it doesn't matter all that much how this projection is carried out since most schemes will produce similar results, and the important thing is that the symbolism be correct – i.e. that both the lunar symbolism (the number seven – and the Chaldean rulerships – are lunar symbols), and the solar symbolism (12-fold day/night division – twelve is a solar symbol), be correct, and not that it necessarily be an accurate astronomical model of anything.

The method adopted here quite arbitrarily utilizes an adaptation of the projection scheme of the Topocentric House System devised by Argentine astrologers Wendel Pollich and Nelson Page. While the Topocentric House System is absurd in its mathematical formulation, nonetheless its conception is rather intriguing, and fertile in its implications (see "The Celestial Hourglass" chapter of my book *Topics in Astrology*). For definitions and explanations of all calculations used here, see my book on celestial sphere geometry *Primary Directions*, downloadable for free from: www.dearbrutus.com/buyprimarydirections.html. AstroApp.com calculates G.P.H. charts this way, and also offers a Campanus solution. However, the Campanus G.P.H. charts have the same distortions as Campanus horoscopes: they tend to stretch the hours near the horizon and compress the ones flanking the meridian. But it really doesn't matter how you do it – all roads lead to Rome (a true astrology based upon cosmic – as opposed to conceptual – principles).

"Topocentric" solution to Generalized Planetary Hours

Using a Topocentric-like solution, the projection circles of planetary positions onto the Sun's diurnal circle are taken to be variable ascension circles: great circles on the celestial sphere whose poles (measure of perpendicular arc from celestial pole to that circle, which also equals 90° – the angle of intersection of that circle with the celestial equator) are arbitrarily defined to equal N * ø / 6, where ø is the latitude of the birthplace and N is an integer from 0 to 6 which depends on the hour (N = 0 for the 7th and 19th hours; N = 6 for the 1st and 13th hours; and N = some intermediate value for hours not coincident with the meridian or horizon).

Hour Poles:

Given Hour number and ø = terrestrial latitude, then:

If Hour < 13 then Pole = |Hour – 7| * ø / 6

If Hour >= 13 then Pole = |Hour – 19| * ø / 6

Planetary Poles:

Given the Meridian Distance of the planet, and the Declinations and Semi-Arcs (NSA and DSA) of the planet and the Sun,

Let Q = Quadrant of planet, then:

If Q = 1 or 2, then let V = 1; let PSA = NSA_{planet}; and let SSA = NSA_{Sun}

If Q = 3 or 4, then let V = -1; let PSA = DSA_{planet}; and let SSA = DSA_{Sun}

Let initial value of Pole = $(MD_{planet} / PSA) * ø$

Let T_{sun} = Arcsin (tan $Declination_{Sun}$ * tan Pole)
Let T_{planet} = Arcsin (tan $Declination_{planet}$ * tan Pole)

Pole = $(MD_{planet} - V * T_{Sun} + V * T_{planet}) * ø / SSA$

And then iterate until successive iterations are sufficiently close (say, within .01). If successive Pole values oscillate, or converge too slowly (which tends to happen with high latitudes and declinations), take the 4th and 5th iterations and average them (all that really matters is being in the ballpark).

Generalized Planetary Hours:
Given a body's Pole and Quadrant Q, to compute its hour position:

Let X = Pole * 6 / ø

If Q = 1 then Hour = 19 + X
If Q = 2 then Hour = 19 – X
If Q = 3 then Hour = 7 + X
If Q = 4 then Hour = 7 – X

Given Day of Week DW (Sunday = 1, Monday = 2, etc.), to compute Day Key (DK):

Let X = 1526374 / (10^(DW-1)) where ^ = exponentiation
DK = INT(X – 10 * INT(X/10)) where INT = Integer Part

Given an hour H, to find its ruler R:

R = (H + 1 – DK – DW) mod 7

"Campanus" solution to Generalized Planetary Hours

A Campanus solution projects the planets onto the Sun's diurnal circle with house circles – great circles which pass through the north and south points on the horizon. To find the position of a planet in the hours (see *Primary Directions*):

1) Compute the RA and declination of the planet
2) Compute the Quadrant of the planet (P.D. book p. 17)
3) Compute Campanus W and pole of the planet (P.D. book pp. 38-39)

4) Compute declination of the Sun and DSA_{Sun} (for day hours) or NSA_{Sun} (for night hours) (P.D. book pages 16-17)
5) Let X = Arcsin (tan $Declination_{Sun}$ * tan $pole_{planet}$)
6) For a planet in the
 1st Quadrant: $RA_{hour} = W_{planet} + X$ and $MD_{hour} = RAIC - RA_{hour}$
 2nd Quadrant: $RA_{hour} = W_{planet} - X$ and $MD_{hour} = RA_{hour} - RAIC$
 3rd Quadrant: $RA_{hour} = W_{planet} + X$ and $MD_{hour} = RAMC - RA_{hour}$
 4th Quadrant: $RA_{hour} = W_{planet} - X$ and $MD_{hour} = RA_{hour} - RAMC$
7) For a planet in the
 1st Quadrant: Hour = $19 + 6 * MD_{hour} / NSA_{Sun}$
 2nd Quadrant: Hour = $19 - 6 * MD_{hour} / NSA_{Sun}$
 3rd Quadrant: Hour = $7 + 6 * MD_{hour} / DSA_{Sun}$
 4th Quadrant: Hour = $7 - 6 * MD_{hour} / DSA_{Sun}$

Once the Hour is known, the ruler is calculated the same as for Topocentric:

Given Day of Week DW, to compute Day Key (DK):
 Let X = 1526374 / (10^(DW-1))
 DK = INT(X – 10 * INT(X/10)) where INT = Integer Part

Given an hour H, to find its ruler R:
 R = (H + 1 – DK – DW) mod 7

The spiritual guardians of astrological knowledge see astrology on a wholly different level than we do. To them it's a beautiful interplay of light fibers; an incredibly intricate harmony of tremendous beauty; a true music of the spheres encompassing sound as well as sight and feeling; an outpouring of cosmic love. But we humans have reduced it to a way of outguessing our fates and making money. The Generalized Planetary Hours, which are a proper combination of the symbolisms of the Sun (dividing the Sun's diurnal circle) and the Moon (assigning rulerships by weekday), allows us to tune into astrology more in the way the spirits do. And this enables us to make exact predictions instead of woolly mumbo-jumbo, because we tune in to a horoscope on a light fiber level rather than a concept level.

How to Use the Tables of Planetary Hours

Using the Planetary Hours Tables seems confusing at first because of all of the time conversions which must be made. However, once you've done it the first time it's easy, because thereafter you are always adding (or subtracting) the same number of minutes to the times listed in the table (as long as you remain at the same latitude and longitude on the earth). You can find the longitude and latitude for the place you are located from a map, or atlas at the local library, or on the internet.

Note that you can also download a free Planetary Hours calculator from my website:

http://www.dearbrutus.com/body_planetaryhours.html

or from the files of my blog:

Magical Almanac: http://groups.yahoo.com/group/MagicalAlmanac/files/How%20to%20use%20Magical%20Almanac/.

This calculator is an Excel worksheet with complete instructions, however when you open it, you will be asked if you want to disable the macros. Since it won't work with macros disabled, click on "Enable Macros" (you may have to have previously reduced the Excel security protocol: Tools => Macro => Security => Low).

To use the Tables: once you have determined on a day and know which planet rules the matter in question, consult the Table of Planetary Hours Rulers to see which hours on that day are ruled by that planet. For example, if you are looking for a Jupiter hour on a Wednesday, then from the Table of Planetary Hours Rulers you note that on Wednesday the 4th, 11th, and 18th hours are ruled by Jupiter.

Next, consult the Planetary Hours Tables for the week (irrespective of year) and scan across the row for the latitude closest to your own to see at what times those hours begin and end. Note that hours 19 – 24 occur in the predawn of the following day.

For example, if you are located at 37° north latitude, then during the week of January 1st through 7th:

the 4th hour begins at 9:40 am and ends at 10:27 am

the 11th hour begins at 3:14 pm and ends at 4:01 pm

the 18th hour begins at 10:51 pm and ends at 12:03 am the next day (Thursday).

If you are in the southern hemisphere, then reverse the daylight and night tables (and read the hours from the bottoms of the columns instead of the tops). Thus, if you are located at 37° south latitude, then during the week of January 1st through 7th:

the 4th hour begins at 8:27 am and ends at 9:38 am
the 11th hour begins at 4:53 pm and ends at 6:04 pm
the 18th hour begins at 11:16 pm and ends at 12:03 am the next day (Thursday)

The times listed in the Planetary Hours Tables are Local Mean Time (LMT), which is the time read on a sundial adjusted for the Sun's daily speed (which varies from month to month throughout the year).* However, unless you are located exactly on one of the world's Standard Time meridians (which are multiples of 15°), to convert the times given in the tables to the Standard Time of your location you must add four minutes of time for each degree of longitude you are west of your Standard Time meridian; or subtract four minutes of time for each degree of longitude you are east of your Standard Time meridian. Examples:

Manchester is located at 2° 15' west of the Greenwich (0°) Standard Time meridian, therefore 9 minutes of time (2¼ x 4) must be added to the times listed in the Planetary Hours tables to obtain Standard Time.

Chicago is located at 87° W 39', which is 2° 21' east of the 90th meridian, therefore 9 minutes 24 seconds (which we round off to 9 minutes) must be subtracted from the times listed in the Planetary Hours tables to obtain Standard Time.

Melbourne is located at 144° E 58', which is 5° 2' west of the 150th meridian, therefore 20 minutes 8 seconds (which we round off to 20 minutes) must be added to the times listed in the Planetary Hours tables to obtain Standard Time.

---

* For the technically minded, the LMT = 15 x (the Sun's Right Ascension – the Right Ascension of the Midheaven) – the Equation of Time. The Equation of Time varies depending on the time of year: +17 minutes in November and –13 minutes in February (but it's not a sine wave – it has minor peaks of +4 in May and –6 in July).

Finally, if Daylight Saving Time or Summertime is in effect, then you must add one hour to the Standard Time to obtain clock time. As of this writing, Daylight Saving Time is in effect in North America from the second Sunday in March until the first Sunday in November; and Summertime is in effect in the European Union from the last Sunday in March until the last Sunday in October.

Table of Planetary Hours Rulers

Hour	Sunday	Monday	Tuesday	Wednesday	Thursday	Friday	Saturday
1	Sun	Moon	Mars	Merc	Jup	Ven	Sat
2	Ven	Sat	Sun	Moon	Mars	Merc	Jup
3	Merc	Jup	Ven	Sat	Sun	Moon	Mars
4	Moon	Mars	Merc	Jup	Ven	Sat	Sun
5	Sat	Sun	Moon	Mars	Merc	Jup	Ven
6	Jup	Ven	Sat	Sun	Moon	Mars	Merc
7	Mars	Merc	Jup	Ven	Sat	Sun	Moon
8	Sun	Moon	Mars	Merc	Jup	Ven	Sat
9	Ven	Sat	Sun	Moon	Mars	Merc	Jup
10	Merc	Jup	Ven	Sat	Sun	Moon	Mars
11	Moon	Mars	Merc	Jup	Ven	Sat	Sun
12	Sat	Sun	Moon	Mars	Merc	Jup	Ven
13	Jup	Ven	Sat	Sun	Moon	Mars	Merc
14	Mars	Merc	Jup	Ven	Sat	Sun	Moon
15	Sun	Moon	Mars	Merc	Jup	Ven	Sat
16	Ven	Sat	Sun	Moon	Mars	Merc	Jup
17	Merc	Jup	Ven	Sat	Sun	Moon	Mars
18	Moon	Mars	Merc	Jup	Ven	Sat	Sun
19	Sat	Sun	Moon	Mars	Merc	Jup	Ven
20	Jup	Ven	Sat	Sun	Moon	Mars	Merc
21	Mars	Merc	Jup	Ven	Sat	Sun	Moon
22	Sun	Moon	Mars	Merc	Jup	Ven	Sat
23	Ven	Sat	Sun	Moon	Mars	Merc	Jup
24	Merc	Jup	Ven	Sat	Sun	Moon	Mars

January 1st to 7th

DAYLIGHT HOURS - DAWN TO DUSK

LAT. N	1	2	3	4	5	6	7	8	9	10	11	12
0	6:04	7:04	8:04	9:04	10:04	11:04	12:04	1:04	2:04	3:04	4:04	5:04
5	6:12	7:11	8:09	9:08	10:06	11:05	12:04	1:02	2:01	2:59	3:58	4:56
10	6:20	7:18	8:15	9:12	10:09	11:06	12:04	1:01	1:58	2:55	3:52	4:49
15	6:29	7:25	8:21	9:16	10:12	11:08	12:04	12:59	1:55	2:51	3:46	4:42
20	6:39	7:33	8:27	9:21	10:15	11:09	12:04	12:58	1:52	2:46	3:40	4:34
25	6:49	7:41	8:34	9:26	10:19	11:11	12:04	12:56	1:48	2:41	3:33	4:26
28	6:55	7:46	8:38	9:29	10:21	11:12	12:04	12:55	1:46	2:38	3:29	4:21
31	7:02	7:52	8:42	9:33	10:23	11:13	12:04	12:54	1:44	2:34	3:25	4:15
34	7:09	7:58	8:47	9:36	10:25	11:14	12:04	12:53	1:42	2:31	3:20	4:09
37	7:17	8:05	8:53	9:40	10:28	11:16	12:04	12:51	1:39	2:27	3:14	4:02
40	7:26	8:12	8:58	9:45	10:31	11:17	12:04	12:50	1:36	2:22	3:09	3:55
42	7:32	8:18	9:03	9:48	10:33	11:18	12:04	12:49	1:34	2:19	3:04	3:50
44	7:39	8:23	9:07	9:51	10:35	11:19	12:04	12:48	1:32	2:16	3:00	3:44
46	7:47	8:29	9:12	9:55	10:38	11:21	12:04	12:46	1:29	2:12	2:55	3:38
48	7:55	8:36	9:18	9:59	10:41	11:22	12:04	12:45	1:26	2:08	2:49	3:31
50	8:04	8:44	9:24	10:04	10:44	11:24	12:04	12:44	1:23	2:03	2:43	3:23
52	8:13	8:52	9:30	10:08	10:47	11:25	12:04	12:42	1:20	1:59	2:37	3:15
54	8:25	9:01	9:38	10:14	10:51	11:27	12:04	12:40	1:16	1:53	2:29	3:06
56	8:37	9:12	9:46	10:20	10:55	11:29	12:04	12:38	1:12	1:47	2:21	2:55
58	8:52	9:24	9:56	10:28	11:00	11:32	12:04	12:35	1:07	1:39	2:11	2:43
S	13	14	15	16	17	18	19	20	21	22	23	24

NIGHT HOURS - DUSK TO DAWN

LAT. N	13	14	15	16	17	18	19	20	21	22	23	24
0	6:04	7:04	8:04	9:04	10:04	11:04	12:04	1:04	2:04	3:04	4:04	5:04
5	5:55	6:56	7:58	8:59	10:01	11:02	12:04	1:05	2:06	3:08	4:09	5:11
10	5:47	6:49	7:52	8:55	9:58	11:01	12:04	1:06	2:09	3:12	4:15	5:18
15	5:38	6:42	7:46	8:51	9:55	10:59	12:04	1:08	2:12	3:16	4:21	5:25
20	5:28	6:34	7:40	8:46	9:52	10:58	12:04	1:09	2:15	3:21	4:27	5:33
25	5:18	6:26	7:33	8:41	9:48	10:56	12:04	1:11	2:19	3:26	4:34	5:41
28	5:12	6:21	7:29	8:38	9:46	10:55	12:04	1:12	2:21	3:29	4:38	5:46
31	5:05	6:15	7:25	8:34	9:44	10:54	12:04	1:13	2:23	3:33	4:42	5:52
34	4:58	6:09	7:20	8:31	9:42	10:53	12:04	1:14	2:25	3:36	4:47	5:58
37	4:50	6:02	7:14	8:27	9:39	10:51	12:04	1:16	2:28	3:40	4:53	6:05
40	4:41	5:55	7:09	8:22	9:36	10:50	12:04	1:17	2:31	3:45	4:58	6:12
42	4:35	5:50	7:04	8:19	9:34	10:49	12:04	1:18	2:33	3:48	5:03	6:18
44	4:28	5:44	7:00	8:16	9:32	10:48	12:04	1:19	2:35	3:51	5:07	6:23
46	4:20	5:38	6:55	8:12	9:29	10:46	12:04	1:21	2:38	3:55	5:12	6:29
48	4:12	5:31	6:49	8:08	9:26	10:45	12:04	1:22	2:41	3:59	5:18	6:36
50	4:03	5:23	6:43	8:03	9:23	10:44	12:04	1:24	2:44	4:04	5:24	6:44
52	3:54	5:15	6:37	7:59	9:20	10:42	12:04	1:25	2:47	4:08	5:30	6:52
54	3:42	5:06	6:29	7:53	9:16	10:40	12:04	1:27	2:51	4:14	5:38	7:01
56	3:30	4:55	6:21	7:47	9:12	10:38	12:04	1:29	2:55	4:20	5:46	7:12
58	3:15	4:43	6:11	7:39	9:07	10:35	12:04	1:32	3:00	4:28	5:56	7:24
S	1	2	3	4	5	6	7	8	9	10	11	12

January 8th to 15th

DAYLIGHT HOURS - DAWN TO DUSK

LAT.

N	1	2	3	4	5	6	7	8	9	10	11	12
0	6:08	7:08	8:08	9:08	10:08	11:08	12:08	1:08	2:08	3:08	4:08	5:08
5	6:16	7:14	8:13	9:12	10:10	11:09	12:08	1:06	2:05	3:04	4:02	5:01
10	6:24	7:21	8:18	9:16	10:13	11:10	12:08	1:05	2:02	2:59	3:57	4:54
15	6:32	7:28	8:24	9:20	10:16	11:12	12:08	1:03	1:59	2:55	3:51	4:47
20	6:41	7:35	8:30	9:24	10:19	11:13	12:08	1:02	1:56	2:51	3:45	4:40
25	6:50	7:43	8:36	9:29	10:22	11:15	12:08	1:00	1:53	2:46	3:39	4:32
28	6:56	7:48	8:40	9:32	10:24	11:16	12:08	12:59	1:51	2:43	3:35	4:27
31	7:03	7:54	8:44	9:35	10:26	11:17	12:08	12:58	1:49	2:40	3:31	4:21
34	7:10	7:59	8:49	9:39	10:28	11:18	12:08	12:57	1:47	2:36	3:26	4:16
37	7:17	8:06	8:54	9:42	10:31	11:19	12:08	12:56	1:44	2:33	3:21	4:09
40	7:26	8:13	9:00	9:47	10:34	11:21	12:08	12:54	1:41	2:28	3:15	4:02
42	7:32	8:18	9:04	9:50	10:36	11:22	12:08	12:53	1:39	2:25	3:11	3:57
44	7:38	8:23	9:08	9:53	10:38	11:23	12:08	12:52	1:37	2:22	3:07	3:52
46	7:45	8:29	9:13	9:56	10:40	11:24	12:08	12:51	1:35	2:19	3:02	3:46
48	7:53	8:35	9:18	10:00	10:43	11:25	12:08	12:50	1:32	2:15	2:57	3:40
50	8:01	8:42	9:23	10:04	10:45	11:26	12:08	12:49	1:30	2:11	2:52	3:33
52	8:10	8:50	9:29	10:09	10:48	11:28	12:08	12:47	1:27	2:06	2:46	3:25
54	8:21	8:58	9:36	10:14	10:52	11:30	12:08	12:45	1:23	2:01	2:39	3:17
56	8:32	9:08	9:44	10:20	10:56	11:32	12:08	12:43	1:19	1:55	2:31	3:07
58	8:46	9:20	9:53	10:27	11:00	11:34	12:08	12:41	1:15	1:48	2:22	2:55
S	13	14	15	16	17	18	19	20	21	22	23	24

NIGHT HOURS - DUSK TO DAWN

LAT.

N	13	14	15	16	17	18	19	20	21	22	23	24
0	6:08	7:08	8:08	9:08	10:08	11:08	12:08	1:08	2:08	3:08	4:08	5:08
5	6:00	7:01	8:02	9:04	10:05	11:06	12:08	1:09	2:10	3:12	4:13	5:14
10	5:51	6:54	7:57	8:59	10:02	11:05	12:08	1:10	2:13	3:16	4:18	5:21
15	5:43	6:47	7:51	8:55	9:59	11:03	12:08	1:12	2:16	3:20	4:24	5:28
20	5:34	6:40	7:45	8:51	9:56	11:02	12:08	1:13	2:19	3:24	4:30	5:35
25	5:25	6:32	7:39	8:46	9:53	11:00	12:08	1:15	2:22	3:29	4:36	5:43
28	5:19	6:27	7:35	8:43	9:51	10:59	12:08	1:16	2:24	3:32	4:40	5:48
31	5:12	6:21	7:31	8:40	9:49	10:58	12:08	1:17	2:26	3:35	4:44	5:54
34	5:05	6:16	7:26	8:36	9:47	10:57	12:08	1:18	2:28	3:39	4:49	5:59
37	4:58	6:09	7:21	8:33	9:44	10:56	12:08	1:19	2:31	3:42	4:54	6:06
40	4:49	6:02	7:15	8:28	9:41	10:54	12:08	1:21	2:34	3:47	5:00	6:13
42	4:43	5:57	7:11	8:25	9:39	10:53	12:08	1:22	2:36	3:50	5:04	6:18
44	4:37	5:52	7:07	8:22	9:37	10:52	12:08	1:23	2:38	3:53	5:08	6:23
46	4:30	5:46	7:02	8:19	9:35	10:51	12:08	1:24	2:40	3:56	5:13	6:29
48	4:22	5:40	6:57	8:15	9:32	10:50	12:08	1:25	2:43	4:00	5:18	6:35
50	4:14	5:33	6:52	8:11	9:30	10:49	12:08	1:26	2:45	4:04	5:23	6:42
52	4:05	5:25	6:46	8:06	9:27	10:47	12:08	1:28	2:48	4:09	5:29	6:50
54	3:54	5:17	6:39	8:01	9:23	10:45	12:08	1:30	2:52	4:14	5:36	6:58
56	3:43	5:07	6:31	7:55	9:19	10:43	12:08	1:32	2:56	4:20	5:44	7:08
58	3:29	4:55	6:22	7:48	9:15	10:41	12:08	1:34	3:00	4:27	5:53	7:20
S	1	2	3	4	5	6	7	8	9	10	11	12

January 16th to 23rd

DAYLIGHT HOURS - DAWN TO DUSK

LAT. N	1	2	3	4	5	6	7	8	9	10	11	12
0	6:10	7:10	8:10	9:10	10:10	11:10	12:10	1:10	2:10	3:10	4:10	5:10
5	6:17	7:16	8:14	9:13	10:12	11:11	12:10	1:08	2:07	3:06	4:05	5:03
10	6:24	7:22	8:19	9:17	10:14	11:12	12:10	1:07	2:05	3:02	4:00	4:57
15	6:32	7:28	8:25	9:21	10:17	11:13	12:10	1:06	2:02	2:58	3:54	4:51
20	6:40	7:35	8:30	9:25	10:20	11:15	12:10	1:04	1:59	2:54	3:49	4:44
25	6:49	7:42	8:36	9:29	10:23	11:16	12:10	1:03	1:56	2:50	3:43	4:37
28	6:55	7:47	8:40	9:32	10:25	11:17	12:10	1:02	1:54	2:47	3:39	4:32
31	7:01	7:52	8:44	9:35	10:27	11:18	12:10	1:01	1:52	2:44	3:35	4:27
34	7:07	7:57	8:48	9:38	10:29	11:19	12:10	1:00	1:50	2:41	3:31	4:22
37	7:14	8:03	8:53	9:42	10:31	11:20	12:10	12:59	1:48	2:37	3:27	4:16
40	7:22	8:10	8:58	9:46	10:34	11:22	12:10	12:57	1:45	2:33	3:21	4:09
42	7:27	8:14	9:01	9:48	10:35	11:22	12:10	12:57	1:44	2:31	3:18	4:05
44	7:33	8:19	9:05	9:51	10:37	11:23	12:10	12:56	1:42	2:28	3:14	4:00
46	7:39	8:24	9:09	9:54	10:39	11:24	12:10	12:55	1:40	2:25	3:10	3:55
48	7:46	8:30	9:14	9:58	10:42	11:26	12:10	12:53	1:37	2:21	3:05	3:49
50	7:54	8:36	9:19	10:02	10:44	11:27	12:10	12:52	1:35	2:17	3:00	3:43
52	8:02	8:43	9:25	10:06	10:47	11:28	12:10	12:51	1:32	2:13	2:54	3:36
54	8:11	8:51	9:31	10:10	10:50	11:30	12:10	12:49	1:29	2:09	2:48	3:28
56	8:22	9:00	9:38	10:16	10:54	11:32	12:10	12:47	1:25	2:03	2:41	3:19
58	8:34	9:10	9:46	10:22	10:58	11:34	12:10	12:45	1:21	1:57	2:33	3:09
S	13	14	15	16	17	18	19	20	21	22	23	24

NIGHT HOURS - DUSK TO DAWN

LAT. N	13	14	15	16	17	18	19	20	21	22	23	24
0	6:10	7:10	8:10	9:10	10:10	11:10	12:10	1:10	2:10	3:10	4:10	5:10
5	6:02	7:03	8:05	9:06	10:07	11:08	12:10	1:11	2:12	3:13	4:14	5:16
10	5:55	6:57	8:00	9:02	10:05	11:07	12:10	1:12	2:14	3:17	4:19	5:22
15	5:47	6:51	7:54	8:58	10:02	11:06	12:10	1:13	2:17	3:21	4:25	5:28
20	5:39	6:44	7:49	8:54	9:59	11:04	12:10	1:15	2:20	3:25	4:30	5:35
25	5:30	6:37	7:43	8:50	9:56	11:03	12:10	1:16	2:23	3:29	4:36	5:42
28	5:24	6:32	7:39	8:47	9:54	11:02	12:10	1:17	2:25	3:32	4:40	5:47
31	5:18	6:27	7:35	8:44	9:52	11:01	12:10	1:18	2:27	3:35	4:44	5:52
34	5:12	6:22	7:31	8:41	9:50	11:00	12:10	1:19	2:29	3:38	4:48	5:57
37	5:05	6:16	7:27	8:37	9:48	10:59	12:10	1:20	2:31	3:42	4:53	6:03
40	4:57	6:09	7:21	8:33	9:45	10:57	12:10	1:22	2:34	3:46	4:58	6:10
42	4:52	6:05	7:18	8:31	9:44	10:57	12:10	1:22	2:35	3:48	5:01	6:14
44	4:46	6:00	7:14	8:28	9:42	10:56	12:10	1:23	2:37	3:51	5:05	6:19
46	4:40	5:55	7:10	8:25	9:40	10:55	12:10	1:24	2:39	3:54	5:09	6:24
48	4:33	5:49	7:05	8:21	9:37	10:53	12:10	1:26	2:42	3:58	5:14	6:30
50	4:25	5:43	7:00	8:17	9:35	10:52	12:10	1:27	2:44	4:02	5:19	6:36
52	4:17	5:36	6:54	8:13	9:32	10:51	12:10	1:28	2:47	4:06	5:25	6:43
54	4:08	5:28	6:48	8:09	9:29	10:49	12:10	1:30	2:50	4:10	5:31	6:51
56	3:57	5:19	6:41	8:03	9:25	10:47	12:10	1:32	2:54	4:16	5:38	7:00
58	3:45	5:09	6:33	7:57	9:21	10:45	12:10	1:34	2:58	4:22	5:46	7:10
S	1	2	3	4	5	6	7	8	9	10	11	12

January 24th to 31st

DAYLIGHT HOURS - DAWN TO DUSK

LAT. N	1	2	3	4	5	6	7	8	9	10	11	12
0	6:12	7:12	8:12	9:12	10:12	11:12	12:12	1:12	2:12	3:12	4:12	5:12
5	6:18	7:17	8:16	9:15	10:14	11:13	12:12	1:10	2:09	3:08	4:07	5:06
10	6:25	7:23	8:20	9:18	10:16	11:14	12:12	1:09	2:07	3:05	4:03	5:00
15	6:32	7:28	8:25	9:22	10:18	11:15	12:12	1:08	2:05	3:01	3:58	4:55
20	6:39	7:35	8:30	9:25	10:21	11:16	12:12	1:07	2:02	2:58	3:53	4:48
25	6:47	7:41	8:35	9:29	10:23	11:17	12:12	1:06	2:00	2:54	3:48	4:42
28	6:52	7:45	8:39	9:32	10:25	11:18	12:12	1:05	1:58	2:51	3:44	4:38
31	6:57	7:50	8:42	9:34	10:27	11:19	12:12	1:04	1:56	2:49	3:41	4:33
34	7:03	7:55	8:46	9:37	10:29	11:20	12:12	1:03	1:54	2:46	3:37	4:28
37	7:09	8:00	8:50	9:40	10:31	11:21	12:12	1:02	1:52	2:43	3:33	4:23
40	7:16	8:05	8:55	9:44	10:33	11:22	12:12	1:01	1:50	2:39	3:28	4:18
42	7:21	8:09	8:58	9:46	10:35	11:23	12:12	1:00	1:48	2:37	3:25	4:14
44	7:26	8:14	9:01	9:49	10:36	11:24	12:12	12:59	1:47	2:34	3:22	4:09
46	7:32	8:18	9:05	9:52	10:38	11:25	12:12	12:58	1:45	2:31	3:18	4:05
48	7:38	8:23	9:09	9:55	10:40	11:26	12:12	12:57	1:43	2:28	3:14	4:00
50	7:45	8:29	9:14	9:58	10:43	11:27	12:12	12:56	1:40	2:25	3:09	3:54
52	7:52	8:35	9:18	10:02	10:45	11:28	12:12	12:55	1:38	2:21	3:05	3:48
54	8:00	8:42	9:24	10:06	10:48	11:30	12:12	12:53	1:35	2:17	2:59	3:41
56	8:09	8:50	9:30	10:10	10:51	11:31	12:12	12:52	1:32	2:13	2:53	3:33
58	8:20	8:58	9:37	10:16	10:54	11:33	12:12	12:50	1:29	2:07	2:46	3:25
S	13	14	15	16	17	18	19	20	21	22	23	24

NIGHT HOURS - DUSK TO DAWN

LAT. N	13	14	15	16	17	18	19	20	21	22	23	24
0	6:12	7:12	8:12	9:12	10:12	11:12	12:12	1:12	2:12	3:12	4:12	5:12
5	6:05	7:06	8:07	9:08	10:09	11:10	12:12	1:13	2:14	3:15	4:16	5:17
10	5:58	7:00	8:03	9:05	10:07	11:09	12:12	1:14	2:16	3:18	4:20	5:23
15	5:51	6:55	7:58	9:01	10:05	11:08	12:12	1:15	2:18	3:22	4:25	5:28
20	5:44	6:48	7:53	8:58	10:02	11:07	12:12	1:16	2:21	3:25	4:30	5:35
25	5:36	6:42	7:48	8:54	10:00	11:06	12:12	1:17	2:23	3:29	4:35	5:41
28	5:31	6:38	7:44	8:51	9:58	11:05	12:12	1:18	2:25	3:32	4:39	5:45
31	5:26	6:33	7:41	8:49	9:56	11:04	12:12	1:19	2:27	3:34	4:42	5:50
34	5:20	6:28	7:37	8:46	9:54	11:03	12:12	1:20	2:29	3:37	4:46	5:55
37	5:14	6:23	7:33	8:43	9:52	11:02	12:12	1:21	2:31	3:40	4:50	6:00
40	5:07	6:18	7:28	8:39	9:50	11:01	12:12	1:22	2:33	3:44	4:55	6:05
42	5:02	6:14	7:25	8:37	9:48	11:00	12:12	1:23	2:35	3:46	4:58	6:09
44	4:57	6:09	7:22	8:34	9:47	10:59	12:12	1:24	2:36	3:49	5:01	6:14
46	4:51	6:05	7:18	8:31	9:45	10:58	12:12	1:25	2:38	3:52	5:05	6:18
48	4:45	6:00	7:14	8:28	9:43	10:57	12:12	1:26	2:40	3:55	5:09	6:23
50	4:38	5:54	7:09	8:25	9:40	10:56	12:12	1:27	2:43	3:58	5:14	6:29
52	4:31	5:48	7:05	8:21	9:38	10:55	12:12	1:28	2:45	4:02	5:18	6:35
54	4:23	5:41	6:59	8:17	9:35	10:53	12:12	1:30	2:48	4:06	5:24	6:42
56	4:14	5:33	6:53	8:13	9:32	10:52	12:12	1:31	2:51	4:10	5:30	6:50
58	4:03	5:25	6:46	8:07	9:29	10:50	12:12	1:33	2:54	4:16	5:37	6:58
S	1	2	3	4	5	6	7	8	9	10	11	12

February 1st to 7th

DAYLIGHT HOURS - DAWN TO DUSK

LAT. N	1	2	3	4	5	6	7	8	9	10	11	12
0	6:13	7:13	8:13	9:13	10:13	11:13	12:13	1:13	2:13	3:13	4:13	5:13
5	6:18	7:17	8:16	9:15	10:14	11:13	12:13	1:12	2:11	3:10	4:09	5:08
10	6:24	7:22	8:20	9:18	10:16	11:14	12:13	1:11	2:09	3:07	4:05	5:03
15	6:31	7:28	8:25	9:22	10:19	11:16	12:13	1:09	2:06	3:03	4:00	4:57
20	6:37	7:33	8:29	9:25	10:21	11:17	12:13	1:08	2:04	3:00	3:56	4:52
25	6:44	7:39	8:34	9:28	10:23	11:18	12:13	1:07	2:02	2:57	3:51	4:46
28	6:48	7:42	8:36	9:30	10:24	11:19	12:13	1:07	2:01	2:55	3:49	4:43
31	6:53	7:46	8:40	9:33	10:26	11:19	12:13	1:06	1:59	2:52	3:45	4:39
34	6:58	7:51	8:43	9:35	10:28	11:20	12:13	1:05	1:57	2:50	3:42	4:34
37	7:04	7:55	8:47	9:38	10:30	11:21	12:13	1:04	1:55	2:47	3:38	4:30
40	7:10	8:00	8:51	9:41	10:32	11:22	12:13	1:03	1:53	2:44	3:34	4:25
42	7:14	8:04	8:53	9:43	10:33	11:23	12:13	1:02	1:52	2:42	3:32	4:21
44	7:18	8:07	8:56	9:45	10:35	11:24	12:13	1:02	1:51	2:40	3:29	4:18
46	7:23	8:12	9:00	9:48	10:36	11:24	12:13	1:01	1:49	2:37	3:25	4:13
48	7:29	8:16	9:03	9:51	10:38	11:25	12:13	1:00	1:47	2:34	3:22	4:09
50	7:35	8:21	9:07	9:54	10:40	11:26	12:13	12:59	1:45	2:31	3:18	4:04
52	7:41	8:26	9:11	9:57	10:42	11:27	12:13	12:58	1:43	2:28	3:14	3:59
54	7:48	8:32	9:16	10:00	10:44	11:28	12:13	12:57	1:41	2:25	3:09	3:53
56	7:56	8:39	9:21	10:04	10:47	11:30	12:13	12:55	1:38	2:21	3:04	3:46
58	8:05	8:46	9:27	10:09	10:50	11:31	12:13	12:54	1:35	2:16	2:58	3:39
S	13	14	15	16	17	18	19	20	21	22	23	24

NIGHT HOURS - DUSK TO DAWN

LAT. N	13	14	15	16	17	18	19	20	21	22	23	24
0	6:13	7:13	8:13	9:13	10:13	11:13	12:13	1:13	2:13	3:13	4:13	5:13
5	6:07	7:08	8:09	9:10	10:11	11:12	12:13	1:13	2:14	3:15	4:16	5:17
10	6:01	7:03	8:05	9:07	10:09	11:11	12:13	1:14	2:16	3:18	4:20	5:22
15	5:54	6:57	8:00	9:03	10:06	11:09	12:13	1:16	2:19	3:22	4:25	5:28
20	5:48	6:52	7:56	9:00	10:04	11:08	12:13	1:17	2:21	3:25	4:29	5:33
25	5:41	6:46	7:51	8:57	10:02	11:07	12:13	1:18	2:23	3:28	4:34	5:39
28	5:37	6:43	7:49	8:55	10:01	11:07	12:13	1:19	2:24	3:30	4:36	5:42
31	5:32	6:39	7:45	8:52	9:59	11:06	12:13	1:19	2:26	3:33	4:40	5:46
34	5:27	6:34	7:42	8:50	9:57	11:05	12:13	1:20	2:28	3:35	4:43	5:51
37	5:21	6:30	7:38	8:47	9:55	11:04	12:13	1:21	2:30	3:38	4:47	5:55
40	5:15	6:25	7:34	8:44	9:53	11:03	12:13	1:22	2:32	3:41	4:51	6:00
42	5:11	6:21	7:32	8:42	9:52	11:02	12:13	1:23	2:33	3:43	4:53	6:04
44	5:07	6:18	7:29	8:40	9:51	11:02	12:13	1:24	2:34	3:45	4:56	6:07
46	5:02	6:13	7:25	8:37	9:49	11:01	12:13	1:24	2:36	3:48	5:00	6:12
48	4:56	6:09	7:22	8:34	9:47	11:00	12:13	1:25	2:38	3:51	5:03	6:16
50	4:50	6:04	7:18	8:31	9:45	10:59	12:13	1:26	2:40	3:54	5:07	6:21
52	4:44	5:59	7:14	8:28	9:43	10:58	12:13	1:27	2:42	3:57	5:11	6:26
54	4:37	5:53	7:09	8:25	9:41	10:57	12:13	1:28	2:44	4:00	5:16	6:32
56	4:29	5:46	7:04	8:21	9:38	10:55	12:13	1:30	2:47	4:04	5:21	6:39
58	4:20	5:39	6:58	8:16	9:35	10:54	12:13	1:31	2:50	4:09	5:27	6:46
S	1	2	3	4	5	6	7	8	9	10	11	12

February 8th to 14th

DAYLIGHT HOURS - DAWN TO DUSK

LAT. N	1	2	3	4	5	6	7	8	9	10	11	12
0	6:14	7:14	8:14	9:14	10:14	11:14	12:14	1:14	2:14	3:14	4:14	5:14
5	6:19	7:18	8:17	9:16	10:15	11:14	12:14	1:13	2:12	3:11	4:10	5:09
10	6:24	7:22	8:20	9:19	10:17	11:15	12:14	1:12	2:10	3:08	4:07	5:05
15	6:29	7:26	8:24	9:21	10:19	11:16	12:14	1:11	2:08	3:06	4:03	5:01
20	6:35	7:31	8:28	9:24	10:21	11:17	12:14	1:10	2:06	3:03	3:59	4:56
25	6:41	7:36	8:32	9:27	10:23	11:18	12:14	1:09	2:04	3:00	3:55	4:51
28	6:44	7:39	8:34	9:29	10:24	11:19	12:14	1:08	2:03	2:58	3:53	4:48
31	6:48	7:43	8:37	9:31	10:25	11:19	12:14	1:08	2:02	2:56	3:50	4:44
34	6:53	7:46	8:40	9:33	10:27	11:20	12:14	1:07	2:00	2:54	3:47	4:41
37	6:57	7:50	8:43	9:35	10:28	11:21	12:14	1:06	1:59	2:52	3:44	4:37
40	7:02	7:54	8:46	9:38	10:30	11:22	12:14	1:05	1:57	2:49	3:41	4:33
42	7:06	7:57	8:49	9:40	10:31	11:22	12:14	1:05	1:56	2:47	3:38	4:30
44	7:10	8:01	8:51	9:42	10:32	11:23	12:14	1:04	1:55	2:45	3:36	4:26
46	7:14	8:04	8:54	9:44	10:34	11:24	12:14	1:03	1:53	2:43	3:33	4:23
48	7:19	8:08	8:57	9:46	10:35	11:24	12:14	1:03	1:52	2:41	3:30	4:19
50	7:24	8:12	9:00	9:49	10:37	11:25	12:14	1:02	1:50	2:38	3:27	4:15
52	7:29	8:16	9:04	9:51	10:39	11:26	12:14	1:01	1:48	2:36	3:23	4:11
54	7:35	8:21	9:08	9:54	10:41	11:27	12:14	1:00	1:46	2:33	3:19	4:06
56	7:42	8:27	9:12	9:58	10:43	11:28	12:14	12:59	1:44	2:29	3:15	4:00
58	7:49	8:33	9:17	10:01	10:45	11:29	12:14	12:58	1:42	2:26	3:10	3:54
S	13	14	15	16	17	18	19	20	21	22	23	24

NIGHT HOURS - DUSK TO DAWN

LAT. N	13	14	15	16	17	18	19	20	21	22	23	24
0	6:14	7:14	8:14	9:14	10:14	11:14	12:14	1:14	2:14	3:14	4:14	5:14
5	6:08	7:09	8:10	9:11	10:12	11:13	12:14	1:14	2:15	3:16	4:17	5:18
10	6:03	7:05	8:07	9:08	10:10	11:12	12:14	1:15	2:17	3:19	4:20	5:22
15	5:58	7:01	8:03	9:06	10:08	11:11	12:14	1:16	2:19	3:21	4:24	5:26
20	5:52	6:56	7:59	9:03	10:06	11:10	12:14	1:17	2:21	3:24	4:28	5:31
25	5:46	6:51	7:55	9:00	10:04	11:09	12:14	1:18	2:23	3:27	4:32	5:36
28	5:43	6:48	7:53	8:58	10:03	11:08	12:14	1:19	2:24	3:29	4:34	5:39
31	5:39	6:44	7:50	8:56	10:02	11:08	12:14	1:19	2:25	3:31	4:37	5:43
34	5:34	6:41	7:47	8:54	10:00	11:07	12:14	1:20	2:27	3:33	4:40	5:46
37	5:30	6:37	7:44	8:52	9:59	11:06	12:14	1:21	2:28	3:35	4:43	5:50
40	5:25	6:33	7:41	8:49	9:57	11:05	12:14	1:22	2:30	3:38	4:46	5:54
42	5:21	6:30	7:38	8:47	9:56	11:05	12:14	1:22	2:31	3:40	4:49	5:57
44	5:17	6:26	7:36	8:45	9:55	11:04	12:14	1:23	2:32	3:42	4:51	6:01
46	5:13	6:23	7:33	8:43	9:53	11:03	12:14	1:24	2:34	3:44	4:54	6:04
48	5:08	6:19	7:30	8:41	9:52	11:03	12:14	1:24	2:35	3:46	4:57	6:08
50	5:03	6:15	7:27	8:38	9:50	11:02	12:14	1:25	2:37	3:49	5:00	6:12
52	4:58	6:11	7:23	8:36	9:48	11:01	12:14	1:26	2:39	3:51	5:04	6:16
54	4:52	6:06	7:19	8:33	9:46	11:00	12:14	1:27	2:41	3:54	5:08	6:21
56	4:45	6:00	7:15	8:29	9:44	10:59	12:14	1:28	2:43	3:58	5:12	6:27
58	4:38	5:54	7:10	8:26	9:42	10:58	12:14	1:29	2:45	4:01	5:17	6:33
S	1	2	3	4	5	6	7	8	9	10	11	12

February 15th to 21st

DAYLIGHT HOURS - DAWN TO DUSK

LAT. N	1	2	3	4	5	6	7	8	9	10	11	12
0	6:14	7:14	8:14	9:14	10:14	11:14	12:14	1:14	2:14	3:14	4:14	5:14
5	6:18	7:17	8:16	9:16	10:15	11:14	12:14	1:13	2:12	3:11	4:11	5:10
10	6:22	7:21	8:19	9:18	10:16	11:15	12:14	1:12	2:11	3:09	4:08	5:06
15	6:26	7:24	8:22	9:20	10:18	11:16	12:14	1:11	2:09	3:07	4:05	5:03
20	6:31	7:28	8:25	9:22	10:19	11:16	12:14	1:11	2:08	3:05	4:02	4:59
25	6:36	7:32	8:28	9:25	10:21	11:17	12:14	1:10	2:06	3:02	3:59	4:55
28	6:39	7:35	8:31	9:26	10:22	11:18	12:14	1:09	2:05	3:01	3:56	4:52
31	6:42	7:38	8:33	9:28	10:23	11:18	12:14	1:09	2:04	2:59	3:54	4:49
34	6:46	7:41	8:35	9:30	10:24	11:19	12:14	1:08	2:03	2:57	3:52	4:46
37	6:50	7:44	8:38	9:32	10:26	11:20	12:14	1:07	2:01	2:55	3:49	4:43
40	6:54	7:47	8:40	9:34	10:27	11:20	12:14	1:07	2:00	2:53	3:47	4:40
42	6:57	7:50	8:42	9:35	10:28	11:21	12:14	1:06	1:59	2:52	3:45	4:37
44	7:00	7:52	8:45	9:37	10:29	11:21	12:14	1:06	1:58	2:50	3:42	4:35
46	7:04	7:55	8:47	9:39	10:30	11:22	12:14	1:05	1:57	2:48	3:40	4:32
48	7:07	7:58	8:49	9:40	10:31	11:22	12:14	1:05	1:56	2:47	3:38	4:29
50	7:11	8:02	8:52	9:42	10:33	11:23	12:14	1:04	1:54	2:45	3:35	4:25
52	7:16	8:05	8:55	9:45	10:34	11:24	12:14	1:03	1:53	2:42	3:32	4:22
54	7:20	8:09	8:58	9:47	10:36	11:25	12:14	1:02	1:51	2:40	3:29	4:18
56	7:26	8:14	9:02	9:50	10:38	11:26	12:14	1:01	1:49	2:37	3:25	4:13
58	7:32	8:19	9:06	9:53	10:40	11:27	12:14	1:00	1:47	2:34	3:21	4:08
S	13	14	15	16	17	18	19	20	21	22	23	24

NIGHT HOURS - DUSK TO DAWN

LAT. N	13	14	15	16	17	18	19	20	21	22	23	24
0	6:14	7:14	8:14	9:14	10:14	11:14	12:14	1:14	2:14	3:14	4:14	5:14
5	6:09	7:10	8:11	9:11	10:12	11:13	12:14	1:14	2:15	3:16	4:16	5:17
10	6:05	7:06	8:08	9:09	10:11	11:12	12:14	1:15	2:16	3:18	4:19	5:21
15	6:01	7:03	8:05	9:07	10:09	11:11	12:14	1:16	2:18	3:20	4:22	5:24
20	5:56	6:59	8:02	9:05	10:08	11:11	12:14	1:16	2:19	3:22	4:25	5:28
25	5:51	6:55	7:59	9:02	10:06	11:10	12:14	1:17	2:21	3:25	4:28	5:32
28	5:48	6:52	7:56	9:01	10:05	11:09	12:14	1:18	2:22	3:26	4:31	5:35
31	5:45	6:49	7:54	8:59	10:04	11:09	12:14	1:18	2:23	3:28	4:33	5:38
34	5:41	6:46	7:52	8:57	10:03	11:08	12:14	1:19	2:24	3:30	4:35	5:41
37	5:37	6:43	7:49	8:55	10:01	11:07	12:14	1:20	2:26	3:32	4:38	5:44
40	5:33	6:40	7:47	8:53	10:00	11:07	12:14	1:20	2:27	3:34	4:40	5:47
42	5:30	6:37	7:45	8:52	9:59	11:06	12:14	1:21	2:28	3:35	4:42	5:50
44	5:27	6:35	7:42	8:50	9:58	11:06	12:14	1:21	2:29	3:37	4:45	5:52
46	5:23	6:32	7:40	8:48	9:57	11:05	12:14	1:22	2:30	3:39	4:47	5:55
48	5:20	6:29	7:38	8:47	9:56	11:05	12:14	1:22	2:31	3:40	4:49	5:58
50	5:16	6:25	7:35	8:45	9:54	11:04	12:14	1:23	2:33	3:42	4:52	6:02
52	5:11	6:22	7:32	8:42	9:53	11:03	12:14	1:24	2:34	3:45	4:55	6:05
54	5:07	6:18	7:29	8:40	9:51	11:02	12:14	1:25	2:36	3:47	4:58	6:09
56	5:01	6:13	7:25	8:37	9:49	11:01	12:14	1:26	2:38	3:50	5:02	6:14
58	4:55	6:08	7:21	8:34	9:47	11:00	12:14	1:27	2:40	3:53	5:06	6:19
S	1	2	3	4	5	6	7	8	9	10	11	12

February 22nd to 28th or 29th

DAYLIGHT HOURS - DAWN TO DUSK

LAT. N	1	2	3	4	5	6	7	8	9	10	11	12
0	6:13	7:13	8:13	9:13	10:13	11:13	12:13	1:13	2:13	3:13	4:13	5:13
5	6:16	7:15	8:15	9:14	10:14	11:13	12:13	1:12	2:11	3:11	4:10	5:10
10	6:19	7:18	8:17	9:16	10:15	11:14	12:13	1:11	2:10	3:09	4:08	5:07
15	6:23	7:21	8:19	9:18	10:16	11:14	12:13	1:11	2:09	3:07	4:06	5:04
20	6:26	7:24	8:22	9:19	10:17	11:15	12:13	1:10	2:08	3:06	4:03	5:01
25	6:30	7:27	8:24	9:21	10:18	11:15	12:13	1:10	2:07	3:04	4:01	4:58
28	6:32	7:29	8:26	9:22	10:19	11:16	12:13	1:09	2:06	3:03	3:59	4:56
31	6:35	7:31	8:28	9:24	10:20	11:16	12:13	1:09	2:05	3:01	3:57	4:54
34	6:38	7:34	8:29	9:25	10:21	11:17	12:13	1:08	2:04	3:00	3:56	4:51
37	6:41	7:36	8:31	9:27	10:22	11:17	12:13	1:08	2:03	2:58	3:54	4:49
40	6:44	7:39	8:34	9:28	10:23	11:18	12:13	1:07	2:02	2:57	3:51	4:46
42	6:46	7:41	8:35	9:29	10:24	11:18	12:13	1:07	2:01	2:56	3:50	4:44
44	6:49	7:43	8:37	9:31	10:25	11:19	12:13	1:06	2:00	2:54	3:48	4:42
46	6:51	7:45	8:38	9:32	10:26	11:19	12:13	1:06	2:00	2:53	3:47	4:40
48	6:54	7:47	8:40	9:33	10:26	11:19	12:13	1:06	1:59	2:52	3:45	4:38
50	6:57	7:50	8:42	9:35	10:27	11:20	12:13	1:05	1:58	2:50	3:43	4:35
52	7:01	7:53	8:45	9:37	10:29	11:21	12:13	1:04	1:56	2:48	3:40	4:32
54	7:05	7:56	8:47	9:39	10:30	11:21	12:13	1:04	1:55	2:47	3:38	4:29
56	7:09	7:59	8:50	9:41	10:31	11:22	12:13	1:03	1:54	2:44	3:35	4:26
58	7:13	8:03	8:53	9:43	10:33	11:23	12:13	1:02	1:52	2:42	3:32	4:22
S	13	14	15	16	17	18	19	20	21	22	23	24

NIGHT HOURS - DUSK TO DAWN

LAT. N	13	14	15	16	17	18	19	20	21	22	23	24
0	6:13	7:13	8:13	9:13	10:13	11:13	12:13	1:13	2:13	3:13	4:13	5:13
5	6:09	7:10	8:10	9:11	10:11	11:12	12:13	1:13	2:14	3:14	4:15	5:15
10	6:06	7:07	8:08	9:09	10:10	11:11	12:13	1:14	2:15	3:16	4:17	5:18
15	6:02	7:04	8:06	9:07	10:09	11:11	12:13	1:14	2:16	3:18	4:19	5:21
20	5:59	7:01	8:03	9:06	10:08	11:10	12:13	1:15	2:17	3:19	4:22	5:24
25	5:55	6:58	8:01	9:04	10:07	11:10	12:13	1:15	2:18	3:21	4:24	5:27
28	5:53	6:56	7:59	9:03	10:06	11:09	12:13	1:16	2:19	3:22	4:26	5:29
31	5:50	6:54	7:57	9:01	10:05	11:09	12:13	1:16	2:20	3:24	4:28	5:31
34	5:47	6:51	7:56	9:00	10:04	11:08	12:13	1:17	2:21	3:25	4:29	5:34
37	5:44	6:49	7:54	8:58	10:03	11:08	12:13	1:17	2:22	3:27	4:31	5:36
40	5:41	6:46	7:51	8:57	10:02	11:07	12:13	1:18	2:23	3:28	4:34	5:39
42	5:39	6:44	7:50	8:56	10:01	11:07	12:13	1:18	2:24	3:29	4:35	5:41
44	5:36	6:42	7:48	8:54	10:00	11:06	12:13	1:19	2:25	3:31	4:37	5:43
46	5:34	6:40	7:47	8:53	10:00	11:06	12:13	1:19	2:26	3:32	4:38	5:45
48	5:31	6:38	7:45	8:52	9:59	11:06	12:13	1:19	2:26	3:33	4:40	5:47
50	5:28	6:35	7:43	8:50	9:58	11:05	12:13	1:20	2:27	3:35	4:42	5:50
52	5:24	6:32	7:40	8:48	9:56	11:04	12:13	1:21	2:29	3:37	4:45	5:53
54	5:21	6:29	7:38	8:47	9:55	11:04	12:13	1:21	2:30	3:39	4:47	5:56
56	5:16	6:26	7:35	8:44	9:54	11:03	12:13	1:22	2:31	3:41	4:50	5:59
58	5:12	6:22	7:32	8:42	9:52	11:02	12:13	1:23	2:33	3:43	4:53	6:03
S	1	2	3	4	5	6	7	8	9	10	11	12

March 1st to 7th

DAYLIGHT HOURS - DAWN TO DUSK

LAT. N	1	2	3	4	5	6	7	8	9	10	11	12
0	6:11	7:11	8:11	9:11	10:11	11:11	12:11	1:11	2:11	3:11	4:11	5:11
5	6:13	7:12	8:12	9:12	10:11	11:11	12:11	1:10	2:10	3:09	4:09	5:09
10	6:15	7:14	8:14	9:13	10:12	11:11	12:11	1:10	2:09	3:08	4:07	5:07
15	6:18	7:16	8:15	9:14	10:13	11:12	12:11	1:09	2:08	3:07	4:06	5:05
20	6:20	7:19	8:17	9:15	10:14	11:12	12:11	1:09	2:07	3:06	4:04	5:02
25	6:23	7:21	8:19	9:17	10:15	11:13	12:11	1:08	2:06	3:04	4:02	5:00
28	6:25	7:22	8:20	9:18	10:15	11:13	12:11	1:08	2:06	3:03	4:01	4:59
31	6:27	7:24	8:21	9:19	10:16	11:13	12:11	1:08	2:05	3:02	4:00	4:57
34	6:29	7:26	8:23	9:20	10:17	11:14	12:11	1:08	2:05	3:02	3:59	4:56
37	6:31	7:27	8:24	9:21	10:17	11:14	12:11	1:07	2:04	3:00	3:57	4:54
40	6:33	7:29	8:25	9:22	10:18	11:14	12:11	1:07	2:03	2:59	3:56	4:52
42	6:35	7:31	8:27	9:23	10:19	11:15	12:11	1:07	2:02	2:58	3:54	4:50
44	6:36	7:32	8:28	9:23	10:19	11:15	12:11	1:06	2:02	2:58	3:53	4:49
46	6:38	7:34	8:29	9:24	10:20	11:15	12:11	1:06	2:01	2:57	3:52	4:47
48	6:40	7:35	8:30	9:25	10:20	11:15	12:11	1:06	2:01	2:56	3:51	4:46
50	6:42	7:37	8:32	9:26	10:21	11:16	12:11	1:05	2:00	2:55	3:49	4:44
52	6:45	7:39	8:33	9:28	10:22	11:16	12:11	1:05	1:59	2:53	3:48	4:42
54	6:47	7:41	8:35	9:29	10:23	11:17	12:11	1:04	1:58	2:52	3:46	4:40
56	6:50	7:44	8:37	9:30	10:24	11:17	12:11	1:04	1:57	2:51	3:44	4:37
58	6:53	7:46	8:39	9:32	10:25	11:18	12:11	1:03	1:56	2:49	3:42	4:35
S	13	14	15	16	17	18	19	20	21	22	23	24

NIGHT HOURS - DUSK TO DAWN

LAT. N	13	14	15	16	17	18	19	20	21	22	23	24
0	6:11	7:11	8:11	9:11	10:11	11:11	12:11	1:11	2:11	3:11	4:11	5:11
5	6:08	7:09	8:09	9:09	10:10	11:10	12:11	1:11	2:11	3:12	4:12	5:12
10	6:06	7:07	8:07	9:08	10:09	11:10	12:11	1:11	2:12	3:13	4:14	5:14
15	6:03	7:05	8:06	9:07	10:08	11:09	12:11	1:12	2:13	3:14	4:15	5:16
20	6:01	7:02	8:04	9:06	10:07	11:09	12:11	1:12	2:14	3:15	4:17	5:19
25	5:58	7:00	8:02	9:04	10:06	11:08	12:11	1:13	2:15	3:17	4:19	5:21
28	5:56	6:59	8:01	9:03	10:06	11:08	12:11	1:13	2:15	3:18	4:20	5:22
31	5:54	6:57	8:00	9:02	10:05	11:08	12:11	1:13	2:16	3:19	4:21	5:24
34	5:53	6:56	7:59	9:02	10:05	11:08	12:11	1:14	2:17	3:20	4:23	5:26
37	5:50	6:54	7:57	9:00	10:04	11:07	12:11	1:14	2:17	3:21	4:24	5:27
40	5:48	6:52	7:56	8:59	10:03	11:07	12:11	1:14	2:18	3:22	4:25	5:29
42	5:46	6:50	7:54	8:58	10:02	11:07	12:11	1:15	2:19	3:23	4:27	5:31
44	5:45	6:49	7:53	8:58	10:02	11:06	12:11	1:15	2:19	3:23	4:28	5:32
46	5:43	6:47	7:52	8:57	10:01	11:06	12:11	1:15	2:20	3:24	4:29	5:34
48	5:41	6:46	7:51	8:56	10:01	11:06	12:11	1:15	2:20	3:25	4:30	5:35
50	5:39	6:44	7:49	8:55	10:00	11:05	12:11	1:16	2:21	3:26	4:32	5:37
52	5:36	6:42	7:48	8:53	9:59	11:05	12:11	1:16	2:22	3:28	4:33	5:39
54	5:34	6:40	7:46	8:52	9:58	11:04	12:11	1:17	2:23	3:29	4:35	5:41
56	5:31	6:37	7:44	8:51	9:57	11:04	12:11	1:17	2:24	3:30	4:37	5:44
58	5:28	6:35	7:42	8:49	9:56	11:03	12:11	1:18	2:25	3:32	4:39	5:46
S	1	2	3	4	5	6	7	8	9	10	11	12

March 8th to 15th

DAYLIGHT HOURS - DAWN TO DUSK

LAT. N	1	2	3	4	5	6	7	8	9	10	11	12
0	6:09	7:09	8:09	9:09	10:09	11:09	12:09	1:09	2:09	3:09	4:09	5:09
5	6:10	7:10	8:09	9:09	10:09	11:09	12:09	1:08	2:08	3:08	4:08	5:07
10	6:11	7:11	8:10	9:10	10:09	11:09	12:09	1:08	2:08	3:07	4:07	5:06
15	6:12	7:12	8:11	9:10	10:10	11:09	12:09	1:08	2:07	3:07	4:06	5:05
20	6:14	7:13	8:12	9:11	10:10	11:09	12:09	1:08	2:07	3:06	4:05	5:04
25	6:15	7:14	8:13	9:12	10:11	11:10	12:09	1:07	2:06	3:05	4:04	5:03
28	6:16	7:15	8:14	9:12	10:11	11:10	12:09	1:07	2:06	3:05	4:04	5:02
31	6:17	7:16	8:14	9:13	10:11	11:10	12:09	1:07	2:06	3:04	4:03	5:01
34	6:18	7:16	8:15	9:13	10:12	11:10	12:09	1:07	2:05	3:04	4:02	5:01
37	6:19	7:17	8:16	9:14	10:12	11:10	12:09	1:07	2:05	3:03	4:01	5:00
40	6:20	7:18	8:16	9:14	10:12	11:10	12:09	1:07	2:05	3:03	4:01	4:59
42	6:21	7:19	8:17	9:15	10:13	11:11	12:09	1:06	2:04	3:02	4:00	4:58
44	6:22	7:20	8:18	9:15	10:13	11:11	12:09	1:06	2:04	3:02	3:59	4:57
46	6:23	7:21	8:18	9:16	10:13	11:11	12:09	1:06	2:04	3:01	3:59	4:56
48	6:24	7:22	8:19	9:16	10:14	11:11	12:09	1:06	2:03	3:01	3:58	4:55
50	6:25	7:23	8:20	9:17	10:14	11:11	12:09	1:06	2:03	3:00	3:57	4:55
52	6:27	7:24	8:21	9:18	10:15	11:12	12:09	1:06	2:02	2:59	3:56	4:53
54	6:28	7:25	8:21	9:18	10:15	11:12	12:09	1:05	2:02	2:59	3:56	4:52
56	6:29	7:26	8:22	9:19	10:15	11:12	12:09	1:05	2:02	2:58	3:55	4:51
58	6:31	7:27	8:24	9:20	10:16	11:12	12:09	1:05	2:01	2:57	3:53	4:50
S	13	14	15	16	17	18	19	20	21	22	23	24

NIGHT HOURS - DUSK TO DAWN

LAT. N	13	14	15	16	17	18	19	20	21	22	23	24
0	6:09	7:09	8:09	9:09	10:09	11:09	12:09	1:09	2:09	3:09	4:09	5:09
5	6:07	7:07	8:08	9:08	10:08	11:08	12:09	1:09	2:09	3:09	4:09	5:10
10	6:06	7:06	8:07	9:07	10:08	11:08	12:09	1:09	2:09	3:10	4:10	5:11
15	6:05	7:05	8:06	9:07	10:07	11:08	12:09	1:09	2:10	3:10	4:11	5:12
20	6:03	7:04	8:05	9:06	10:07	11:08	12:09	1:09	2:10	3:11	4:12	5:13
25	6:02	7:03	8:04	9:05	10:06	11:07	12:09	1:10	2:11	3:12	4:13	5:14
28	6:01	7:02	8:04	9:05	10:06	11:07	12:09	1:10	2:11	3:12	4:14	5:15
31	6:00	7:01	8:03	9:04	10:06	11:07	12:09	1:10	2:11	3:13	4:14	5:16
34	5:59	7:01	8:02	9:04	10:05	11:07	12:09	1:10	2:12	3:13	4:15	5:16
37	5:58	7:00	8:01	9:03	10:05	11:07	12:09	1:10	2:12	3:14	4:16	5:17
40	5:57	6:59	8:01	9:03	10:05	11:07	12:09	1:10	2:12	3:14	4:16	5:18
42	5:56	6:58	8:00	9:02	10:04	11:06	12:09	1:11	2:13	3:15	4:17	5:19
44	5:55	6:57	7:59	9:02	10:04	11:06	12:09	1:11	2:13	3:15	4:18	5:20
46	5:54	6:56	7:59	9:01	10:04	11:06	12:09	1:11	2:13	3:16	4:18	5:21
48	5:53	6:55	7:58	9:01	10:03	11:06	12:09	1:11	2:14	3:16	4:19	5:22
50	5:52	6:55	7:57	9:00	10:03	11:06	12:09	1:11	2:14	3:17	4:20	5:23
52	5:50	6:53	7:56	8:59	10:02	11:06	12:09	1:12	2:15	3:18	4:21	5:24
54	5:49	6:52	7:56	8:59	10:02	11:05	12:09	1:12	2:15	3:18	4:21	5:25
56	5:48	6:51	7:55	8:58	10:02	11:05	12:09	1:12	2:15	3:19	4:22	5:26
58	5:46	6:50	7:53	8:57	10:01	11:05	12:09	1:12	2:16	3:20	4:24	5:27
S	1	2	3	4	5	6	7	8	9	10	11	12

March 16th to 23rd

DAYLIGHT HOURS - DAWN TO DUSK

LAT. N	1	2	3	4	5	6	7	8	9	10	11	12
0	6:07	7:07	8:07	9:07	10:07	11:07	12:07	1:07	2:07	3:07	4:07	5:07
5	6:07	7:07	8:07	9:07	10:07	11:07	12:07	1:06	2:06	3:06	4:06	5:06
10	6:07	7:07	8:07	9:07	10:07	11:07	12:07	1:06	2:06	3:06	4:06	5:06
15	6:07	7:07	8:07	9:07	10:07	11:07	12:07	1:06	2:06	3:06	4:06	5:06
20	6:07	7:07	8:07	9:07	10:07	11:07	12:07	1:06	2:06	3:06	4:06	5:06
25	6:07	7:07	8:07	9:07	10:07	11:07	12:07	1:06	2:06	3:06	4:06	5:06
28	6:07	7:07	8:07	9:07	10:07	11:07	12:07	1:06	2:06	3:06	4:06	5:06
31	6:07	7:07	8:07	9:07	10:07	11:07	12:07	1:06	2:06	3:06	4:06	5:06
34	6:07	7:07	8:07	9:07	10:07	11:07	12:07	1:06	2:06	3:06	4:06	5:06
37	6:08	7:07	8:07	9:07	10:07	11:07	12:07	1:06	2:06	3:06	4:06	5:06
40	6:08	7:08	8:07	9:07	10:07	11:07	12:07	1:06	2:06	3:06	4:06	5:05
42	6:08	7:08	8:07	9:07	10:07	11:07	12:07	1:06	2:06	3:06	4:06	5:05
44	6:08	7:08	8:07	9:07	10:07	11:07	12:07	1:06	2:06	3:06	4:06	5:05
46	6:08	7:08	8:08	9:07	10:07	11:07	12:07	1:06	2:06	3:06	4:05	5:05
48	6:08	7:08	8:08	9:07	10:07	11:07	12:07	1:06	2:06	3:06	4:05	5:05
50	6:08	7:08	8:08	9:07	10:07	11:07	12:07	1:06	2:06	3:06	4:05	5:05
52	6:08	7:08	8:08	9:07	10:07	11:07	12:07	1:06	2:06	3:06	4:05	5:05
54	6:09	7:08	8:08	9:08	10:07	11:07	12:07	1:06	2:06	3:05	4:05	5:05
56	6:09	7:08	8:08	9:08	10:07	11:07	12:07	1:06	2:06	3:05	4:05	5:05
58	6:09	7:08	8:08	9:08	10:07	11:07	12:07	1:06	2:06	3:05	4:05	5:05
S	13	14	15	16	17	18	19	20	21	22	23	24

NIGHT HOURS - DUSK TO DAWN

LAT. N	13	14	15	16	17	18	19	20	21	22	23	24
0	6:07	7:07	8:07	9:07	10:07	11:07	12:07	1:07	2:07	3:07	4:07	5:07
5	6:06	7:06	8:06	9:06	10:06	11:06	12:07	1:07	2:07	3:07	4:07	5:07
10	6:06	7:06	8:06	9:06	10:06	11:06	12:07	1:07	2:07	3:07	4:07	5:07
15	6:06	7:06	8:06	9:06	10:06	11:06	12:07	1:07	2:07	3:07	4:07	5:07
20	6:06	7:06	8:06	9:06	10:06	11:06	12:07	1:07	2:07	3:07	4:07	5:07
25	6:06	7:06	8:06	9:06	10:06	11:06	12:07	1:07	2:07	3:07	4:07	5:07
28	6:06	7:06	8:06	9:06	10:06	11:06	12:07	1:07	2:07	3:07	4:07	5:07
31	6:06	7:06	8:06	9:06	10:06	11:06	12:07	1:07	2:07	3:07	4:07	5:07
34	6:06	7:06	8:06	9:06	10:06	11:06	12:07	1:07	2:07	3:07	4:07	5:07
37	6:05	7:06	8:06	9:06	10:06	11:06	12:07	1:07	2:07	3:07	4:07	5:07
40	6:05	7:05	8:06	9:06	10:06	11:06	12:07	1:07	2:07	3:07	4:07	5:08
42	6:05	7:05	8:06	9:06	10:06	11:06	12:07	1:07	2:07	3:07	4:07	5:08
44	6:05	7:05	8:06	9:06	10:06	11:06	12:07	1:07	2:07	3:07	4:07	5:08
46	6:05	7:05	8:05	9:06	10:06	11:06	12:07	1:07	2:07	3:07	4:08	5:08
48	6:05	7:05	8:05	9:06	10:06	11:06	12:07	1:07	2:07	3:07	4:08	[illegible]
50	6:05	7:05	8:05	9:06	10:06	11:06	12:07	1:07	2:07	3:07	4:08	[illegible]
52	6:05	7:05	8:05	9:06	10:06	11:06	12:07	1:07	2:07	3:07	4:08	[illegible]
54	6:04	7:05	8:05	9:05	10:06	11:06	12:07	1:07	2:07	3:08	4:08	[illegible]
56	6:04	7:05	8:05	9:05	10:06	11:06	12:07	1:07	2:07	3:08	4:08	[illegible]
58	6:04	7:05	8:05	9:05	10:06	11:06	12:07	1:07	2:07	3:08	4:08	[illegible]
S	1	2	3	4	5	6	7	8	9	10	11	[illegible]

March 24th to 31st

DAYLIGHT HOURS - DAWN TO DUSK

LAT. N	1	2	3	4	5	6	7	8	9	10	11	12
0	6:04	7:04	8:04	9:04	10:04	11:04	12:04	1:04	2:04	3:04	4:04	5:04
5	6:03	7:03	8:03	9:03	10:03	11:03	12:04	1:04	2:04	3:04	4:04	5:04
10	6:02	7:02	8:02	9:03	10:03	11:03	12:04	1:04	2:04	3:04	4:05	5:05
15	6:01	7:01	8:02	9:02	10:03	11:03	12:04	1:04	2:04	3:05	4:05	5:06
20	6:00	7:00	8:01	9:02	10:02	11:03	12:04	1:04	2:05	3:05	4:06	5:07
25	5:58	6:59	8:00	9:01	10:02	11:03	12:04	1:04	2:05	3:06	4:07	5:08
28	5:58	6:59	8:00	9:01	10:02	11:03	12:04	1:04	2:05	3:06	4:07	5:08
31	5:57	6:58	7:59	9:00	10:01	11:02	12:04	1:05	2:06	3:07	4:08	5:09
34	5:56	6:57	7:59	9:00	10:01	11:02	12:04	1:05	2:06	3:07	4:08	5:10
37	5:55	6:57	7:58	8:59	10:01	11:02	12:04	1:05	2:06	3:08	4:09	5:10
40	5:54	6:56	7:57	8:59	10:00	11:02	12:04	1:05	2:07	3:08	4:10	5:11
42	5:54	6:55	7:57	8:59	10:00	11:02	12:04	1:05	2:07	3:08	4:10	5:12
44	5:53	6:55	7:56	8:58	10:00	11:02	12:04	1:05	2:07	3:09	4:11	5:12
46	5:52	6:54	7:56	8:58	10:00	11:02	12:04	1:05	2:07	3:09	4:11	5:13
48	5:51	6:53	7:55	8:57	9:59	11:01	12:04	1:06	2:08	3:10	4:12	5:14
50	5:50	6:53	7:55	8:57	9:59	11:01	12:04	1:06	2:08	3:10	4:12	5:14
52	5:49	6:52	7:54	8:57	9:59	11:01	12:04	1:06	2:08	3:11	4:13	5:15
54	5:48	6:51	7:53	8:56	9:58	11:01	12:04	1:06	2:09	3:11	4:14	5:16
56	5:47	6:50	7:53	8:55	9:58	11:01	12:04	1:06	2:09	3:12	4:14	5:17
58	5:46	6:49	7:52	8:55	9:58	11:01	12:04	1:06	2:09	3:12	4:15	5:18
S	13	14	15	16	17	18	19	20	21	22	23	24

NIGHT HOURS - DUSK TO DAWN

LAT. N	13	14	15	16	17	18	19	20	21	22	23	24
0	6:04	7:04	8:04	9:04	10:04	11:04	12:04	1:04	2:04	3:04	4:04	5:04
5	6:04	7:04	8:04	9:04	10:04	11:04	12:04	1:03	2:03	3:03	4:03	5:03
10	6:05	7:05	8:05	9:04	10:04	11:04	12:04	1:03	2:03	3:03	4:02	5:02
15	6:06	7:06	8:05	9:05	10:04	11:04	12:04	1:03	2:03	3:02	4:02	5:01
20	6:07	7:07	8:06	9:06	10:05	11:04	12:04	1:03	2:02	3:02	4:01	5:00
25	6:09	7:08	8:07	9:06	10:05	11:04	12:04	1:03	2:02	3:01	4:00	4:59
28	6:09	7:08	8:07	9:06	10:05	11:04	12:04	1:03	2:02	3:01	4:00	4:59
31	6:10	7:09	8:08	9:07	10:06	11:05	12:04	1:02	2:01	3:00	3:59	4:58
34	6:11	7:10	8:08	9:07	10:06	11:05	12:04	1:02	2:01	3:00	3:59	4:57
37	6:12	7:10	8:09	9:08	10:06	11:05	12:04	1:02	2:01	2:59	3:58	4:57
40	6:13	7:11	8:10	9:08	10:07	11:05	12:04	1:02	2:00	2:59	3:57	4:56
42	6:13	7:12	8:10	9:08	10:07	11:05	12:04	1:02	2:00	2:59	3:57	4:55
44	6:14	7:12	8:11	9:09	10:07	11:05	12:04	1:02	2:00	2:58	3:56	4:55
46	6:15	7:13	8:11	9:09	10:07	11:05	12:04	1:02	2:00	2:58	3:56	4:54
48	6:16	7:14	8:12	9:10	10:08	11:06	12:04	1:01	1:59	2:57	3:55	4:53
50	6:17	7:14	8:12	9:10	10:08	11:06	12:04	1:01	1:59	2:57	3:55	4:53
52	6:18	7:15	8:13	9:11	10:08	11:06	12:04	1:01	1:59	2:57	3:54	4:52
54	6:19	7:16	8:14	9:11	10:09	11:06	12:04	1:01	1:58	2:56	3:53	4:51
56	6:20	7:17	8:14	9:12	10:09	11:06	12:04	1:01	1:58	2:55	3:53	4:50
58	6:21	7:18	8:15	9:12	10:09	11:06	12:04	1:01	1:58	2:55	3:52	4:49
S	1	2	3	4	5	6	7	8	9	10	11	12

April 1st to 7th

DAYLIGHT HOURS - DAWN TO DUSK

LAT. N	1	2	3	4	5	6	7	8	9	10	11	12
0	6:03	7:03	8:03	9:03	10:03	11:03	12:03	1:03	2:03	3:03	4:03	5:03
5	6:01	7:01	8:01	9:02	10:02	11:02	12:03	1:03	2:03	3:03	4:04	5:04
10	5:59	6:59	8:00	9:01	10:01	11:02	12:03	1:03	2:04	3:04	4:05	5:06
15	5:57	6:58	7:59	9:00	10:01	11:02	12:03	1:03	2:04	3:05	4:06	5:07
20	5:54	6:56	7:57	8:58	10:00	11:01	12:03	1:04	2:05	3:07	4:08	5:09
25	5:52	6:54	7:56	8:57	9:59	11:01	12:03	1:04	2:06	3:08	4:09	5:11
28	5:51	6:53	7:55	8:57	9:59	11:01	12:03	1:04	2:06	3:08	4:10	5:12
31	5:49	6:51	7:54	8:56	9:58	11:00	12:03	1:05	2:07	3:09	4:11	5:14
34	5:48	6:50	7:53	8:55	9:58	11:00	12:03	1:05	2:07	3:10	4:12	5:15
37	5:46	6:49	7:51	8:54	9:57	11:00	12:03	1:05	2:08	3:11	4:14	5:16
40	5:44	6:47	7:50	8:53	9:56	10:59	12:03	1:06	2:09	3:12	4:15	5:18
42	5:43	6:46	7:49	8:53	9:56	10:59	12:03	1:06	2:09	3:12	4:16	5:19
44	5:41	6:45	7:48	8:52	9:55	10:59	12:03	1:06	2:10	3:13	4:17	5:20
46	5:40	6:43	7:47	8:51	9:55	10:59	12:03	1:06	2:10	3:14	4:18	5:22
48	5:38	6:42	7:46	8:50	9:54	10:58	12:03	1:07	2:11	3:15	4:19	5:23
50	5:36	6:41	7:45	8:49	9:54	10:58	12:03	1:07	2:11	3:16	4:20	5:24
52	5:34	6:39	7:44	8:48	9:53	10:58	12:03	1:07	2:12	3:17	4:21	5:26
54	5:32	6:37	7:42	8:47	9:52	10:57	12:03	1:08	2:13	3:18	4:23	5:28
56	5:30	6:35	7:41	8:46	9:52	10:57	12:03	1:08	2:13	3:19	4:24	5:30
58	5:27	6:33	7:39	8:45	9:51	10:57	12:03	1:08	2:14	3:20	4:26	5:32
S	13	14	15	16	17	18	19	20	21	22	23	24

NIGHT HOURS - DUSK TO DAWN

LAT. N	13	14	15	16	17	18	19	20	21	22	23	24
0	6:03	7:03	8:03	9:03	10:03	11:03	12:03	1:03	2:03	3:03	4:03	5:03
5	6:04	7:04	8:04	9:03	10:03	11:03	12:03	1:02	2:02	3:02	4:01	5:01
10	6:06	7:06	8:05	9:04	10:04	11:03	12:03	1:02	2:01	3:01	4:00	4:59
15	6:08	7:07	8:06	9:05	10:04	11:03	12:03	1:02	2:01	3:00	3:59	4:58
20	6:11	7:09	8:08	9:07	10:05	11:04	12:03	1:01	2:00	2:58	3:57	4:56
25	6:13	7:11	8:09	9:08	10:06	11:04	12:03	1:01	1:59	2:57	3:56	4:54
28	6:14	7:12	8:10	9:08	10:06	11:04	12:03	1:01	1:59	2:57	3:55	4:53
31	6:16	7:14	8:11	9:09	10:07	11:05	12:03	1:00	1:58	2:56	3:54	4:51
34	6:17	7:15	8:12	9:10	10:07	11:05	12:03	1:00	1:58	2:55	3:53	4:50
37	6:19	7:16	8:14	9:11	10:08	11:05	12:03	1:00	1:57	2:54	3:51	4:49
40	6:21	7:18	8:15	9:12	10:09	11:06	12:03	12:59	1:56	2:53	3:50	4:47
42	6:22	7:19	8:16	9:12	10:09	11:06	12:03	12:59	1:56	2:53	3:49	4:46
44	6:24	7:20	8:17	9:13	10:10	11:06	12:03	12:59	1:55	2:52	3:48	4:45
46	6:25	7:22	8:18	9:14	10:10	11:06	12:03	12:59	1:55	2:51	3:47	4:43
48	6:27	7:23	8:19	9:15	10:11	11:07	12:03	12:58	1:54	2:50	3:46	4:42
50	6:29	7:24	8:20	9:16	10:11	11:07	12:03	12:58	1:54	2:49	3:45	4:41
52	6:31	7:26	8:21	9:17	10:12	11:07	12:03	12:58	1:53	2:48	3:44	4:39
54	6:33	7:28	8:23	9:18	10:13	11:08	12:03	12:57	1:52	2:47	3:42	4:37
56	6:35	7:30	8:24	9:19	10:13	11:08	12:03	12:57	1:52	2:46	3:41	4:35
58	6:38	7:32	8:26	9:20	10:14	11:08	12:03	12:57	1:51	2:45	3:39	4:33
S	1	2	3	4	5	6	7	8	9	10	11	12

April 8th to 14th

DAYLIGHT HOURS - DAWN TO DUSK

LAT. N	1	2	3	4	5	6	7	8	9	10	11	12
0	6:00	7:00	8:00	9:00	10:00	11:00	12:00	13:00	2:00	3:00	4:00	5:00
5	5:57	6:57	7:58	8:58	9:59	10:59	12:00	1:00	2:01	3:01	4:02	5:02
10	5:53	6:54	7:55	8:56	9:57	10:59	12:00	1:01	2:02	3:03	4:04	5:05
15	5:50	6:52	7:53	8:55	9:56	10:58	12:00	1:01	2:03	3:04	4:06	5:07
20	5:47	6:49	7:51	8:53	9:55	10:57	12:00	1:02	2:04	3:06	4:08	5:10
25	5:44	6:46	7:49	8:52	9:54	10:57	12:00	1:02	2:05	3:08	4:10	5:13
28	5:41	6:44	7:47	8:50	9:53	10:56	12:00	1:03	2:06	3:09	4:12	5:15
31	5:39	6:42	7:46	8:49	9:53	10:56	12:00	1:03	2:06	3:10	4:13	5:17
34	5:36	6:40	7:44	8:48	9:52	10:56	12:00	1:03	2:07	3:11	4:15	5:19
37	5:34	6:38	7:42	8:47	9:51	10:55	12:00	1:04	2:08	3:12	4:17	5:21
40	5:31	6:35	7:40	8:45	9:50	10:55	12:00	1:04	2:09	3:14	4:19	5:24
42	5:29	6:34	7:39	8:44	9:49	10:54	12:00	1:05	2:10	3:15	4:20	5:25
44	5:26	6:32	7:37	8:43	9:48	10:54	12:00	1:05	2:11	3:16	4:22	5:27
46	5:24	6:30	7:36	8:42	9:48	10:54	12:00	1:05	2:11	3:17	4:23	5:29
48	5:21	6:28	7:34	8:40	9:47	10:53	12:00	1:06	2:12	3:19	4:25	5:31
50	5:18	6:25	7:32	8:39	9:46	10:53	12:00	1:06	2:13	3:20	4:27	5:34
52	5:15	6:23	7:30	8:37	9:45	10:52	12:00	1:07	2:14	3:22	4:29	5:36
54	5:12	6:20	7:28	8:36	9:44	10:52	12:00	1:07	2:15	3:23	4:31	5:39
56	5:08	6:17	7:25	8:34	9:42	10:51	12:00	1:08	2:17	3:25	4:34	5:42
58	5:04	6:13	7:23	8:32	9:41	10:50	12:00	1:09	2:18	3:27	4:36	5:46
S	13	14	15	16	17	18	19	20	21	22	23	24

NIGHT HOURS - DUSK TO DAWN

LAT. N	13	14	15	16	17	18	19	20	21	22	23	24
0	6:00	7:00	8:00	9:00	10:00	11:00	12:00	13:00	2:00	3:00	4:00	5:00
5	6:03	7:02	8:02	9:01	10:01	11:00	12:00	12:59	1:59	2:58	3:58	4:57
10	6:06	7:05	8:04	9:03	10:02	11:01	12:00	12:59	1:57	2:56	3:55	4:54
15	6:09	7:07	8:06	9:04	10:03	11:01	12:00	12:58	1:56	2:55	3:53	4:52
20	6:12	7:10	8:08	9:06	10:04	11:02	12:00	12:57	1:55	2:53	3:51	4:49
25	6:15	7:13	8:10	9:08	10:05	11:02	12:00	12:57	1:54	2:52	3:49	4:46
28	6:18	7:15	8:12	9:09	10:06	11:03	12:00	12:56	1:53	2:50	3:47	4:44
31	6:20	7:17	8:13	9:10	10:06	11:03	12:00	12:56	1:53	2:49	3:46	4:42
34	6:23	7:19	8:15	9:11	10:07	11:03	12:00	12:56	1:52	2:48	3:44	4:40
37	6:25	7:21	8:17	9:12	10:08	11:04	12:00	12:55	1:51	2:47	3:42	4:38
40	6:28	7:24	8:19	9:14	10:09	11:04	12:00	12:55	1:50	2:45	3:40	4:35
42	6:30	7:25	8:20	9:15	10:10	11:05	12:00	12:54	1:49	2:44	3:39	4:34
44	6:33	7:27	8:22	9:16	10:11	11:05	12:00	12:54	1:48	2:43	3:37	4:32
46	6:35	7:29	8:23	9:17	10:11	11:05	12:00	12:54	1:48	2:42	3:36	4:30
48	6:38	7:31	8:25	9:19	10:12	11:06	12:00	12:53	1:47	2:40	3:34	4:28
50	6:41	7:34	8:27	9:20	10:13	11:06	12:00	12:53	1:46	2:39	3:32	4:25
52	6:44	7:36	8:29	9:22	10:14	11:07	12:00	12:52	1:45	2:37	3:30	4:23
54	6:47	7:39	8:31	9:23	10:15	11:07	12:00	12:52	1:44	2:36	3:28	4:20
56	6:51	7:42	8:34	9:25	10:17	11:08	12:00	12:51	1:42	2:34	3:25	4:17
58	6:55	7:46	8:36	9:27	10:18	11:09	12:00	12:50	1:41	2:32	3:23	4:13
S	1	2	3	4	5	6	7	8	9	10	11	12

April 15th to 22nd

DAYLIGHT HOURS - DAWN TO DUSK

LAT. N	1	2	3	4	5	6	7	8	9	10	11	12
0	5:59	6:59	7:59	8:59	9:59	10:59	11:59	12:59	1:59	2:59	3:59	4:59
5	5:54	6:55	7:56	8:56	9:57	10:58	11:59	12:59	2:00	3:01	4:01	5:02
10	5:50	6:52	7:53	8:54	9:56	10:57	11:59	1:00	2:01	3:03	4:04	5:05
15	5:46	6:48	7:50	8:52	9:54	10:56	11:59	1:01	2:03	3:05	4:07	5:09
20	5:42	6:45	7:47	8:50	9:53	10:56	11:59	1:01	2:04	3:07	4:10	5:12
25	5:37	6:41	7:44	8:48	9:51	10:55	11:59	1:02	2:06	3:09	4:13	5:16
28	5:34	6:38	7:42	8:46	9:50	10:54	11:59	1:03	2:07	3:11	4:15	5:19
31	5:31	6:35	7:40	8:45	9:49	10:54	11:59	1:03	2:08	3:12	4:17	5:22
34	5:27	6:33	7:38	8:43	9:48	10:53	11:59	1:04	2:09	3:14	4:19	5:24
37	5:24	6:30	7:35	8:41	9:47	10:53	11:59	1:04	2:10	3:16	4:22	5:27
40	5:20	6:26	7:33	8:39	9:46	10:52	11:59	1:05	2:11	3:18	4:24	5:31
42	5:17	6:24	7:31	8:38	9:45	10:52	11:59	1:05	2:12	3:19	4:26	5:33
44	5:14	6:21	7:29	8:36	9:44	10:51	11:59	1:06	2:13	3:21	4:28	5:36
46	5:11	6:19	7:27	8:35	9:43	10:51	11:59	1:06	2:14	3:22	4:30	5:38
48	5:07	6:16	7:24	8:33	9:41	10:50	11:59	1:07	2:16	3:24	4:33	5:41
50	5:03	6:12	7:22	8:31	9:40	10:49	11:59	1:08	2:17	3:26	4:35	5:45
52	4:59	6:09	7:19	8:29	9:39	10:49	11:59	1:08	2:18	3:28	4:38	5:48
54	4:54	6:05	7:16	8:26	9:37	10:48	11:59	1:09	2:20	3:31	4:41	5:52
56	4:49	6:01	7:12	8:24	9:35	10:47	11:59	1:10	2:22	3:33	4:45	5:56
58	4:44	5:56	7:09	8:21	9:34	10:46	11:59	1:11	2:23	3:36	4:48	6:01
S	13	14	15	16	17	18	19	20	21	22	23	24

NIGHT HOURS - DUSK TO DAWN

LAT. N	13	14	15	16	17	18	19	20	21	22	23	24
0	5:59	6:59	7:59	8:59	9:59	10:59	11:59	12:59	1:59	2:59	3:59	4:59
5	6:03	7:02	8:01	9:01	10:00	10:59	11:59	12:58	1:57	2:56	3:56	4:55
10	6:07	7:05	8:04	9:03	10:01	11:00	11:59	12:57	1:56	2:54	3:53	4:52
15	6:11	7:09	8:07	9:05	10:03	11:01	11:59	12:56	1:54	2:52	3:50	4:48
20	6:15	7:12	8:10	9:07	10:04	11:01	11:59	12:56	1:53	2:50	3:47	4:45
25	6:20	7:16	8:13	9:09	10:06	11:02	11:59	12:55	1:51	2:48	3:44	4:41
28	6:23	7:19	8:15	9:11	10:07	11:03	11:59	12:54	1:50	2:46	3:42	4:38
31	6:26	7:22	8:17	9:12	10:08	11:03	11:59	12:54	1:49	2:45	3:40	4:35
34	6:30	7:24	8:19	9:14	10:09	11:04	11:59	12:53	1:48	2:43	3:38	4:33
37	6:33	7:27	8:22	9:16	10:10	11:04	11:59	12:53	1:47	2:41	3:35	4:30
40	6:37	7:31	8:24	9:18	10:11	11:05	11:59	12:52	1:46	2:39	3:33	4:26
42	6:40	7:33	8:26	9:19	10:12	11:05	11:59	12:52	1:45	2:38	3:31	4:24
44	6:43	7:36	8:28	9:21	10:13	11:06	11:59	12:51	1:44	2:36	3:29	4:21
46	6:46	7:38	8:30	9:22	10:14	11:06	11:59	12:51	1:43	2:35	3:27	4:19
48	6:50	7:41	8:33	9:24	10:16	11:07	11:59	12:50	1:41	2:33	3:24	4:16
50	6:54	7:45	8:35	9:26	10:17	11:08	11:59	12:49	1:40	2:31	3:22	4:12
52	6:58	7:48	8:38	9:28	10:18	11:08	11:59	12:49	1:39	2:29	3:19	4:09
54	7:03	7:52	8:41	9:31	10:20	11:09	11:59	12:48	1:37	2:26	3:16	4:05
56	7:08	7:56	8:45	9:33	10:22	11:10	11:59	12:47	1:35	2:24	3:12	4:01
58	7:13	8:01	8:48	9:36	10:23	11:11	11:59	12:46	1:34	2:21	3:09	3:56
S	1	2	3	4	5	6	7	8	9	10	11	12

April 23rd to 30th

DAYLIGHT HOURS - DAWN TO DUSK

LAT. N	1	2	3	4	5	6	7	8	9	10	11	12
0	5:57	6:57	7:57	8:57	9:57	10:57	11:57	12:57	1:57	2:57	3:57	4:57
5	5:52	6:52	7:53	8:54	9:55	10:56	11:57	12:57	1:58	2:59	4:00	5:01
10	5:47	6:48	7:50	8:52	9:53	10:55	11:57	12:58	2:00	3:01	4:03	5:05
15	5:42	6:44	7:47	8:49	9:52	10:54	11:57	12:59	2:01	3:04	4:06	5:09
20	5:36	6:40	7:43	8:46	9:50	10:53	11:57	1:00	2:03	3:07	4:10	5:13
25	5:30	6:35	7:39	8:43	9:48	10:52	11:57	1:01	2:05	3:10	4:14	5:18
28	5:27	6:32	7:37	8:42	9:47	10:52	11:57	1:01	2:06	3:11	4:16	5:21
31	5:23	6:29	7:34	8:40	9:45	10:51	11:57	1:02	2:08	3:13	4:19	5:25
34	5:19	6:25	7:31	8:38	9:44	10:50	11:57	1:03	2:09	3:15	4:22	5:28
37	5:14	6:21	7:28	8:35	9:42	10:49	11:57	1:04	2:11	3:18	4:25	5:32
40	5:09	6:17	7:25	8:33	9:41	10:49	11:57	1:04	2:12	3:20	4:28	5:36
42	5:06	6:14	7:23	8:31	9:40	10:48	11:57	1:05	2:13	3:22	4:30	5:39
44	5:02	6:11	7:20	8:29	9:38	10:47	11:57	1:06	2:15	3:24	4:33	5:42
46	4:58	6:08	7:18	8:27	9:37	10:47	11:57	1:06	2:16	3:26	4:35	5:45
48	4:54	6:04	7:15	8:25	9:36	10:46	11:57	1:07	2:17	3:28	4:38	5:49
50	4:49	6:00	7:12	8:23	9:34	10:45	11:57	1:08	2:19	3:30	4:41	5:53
52	4:44	5:56	7:08	8:20	9:32	10:44	11:57	1:09	2:21	3:33	4:45	5:57
54	4:38	5:51	7:04	8:17	9:30	10:43	11:57	1:10	2:23	3:36	4:49	6:02
56	4:32	5:46	7:00	8:14	9:28	10:42	11:57	1:11	2:25	3:39	4:53	6:07
58	4:25	5:40	6:55	8:11	9:26	10:41	11:57	1:12	2:27	3:42	4:58	6:13
S	13	14	15	16	17	18	19	20	21	22	23	24

NIGHT HOURS - DUSK TO DAWN

LAT. N	13	14	15	16	17	18	19	20	21	22	23	24
0	5:57	6:57	7:57	8:57	9:57	10:57	11:57	12:57	1:57	2:57	3:57	4:57
5	6:01	7:01	8:00	8:59	9:58	10:57	11:57	12:56	1:55	2:54	3:53	4:52
10	6:06	7:05	8:03	9:01	10:00	10:58	11:57	12:55	1:53	2:52	3:50	4:48
15	6:11	7:09	8:06	9:04	10:01	10:59	11:57	12:54	1:52	2:49	3:47	4:44
20	6:17	7:13	8:10	9:07	10:03	11:00	11:57	12:53	1:50	2:46	3:43	4:40
25	6:23	7:18	8:14	9:10	10:05	11:01	11:57	12:52	1:48	2:43	3:39	4:35
28	6:26	7:21	8:16	9:11	10:06	11:01	11:57	12:52	1:47	2:42	3:37	4:32
31	6:30	7:25	8:19	9:13	10:08	11:02	11:57	12:51	1:45	2:40	3:34	4:29
34	6:34	7:28	8:22	9:15	10:09	11:03	11:57	12:50	1:44	2:38	3:31	4:25
37	6:39	7:32	8:25	9:18	10:11	11:04	11:57	12:49	1:42	2:35	3:28	4:21
40	6:44	7:36	8:28	9:20	10:12	11:04	11:57	12:49	1:41	2:33	3:25	4:17
42	6:47	7:39	8:30	9:22	10:13	11:05	11:57	12:48	1:40	2:31	3:23	4:14
44	6:51	7:42	8:33	9:24	10:15	11:06	11:57	12:47	1:38	2:29	3:20	4:11
46	6:55	7:45	8:35	9:26	10:16	11:06	11:57	12:47	1:37	2:27	3:18	4:08
48	6:59	7:49	8:38	9:28	10:17	11:07	11:57	12:46	1:36	2:25	3:15	4:04
50	7:04	7:53	8:41	9:30	10:19	11:08	11:57	12:45	1:34	2:23	3:12	4:00
52	7:09	7:57	8:45	9:33	10:21	11:09	11:57	12:44	1:32	2:20	3:08	3:56
54	7:15	8:02	8:49	9:36	10:23	11:10	11:57	12:43	1:30	2:17	3:04	3:51
56	7:21	8:07	8:53	9:39	10:25	11:11	11:57	12:42	1:28	2:14	3:00	3:46
58	7:28	8:13	8:58	9:42	10:27	11:12	11:57	12:41	1:26	2:11	2:55	3:40
S	1	2	3	4	5	6	7	8	9	10	11	12

May 1st to 7th

DAYLIGHT HOURS - DAWN TO DUSK

LAT. N	1	2	3	4	5	6	7	8	9	10	11	12
0	5:56	6:56	7:56	8:56	9:56	10:56	11:56	12:56	1:56	2:56	3:56	4:56
5	5:50	6:51	7:52	8:53	9:54	10:55	11:56	12:56	1:57	2:58	3:59	5:00
10	5:44	6:46	7:48	8:50	9:52	10:54	11:56	12:57	1:59	3:01	4:03	5:05
15	5:38	6:41	7:44	8:47	9:50	10:53	11:56	12:58	2:01	3:04	4:07	5:10
20	5:32	6:36	7:40	8:44	9:48	10:52	11:56	12:59	2:03	3:07	4:11	5:15
25	5:25	6:30	7:35	8:40	9:45	10:50	11:56	1:01	2:06	3:11	4:16	5:21
28	5:21	6:27	7:32	8:38	9:44	10:50	11:56	1:01	2:07	3:13	4:19	5:24
31	5:16	6:23	7:29	8:36	9:42	10:49	11:56	1:02	2:09	3:15	4:22	5:28
34	5:11	6:19	7:26	8:33	9:41	10:48	11:56	1:03	2:10	3:18	4:25	5:32
37	5:06	6:14	7:23	8:31	9:39	10:47	11:56	1:04	2:12	3:20	4:28	5:37
40	5:01	6:10	7:19	8:28	9:37	10:46	11:56	1:05	2:14	3:23	4:32	5:41
42	4:56	6:06	7:16	8:26	9:36	10:46	11:56	1:05	2:15	3:25	4:35	5:45
44	4:52	6:03	7:13	8:24	9:34	10:45	11:56	1:06	2:17	3:27	4:38	5:48
46	4:47	5:59	7:10	8:21	9:33	10:44	11:56	1:07	2:18	3:30	4:41	5:52
48	4:42	5:54	7:07	8:19	9:31	10:43	11:56	1:08	2:20	3:32	4:44	5:57
50	4:37	5:50	7:03	8:16	9:29	10:42	11:56	1:09	2:22	3:35	4:48	6:01
52	4:30	5:45	6:59	8:13	9:27	10:41	11:56	1:10	2:24	3:38	4:52	6:06
54	4:24	5:39	6:54	8:10	9:25	10:40	11:56	1:11	2:26	3:41	4:57	6:12
56	4:16	5:33	6:49	8:06	9:22	10:39	11:56	1:12	2:29	3:45	5:02	6:18
58	4:08	5:26	6:44	8:02	9:20	10:38	11:56	1:13	2:31	3:49	5:07	6:25
S	13	14	15	16	17	18	19	20	21	22	23	24

NIGHT HOURS - DUSK TO DAWN

LAT. N	13	14	15	16	17	18	19	20	21	22	23	24
0	5:56	6:56	7:56	8:56	9:56	10:56	11:56	12:56	1:56	2:56	3:56	4:56
5	6:01	7:00	7:59	8:58	9:57	10:56	11:56	12:55	1:54	2:53	3:52	4:51
10	6:07	7:05	8:03	9:01	9:59	10:57	11:56	12:54	1:52	2:50	3:48	4:46
15	6:13	7:10	8:07	9:04	10:01	10:58	11:56	12:53	1:50	2:47	3:44	4:41
20	6:19	7:15	8:11	9:07	10:03	10:59	11:56	12:52	1:48	2:44	3:40	4:36
25	6:26	7:21	8:16	9:11	10:06	11:01	11:56	12:50	1:45	2:40	3:35	4:30
28	6:30	7:24	8:19	9:13	10:07	11:01	11:56	12:50	1:44	2:38	3:32	4:27
31	6:35	7:28	8:22	9:15	10:09	11:02	11:56	12:49	1:42	2:36	3:29	4:23
34	6:40	7:32	8:25	9:18	10:10	11:03	11:56	12:48	1:41	2:33	3:26	4:19
37	6:45	7:37	8:28	9:20	10:12	11:04	11:56	12:47	1:39	2:31	3:23	4:14
40	6:51	7:41	8:32	9:23	10:14	11:05	11:56	12:46	1:37	2:28	3:19	4:10
42	6:55	7:45	8:35	9:25	10:15	11:05	11:56	12:46	1:36	2:26	3:16	4:06
44	6:59	7:48	8:38	9:27	10:17	11:06	11:56	12:45	1:34	2:24	3:13	4:03
46	7:04	7:52	8:41	9:30	10:18	11:07	11:56	12:44	1:33	2:21	3:10	3:59
48	7:09	7:57	8:44	9:32	10:20	11:08	11:56	12:43	1:31	2:19	3:07	3:54
50	7:14	8:01	8:48	9:35	10:22	11:09	11:56	12:42	1:29	2:16	3:03	3:50
52	7:21	8:06	8:52	9:38	10:24	11:10	11:56	12:41	1:27	2:13	2:59	3:45
54	7:27	8:12	8:57	9:41	10:26	11:11	11:56	12:40	1:25	2:10	2:54	3:39
56	7:35	8:18	9:02	9:45	10:29	11:12	11:56	12:39	1:22	2:06	2:49	3:33
58	7:43	8:25	9:07	9:49	10:31	11:13	11:56	12:38	1:20	2:02	2:44	3:26
S	1	2	3	4	5	6	7	8	9	10	11	12

May 8th to 15th

DAYLIGHT HOURS - DAWN TO DUSK

LAT. N	1	2	3	4	5	6	7	8	9	10	11	12
0	5:56	6:56	7:56	8:56	9:56	10:56	11:56	12:56	1:56	2:56	3:56	4:56
5	5:49	6:50	7:51	8:52	9:53	10:54	11:56	12:57	1:58	2:59	4:00	5:01
10	5:42	6:45	7:47	8:49	9:51	10:53	11:56	12:58	2:00	3:02	4:04	5:06
15	5:36	6:39	7:42	8:46	9:49	10:52	11:56	12:59	2:02	3:05	4:09	5:12
20	5:28	6:33	7:37	8:42	9:46	10:51	11:56	1:00	2:05	3:09	4:14	5:18
25	5:21	6:26	7:32	8:38	9:44	10:50	11:56	1:01	2:07	3:13	4:19	5:25
28	5:16	6:22	7:29	8:36	9:42	10:49	11:56	1:02	2:09	3:15	4:22	5:29
31	5:10	6:18	7:25	8:33	9:40	10:48	11:56	1:03	2:11	3:18	4:26	5:33
34	5:05	6:13	7:22	8:30	9:39	10:47	11:56	1:04	2:12	3:21	4:29	5:38
37	4:59	6:08	7:18	8:27	9:37	10:46	11:56	1:05	2:14	3:24	4:33	5:43
40	4:52	6:03	7:13	8:24	9:34	10:45	11:56	1:06	2:17	3:27	4:38	5:48
42	4:47	5:59	7:10	8:21	9:33	10:44	11:56	1:07	2:18	3:30	4:41	5:52
44	4:42	5:55	7:07	8:19	9:31	10:43	11:56	1:08	2:20	3:32	4:44	5:56
46	4:37	5:50	7:03	8:16	9:29	10:42	11:56	1:09	2:22	3:35	4:48	6:01
48	4:31	5:45	6:59	8:13	9:27	10:41	11:56	1:10	2:24	3:38	4:52	6:06
50	4:24	5:40	6:55	8:10	9:25	10:40	11:56	1:11	2:26	3:41	4:56	6:11
52	4:17	5:34	6:50	8:06	9:23	10:39	11:56	1:12	2:28	3:45	5:01	6:17
54	4:09	5:27	6:45	8:02	9:20	10:38	11:56	1:13	2:31	3:49	5:06	6:24
56	4:00	5:20	6:39	7:58	9:17	10:36	11:56	1:15	2:34	3:53	5:12	6:31
58	3:50	5:11	6:32	7:53	9:14	10:35	11:56	1:16	2:37	3:58	5:19	6:40
S	13	14	15	16	17	18	19	20	21	22	23	24

NIGHT HOURS - DUSK TO DAWN

LAT. N	13	14	15	16	17	18	19	20	21	22	23	24
0	5:56	6:56	7:56	8:56	9:56	10:56	11:56	12:56	1:56	2:56	3:56	4:56
5	6:02	7:01	8:00	8:59	9:58	10:57	11:56	12:54	1:53	2:52	3:51	4:50
10	6:09	7:06	8:04	9:02	10:00	10:58	11:56	12:53	1:51	2:49	3:47	4:45
15	6:15	7:12	8:09	9:05	10:02	10:59	11:56	12:52	1:49	2:46	3:42	4:39
20	6:23	7:18	8:14	9:09	10:05	11:00	11:56	12:51	1:46	2:42	3:37	4:33
25	6:30	7:25	8:19	9:13	10:07	11:01	11:56	12:50	1:44	2:38	3:32	4:26
28	6:35	7:29	8:22	9:15	10:09	11:02	11:56	12:49	1:42	2:36	3:29	4:22
31	6:41	7:33	8:26	9:18	10:11	11:03	11:56	12:48	1:40	2:33	3:25	4:18
34	6:46	7:38	8:29	9:21	10:12	11:04	11:56	12:47	1:39	2:30	3:22	4:13
37	6:52	7:43	8:33	9:24	10:14	11:05	11:56	12:46	1:37	2:27	3:18	4:08
40	6:59	7:48	8:38	9:27	10:17	11:06	11:56	12:45	1:34	2:24	3:13	4:03
42	7:04	7:52	8:41	9:30	10:18	11:07	11:56	12:44	1:33	2:21	3:10	3:59
44	7:09	7:56	8:44	9:32	10:20	11:08	11:56	12:43	1:31	2:19	3:07	3:55
46	7:14	8:01	8:48	9:35	10:22	11:09	11:56	12:42	1:29	2:16	3:03	3:50
48	7:20	8:06	8:52	9:38	10:24	11:10	11:56	12:41	1:27	2:13	2:59	3:45
50	7:27	8:11	8:56	9:41	10:26	11:11	11:56	12:40	1:25	2:10	2:55	3:40
52	7:34	8:17	9:01	9:45	10:28	11:12	11:56	12:39	1:23	2:06	2:50	3:34
54	7:42	8:24	9:06	9:49	10:31	11:13	11:56	12:38	1:20	2:02	2:45	3:27
56	7:51	8:31	9:12	9:53	10:34	11:15	11:56	12:36	1:17	1:58	2:39	3:20
58	8:01	8:40	9:19	9:58	10:37	11:16	11:56	12:35	1:14	1:53	2:32	3:11
S	1	2	3	4	5	6	7	8	9	10	11	12

May 16th to 23rd

DAYLIGHT HOURS - DAWN TO DUSK

LAT. N	1	2	3	4	5	6	7	8	9	10	11	12
0	5:56	6:56	7:56	8:56	9:56	10:56	11:56	12:56	1:56	2:56	3:56	4:56
5	5:48	6:49	7:51	8:52	9:53	10:54	11:56	12:57	1:58	2:59	4:00	5:02
10	5:41	6:43	7:46	8:48	9:51	10:53	11:56	12:58	2:00	3:03	4:05	5:08
15	5:33	6:37	7:41	8:44	9:48	10:52	11:56	12:59	2:03	3:07	4:10	5:14
20	5:25	6:30	7:35	8:40	9:45	10:50	11:56	1:01	2:06	3:11	4:16	5:21
25	5:17	6:23	7:30	8:36	9:43	10:49	11:56	1:02	2:08	3:15	4:21	5:28
28	5:11	6:19	7:26	8:33	9:41	10:48	11:56	1:03	2:10	3:18	4:25	5:32
31	5:05	6:14	7:22	8:30	9:39	10:47	11:56	1:04	2:12	3:21	4:29	5:37
34	4:59	6:08	7:18	8:27	9:37	10:46	11:56	1:05	2:14	3:24	4:33	5:43
37	4:52	6:03	7:13	8:24	9:34	10:45	11:56	1:06	2:17	3:27	4:38	5:48
40	4:45	5:57	7:08	8:20	9:32	10:44	11:56	1:07	2:19	3:31	4:43	5:54
42	4:40	5:52	7:05	8:18	9:30	10:43	11:56	1:08	2:21	3:33	4:46	5:59
44	4:34	5:47	7:01	8:15	9:28	10:42	11:56	1:09	2:23	3:36	4:50	6:04
46	4:28	5:42	6:57	8:12	9:26	10:41	11:56	1:10	2:25	3:39	4:54	6:09
48	4:21	5:37	6:52	8:08	9:24	10:40	11:56	1:11	2:27	3:43	4:59	6:14
50	4:13	5:30	6:47	8:04	9:21	10:39	11:56	1:13	2:30	3:47	5:04	6:21
52	4:05	5:24	6:42	8:00	9:19	10:37	11:56	1:14	2:32	3:51	5:09	6:27
54	3:56	5:16	6:36	7:56	9:16	10:36	11:56	1:15	2:35	3:55	5:15	6:35
56	3:46	5:08	6:29	7:51	9:12	10:34	11:56	1:17	2:39	4:00	5:22	6:43
58	3:34	4:58	6:21	7:45	9:08	10:32	11:56	1:19	2:43	4:06	5:30	6:53
S	13	14	15	16	17	18	19	20	21	22	23	24

NIGHT HOURS - DUSK TO DAWN

LAT. N	13	14	15	16	17	18	19	20	21	22	23	24
0	5:56	6:56	7:56	8:56	9:56	10:56	11:56	12:56	1:56	2:56	3:56	4:56
5	6:03	7:02	8:00	8:59	9:58	10:57	11:56	12:54	1:53	2:52	3:51	4:49
10	6:10	7:08	8:05	9:03	10:00	10:58	11:56	12:53	1:51	2:48	3:46	4:43
15	6:18	7:14	8:10	9:07	10:03	10:59	11:56	12:52	1:48	2:44	3:41	4:37
20	6:26	7:21	8:16	9:11	10:06	11:01	11:56	12:50	1:45	2:40	3:35	4:30
25	6:34	7:28	8:21	9:15	10:08	11:02	11:56	12:49	1:43	2:36	3:30	4:23
28	6:40	7:32	8:25	9:18	10:10	11:03	11:56	12:48	1:41	2:33	3:26	4:19
31	6:46	7:37	8:29	9:21	10:12	11:04	11:56	12:47	1:39	2:30	3:22	4:14
34	6:52	7:43	8:33	9:24	10:14	11:05	11:56	12:46	1:37	2:27	3:18	4:08
37	6:59	7:48	8:38	9:27	10:17	11:06	11:56	12:45	1:34	2:24	3:13	4:03
40	7:06	7:54	8:43	9:31	10:19	11:07	11:56	12:44	1:32	2:20	3:08	3:57
42	7:11	7:59	8:46	9:33	10:21	11:08	11:56	12:43	1:30	2:18	3:05	3:52
44	7:17	8:04	8:50	9:36	10:23	11:09	11:56	12:42	1:28	2:15	3:01	3:47
46	7:23	8:09	8:54	9:39	10:25	11:10	11:56	12:41	1:26	2:12	2:57	3:42
48	7:30	8:14	8:59	9:43	10:27	11:11	11:56	12:40	1:24	2:08	2:52	3:37
50	7:38	8:21	9:04	9:47	10:30	11:13	11:56	12:39	1:21	2:04	2:47	3:30
52	7:46	8:27	9:09	9:51	10:32	11:14	11:56	12:37	1:19	2:00	2:42	3:24
54	7:55	8:35	9:15	9:55	10:35	11:15	11:56	12:36	1:16	1:56	2:36	3:16
56	8:05	8:43	9:22	10:00	10:39	11:17	11:56	12:34	1:12	1:51	2:29	3:08
58	8:17	8:53	9:30	10:06	10:43	11:19	11:56	12:32	1:08	1:45	2:21	2:58
S	1	2	3	4	5	6	7	8	9	10	11	12

May 24th to 31st

DAYLIGHT HOURS - DAWN TO DUSK

LAT. N	1	2	3	4	5	6	7	8	9	10	11	12
0	5:57	6:57	7:57	8:57	9:57	10:57	11:57	12:57	1:57	2:57	3:57	4:57
5	5:49	6:50	7:51	8:53	9:54	10:55	11:57	12:58	1:59	3:00	4:02	5:03
10	5:41	6:43	7:46	8:49	9:51	10:54	11:57	12:59	2:02	3:04	4:07	5:10
15	5:32	6:36	7:40	8:44	9:48	10:52	11:57	1:01	2:05	3:09	4:13	5:17
20	5:24	6:29	7:35	8:40	9:46	10:51	11:57	1:02	2:07	3:13	4:18	5:24
25	5:14	6:21	7:28	8:35	9:42	10:49	11:57	1:04	2:11	3:18	4:25	5:32
28	5:08	6:16	7:24	8:32	9:40	10:48	11:57	1:05	2:13	3:21	4:29	5:37
31	5:02	6:11	7:20	8:29	9:38	10:47	11:57	1:06	2:15	3:24	4:33	5:42
34	4:55	6:05	7:16	8:26	9:36	10:46	11:57	1:07	2:17	3:27	4:37	5:48
37	4:48	5:59	7:11	8:22	9:34	10:45	11:57	1:08	2:19	3:31	4:42	5:54
40	4:40	5:53	7:05	8:18	9:31	10:44	11:57	1:09	2:22	3:35	4:48	6:00
42	4:34	5:48	7:01	8:15	9:29	10:43	11:57	1:10	2:24	3:38	4:52	6:05
44	4:28	5:42	6:57	8:12	9:27	10:42	11:57	1:11	2:26	3:41	4:56	6:11
46	4:21	5:37	6:53	8:09	9:25	10:41	11:57	1:12	2:28	3:44	5:00	6:16
48	4:13	5:31	6:48	8:05	9:22	10:39	11:57	1:14	2:31	3:48	5:05	6:22
50	4:05	5:24	6:42	8:01	9:19	10:38	11:57	1:15	2:34	3:52	5:11	6:29
52	3:56	5:16	6:36	7:56	9:16	10:36	11:57	1:17	2:37	3:57	5:17	6:37
54	3:46	5:08	6:30	7:51	9:13	10:35	11:57	1:18	2:40	4:02	5:23	6:45
56	3:35	4:58	6:22	7:46	9:09	10:33	11:57	1:20	2:44	4:07	5:31	6:55
58	3:21	4:47	6:13	7:39	9:05	10:31	11:57	1:22	2:48	4:14	5:40	7:06
S	13	14	15	16	17	18	19	20	21	22	23	24

NIGHT HOURS - DUSK TO DAWN

LAT. N	13	14	15	16	17	18	19	20	21	22	23	24
0	5:57	6:57	7:57	8:57	9:57	10:57	11:57	12:57	1:57	2:57	3:57	4:57
5	6:04	7:03	8:02	9:00	9:59	10:58	11:57	12:55	1:54	2:53	3:51	4:50
10	6:12	7:10	8:07	9:04	10:02	10:59	11:57	12:54	1:51	2:49	3:46	4:43
15	6:21	7:17	8:13	9:09	10:05	11:01	11:57	12:52	1:48	2:44	3:40	4:36
20	6:29	7:24	8:18	9:13	10:07	11:02	11:57	12:51	1:46	2:40	3:35	4:29
25	6:39	7:32	8:25	9:18	10:11	11:04	11:57	12:49	1:42	2:35	3:28	4:21
28	6:45	7:37	8:29	9:21	10:13	11:05	11:57	12:48	1:40	2:32	3:24	4:16
31	6:51	7:42	8:33	9:24	10:15	11:06	11:57	12:47	1:38	2:29	3:20	4:11
34	6:58	7:48	8:37	9:27	10:17	11:07	11:57	12:46	1:36	2:26	3:16	4:05
37	7:05	7:54	8:42	9:31	10:19	11:08	11:57	12:45	1:34	2:22	3:11	3:59
40	7:13	8:00	8:48	9:35	10:22	11:09	11:57	12:44	1:31	2:18	3:05	3:53
42	7:19	8:05	8:52	9:38	10:24	11:10	11:57	12:43	1:29	2:15	3:01	3:48
44	7:25	8:11	8:56	9:41	10:26	11:11	11:57	12:42	1:27	2:12	2:57	3:42
46	7:32	8:16	9:00	9:44	10:28	11:12	11:57	12:41	1:25	2:09	2:53	3:37
48	7:40	8:22	9:05	9:48	10:31	11:14	11:57	12:39	1:22	2:05	2:48	3:31
50	7:48	8:29	9:11	9:52	10:34	11:15	11:57	12:38	1:19	2:01	2:42	3:24
52	7:57	8:37	9:17	9:57	10:37	11:17	11:57	12:36	1:16	1:56	2:36	3:16
54	8:07	8:45	9:23	10:02	10:40	11:18	11:57	12:35	1:13	1:51	2:30	3:08
56	8:18	8:55	9:31	10:07	10:44	11:20	11:57	12:33	1:09	1:46	2:22	2:58
58	8:32	9:06	9:40	10:14	10:48	11:22	11:57	12:31	1:05	1:39	2:13	2:47
S	1	2	3	4	5	6	7	8	9	10	11	12

June 1st to 7th

DAYLIGHT HOURS - DAWN TO DUSK

LAT. N	1	2	3	4	5	6	7	8	9	10	11	12
0	5:58	6:58	7:58	8:58	9:58	10:58	11:58	12:58	1:58	2:58	3:58	4:58
5	5:49	6:51	7:52	8:53	9:55	10:56	11:58	12:59	2:00	3:02	4:03	5:04
10	5:41	6:44	7:46	8:49	9:52	10:55	11:58	1:00	2:03	3:06	4:09	5:11
15	5:32	6:36	7:41	8:45	9:49	10:53	11:58	1:02	2:06	3:10	4:14	5:19
20	5:23	6:29	7:35	8:40	9:46	10:52	11:58	1:03	2:09	3:15	4:20	5:26
25	5:13	6:21	7:28	8:35	9:43	10:50	11:58	1:05	2:12	3:20	4:27	5:34
28	5:07	6:15	7:24	8:32	9:41	10:49	11:58	1:06	2:14	3:23	4:31	5:40
31	5:00	6:10	7:19	8:29	9:38	10:48	11:58	1:07	2:17	3:26	4:36	5:45
34	4:53	6:04	7:15	8:25	9:36	10:47	11:58	1:08	2:19	3:30	4:40	5:51
37	4:45	5:57	7:09	8:21	9:33	10:45	11:58	1:10	2:22	3:34	4:46	5:58
40	4:37	5:50	7:04	8:17	9:31	10:44	11:58	1:11	2:24	3:38	4:51	6:05
42	4:31	5:45	7:00	8:14	9:29	10:43	11:58	1:12	2:27	3:41	4:55	6:10
44	4:24	5:39	6:55	8:11	9:26	10:42	11:58	1:13	2:29	3:44	5:00	6:16
46	4:17	5:33	6:50	8:07	9:24	10:41	11:58	1:14	2:31	3:48	5:05	6:22
48	4:09	5:27	6:45	8:03	9:21	10:39	11:58	1:16	2:34	3:52	5:10	6:28
50	4:00	5:20	6:39	7:59	9:18	10:38	11:58	1:17	2:37	3:56	5:16	6:35
52	3:50	5:12	6:33	7:54	9:15	10:36	11:58	1:19	2:40	4:01	5:22	6:43
54	3:40	5:03	6:26	7:49	9:12	10:35	11:58	1:21	2:44	4:07	5:30	6:52
56	3:27	4:52	6:17	7:42	9:07	10:32	11:58	1:23	2:48	4:13	5:38	7:03
58	3:13	4:40	6:08	7:35	9:03	10:30	11:58	1:25	2:52	4:20	5:47	7:15
S	13	14	15	16	17	18	19	20	21	22	23	24

NIGHT HOURS - DUSK TO DAWN

LAT. N	13	14	15	16	17	18	19	20	21	22	23	24
0	5:58	6:58	7:58	8:58	9:58	10:58	11:58	12:58	1:58	2:58	3:58	4:58
5	6:06	7:04	8:03	9:02	10:00	10:59	11:58	12:56	1:55	2:53	3:52	4:51
10	6:14	7:11	8:09	9:06	10:03	11:00	11:58	12:55	1:52	2:49	3:46	4:44
15	6:23	7:19	8:14	9:10	10:06	11:02	11:58	12:53	1:49	2:45	3:41	4:36
20	6:32	7:26	8:20	9:15	10:09	11:03	11:58	12:52	1:46	2:40	3:35	4:29
25	6:42	7:34	8:27	9:20	10:12	11:05	11:58	12:50	1:43	2:35	3:28	4:21
28	6:48	7:40	8:31	9:23	10:14	11:06	11:58	12:49	1:41	2:32	3:24	4:15
31	6:55	7:45	8:36	9:26	10:17	11:07	11:58	12:48	1:38	2:29	3:19	4:10
34	7:02	7:51	8:40	9:30	10:19	11:08	11:58	12:47	1:36	2:25	3:15	4:04
37	7:10	7:58	8:46	9:34	10:22	11:10	11:58	12:45	1:33	2:21	3:09	3:57
40	7:18	8:05	8:51	9:38	10:24	11:11	11:58	12:44	1:31	2:17	3:04	3:50
42	7:24	8:10	8:56	9:41	10:27	11:12	11:58	12:43	1:29	2:14	3:00	3:45
44	7:31	8:16	9:00	9:44	10:29	11:13	11:58	12:42	1:26	2:11	2:55	3:39
46	7:38	8:22	9:05	9:48	10:31	11:14	11:58	12:41	1:24	2:07	2:50	3:33
48	7:46	8:28	9:10	9:52	10:34	11:16	11:58	12:39	1:21	2:03	2:45	3:27
50	7:55	8:35	9:16	9:56	10:37	11:17	11:58	12:38	1:18	1:59	2:39	3:20
52	8:05	8:43	9:22	10:01	10:40	11:19	11:58	12:36	1:15	1:54	2:33	3:12
54	8:15	8:52	9:30	10:07	10:44	11:21	11:58	12:35	1:12	1:49	2:26	3:03
56	8:28	9:03	9:38	10:13	10:48	11:23	11:58	12:32	1:07	1:42	2:17	2:52
58	8:42	9:15	9:47	10:20	10:52	11:25	11:58	12:30	1:03	1:35	2:08	2:40
S	1	2	3	4	5	6	7	8	9	10	11	12

June 8th to 14th

DAYLIGHT HOURS - DAWN TO DUSK

LAT. N	1	2	3	4	5	6	7	8	9	10	11	12
0	5:59	6:59	7:59	8:59	9:59	10:59	11:59	12:59	1:59	2:59	3:59	4:59
5	5:50	6:51	7:53	8:54	9:56	10:57	11:59	1:00	2:01	3:03	4:04	5:06
10	5:41	6:44	7:47	8:50	9:53	10:56	11:59	1:01	2:04	3:07	4:10	5:13
15	5:32	6:37	7:41	8:45	9:50	10:54	11:59	1:03	2:07	3:12	4:16	5:20
20	5:23	6:29	7:35	8:41	9:47	10:53	11:59	1:04	2:10	3:16	4:22	5:28
25	5:13	6:20	7:28	8:36	9:43	10:51	11:59	1:06	2:14	3:21	4:29	5:37
28	5:06	6:15	7:24	8:32	9:41	10:50	11:59	1:07	2:16	3:25	4:33	5:42
31	4:59	6:09	7:19	8:29	9:39	10:49	11:59	1:08	2:18	3:28	4:38	5:48
34	4:52	6:03	7:14	8:25	9:36	10:47	11:59	1:10	2:21	3:32	4:43	5:54
37	4:43	5:56	7:08	8:21	9:33	10:46	11:59	1:11	2:24	3:36	4:49	6:01
40	4:35	5:49	7:03	8:17	9:31	10:45	11:59	1:13	2:26	3:40	4:54	6:08
42	4:28	5:43	6:58	8:13	9:28	10:43	11:59	1:14	2:29	3:44	4:59	6:14
44	4:21	5:37	6:54	8:10	9:26	10:42	11:59	1:15	2:31	3:47	5:03	6:20
46	4:14	5:31	6:49	8:06	9:24	10:41	11:59	1:16	2:33	3:51	5:08	6:26
48	4:05	5:24	6:43	8:02	9:21	10:40	11:59	1:17	2:36	3:55	5:14	6:33
50	3:56	5:17	6:37	7:57	9:18	10:38	11:59	1:19	2:39	4:00	5:20	6:40
52	3:46	5:08	6:30	7:52	9:14	10:36	11:59	1:21	2:43	4:05	5:27	6:49
54	3:35	4:59	6:23	7:47	9:11	10:35	11:59	1:22	2:46	4:10	5:34	6:58
56	3:21	4:48	6:14	7:40	9:06	10:32	11:59	1:25	2:51	4:17	5:43	7:09
58	3:06	4:35	6:04	7:32	9:01	10:30	11:59	1:27	2:56	4:25	5:53	7:22
S	13	14	15	16	17	18	19	20	21	22	23	24

NIGHT HOURS - DUSK TO DAWN

LAT. N	13	14	15	16	17	18	19	20	21	22	23	24
0	5:59	6:59	7:59	8:59	9:59	10:59	11:59	12:59	1:59	2:59	3:59	4:59
5	6:07	7:06	8:04	9:03	10:01	11:00	11:59	12:57	1:56	2:54	3:53	4:51
10	6:16	7:13	8:10	9:07	10:04	11:01	11:59	12:56	1:53	2:50	3:47	4:44
15	6:25	7:20	8:16	9:12	10:07	11:03	11:59	12:54	1:50	2:45	3:41	4:37
20	6:34	7:28	8:22	9:16	10:10	11:04	11:59	12:53	1:47	2:41	3:35	4:29
25	6:44	7:37	8:29	9:21	10:14	11:06	11:59	12:51	1:43	2:36	3:28	4:20
28	6:51	7:42	8:33	9:25	10:16	11:07	11:59	12:50	1:41	2:32	3:24	4:15
31	6:58	7:48	8:38	9:28	10:18	11:08	11:59	12:49	1:39	2:29	3:19	4:09
34	7:05	7:54	8:43	9:32	10:21	11:10	11:59	12:47	1:36	2:25	3:14	4:03
37	7:14	8:01	8:49	9:36	10:24	11:11	11:59	12:46	1:33	2:21	3:08	3:56
40	7:22	8:08	8:54	9:40	10:26	11:13	11:59	12:45	1:31	2:17	3:03	3:49
42	7:29	8:14	8:59	9:44	10:29	11:14	11:59	12:43	1:28	2:13	2:58	3:43
44	7:36	8:20	9:03	9:47	10:31	11:15	11:59	12:42	1:26	2:10	2:54	3:37
46	7:43	8:26	9:08	9:51	10:33	11:16	11:59	12:41	1:24	2:06	2:49	3:31
48	7:52	8:33	9:14	9:55	10:36	11:17	11:59	12:40	1:21	2:02	2:43	3:24
50	8:01	8:40	9:20	10:00	10:39	11:19	11:59	12:38	1:18	1:57	2:37	3:17
52	8:11	8:49	9:27	10:05	10:43	11:21	11:59	12:36	1:14	1:52	2:30	3:08
54	8:22	8:58	9:34	10:10	10:46	11:22	11:59	12:35	1:11	1:47	2:23	2:59
56	8:36	9:09	9:43	10:17	10:51	11:25	11:59	12:32	1:06	1:40	2:14	2:48
58	8:51	9:22	9:53	10:25	10:56	11:27	11:59	12:30	1:01	1:32	2:04	2:35
S	1	2	3	4	5	6	7	8	9	10	11	12

June 15th to 22nd

DAYLIGHT HOURS - DAWN TO DUSK

LAT. N	1	2	3	4	5	6	7	8	9	10	11	12
0	6:01	7:01	8:01	9:01	10:01	11:01	12:01	1:01	2:01	3:01	4:01	5:01
5	5:52	6:53	7:55	8:56	9:58	10:59	12:01	1:02	2:03	3:05	4:06	5:08
10	5:43	6:46	7:49	8:52	9:55	10:58	12:01	1:03	2:06	3:09	4:12	5:15
15	5:34	6:38	7:43	8:47	9:52	10:56	12:01	1:05	2:09	3:14	4:18	5:23
20	5:24	6:30	7:36	8:42	9:48	10:54	12:01	1:07	2:13	3:19	4:25	5:31
25	5:14	6:22	7:29	8:37	9:45	10:53	12:01	1:08	2:16	3:24	4:32	5:39
28	5:07	6:16	7:25	8:34	9:43	10:52	12:01	1:09	2:18	3:27	4:36	5:45
31	5:00	6:10	7:20	8:30	9:40	10:50	12:01	1:11	2:21	3:31	4:41	5:51
34	4:53	6:04	7:15	8:27	9:38	10:49	12:01	1:12	2:23	3:35	4:46	5:57
37	4:44	5:57	7:10	8:22	9:35	10:48	12:01	1:13	2:26	3:39	4:51	6:04
40	4:35	5:49	7:04	8:18	9:32	10:46	12:01	1:15	2:29	3:43	4:57	6:12
42	4:29	5:44	6:59	8:15	9:30	10:45	12:01	1:16	2:31	3:46	5:02	6:17
44	4:22	5:38	6:55	8:11	9:28	10:44	12:01	1:17	2:33	3:50	5:06	6:23
46	4:14	5:32	6:49	8:07	9:25	10:43	12:01	1:18	2:36	3:54	5:12	6:29
48	4:05	5:25	6:44	8:03	9:22	10:41	12:01	1:20	2:39	3:58	5:17	6:36
50	3:56	5:17	6:38	7:58	9:19	10:40	12:01	1:21	2:42	4:03	5:23	6:44
52	3:46	5:08	6:31	7:53	9:16	10:38	12:01	1:23	2:45	4:08	5:30	6:53
54	3:34	4:58	6:23	7:47	9:12	10:36	12:01	1:25	2:49	4:14	5:38	7:03
56	3:21	4:47	6:14	7:41	9:07	10:34	12:01	1:27	2:54	4:20	5:47	7:14
58	3:05	4:34	6:03	7:33	9:02	10:31	12:01	1:30	2:59	4:28	5:58	7:27
S	13	14	15	16	17	18	19	20	21	22	23	24

NIGHT HOURS - DUSK TO DAWN

LAT. N	13	14	15	16	17	18	19	20	21	22	23	24
0	6:01	7:01	8:01	9:01	10:01	11:01	12:01	1:01	2:01	3:01	4:01	5:01
5	6:09	7:08	8:06	9:05	10:03	11:02	12:01	12:59	1:58	2:56	3:55	4:53
10	6:18	7:15	8:12	9:09	10:06	11:03	12:01	12:58	1:55	2:52	3:49	4:46
15	6:27	7:23	8:18	9:14	10:09	11:05	12:01	12:56	1:52	2:47	3:43	4:38
20	6:37	7:31	8:25	9:19	10:13	11:07	12:01	12:54	1:48	2:42	3:36	4:30
25	6:47	7:39	8:32	9:24	10:16	11:08	12:01	12:53	1:45	2:37	3:29	4:22
28	6:54	7:45	8:36	9:27	10:18	11:09	12:01	12:52	1:43	2:34	3:25	4:16
31	7:01	7:51	8:41	9:31	10:21	11:11	12:01	12:50	1:40	2:30	3:20	4:10
34	7:09	7:57	8:46	9:35	10:23	11:12	12:01	12:49	1:38	2:27	3:15	4:04
37	7:17	8:04	8:51	9:39	10:26	11:13	12:01	12:48	1:35	2:22	3:10	3:57
40	7:26	8:12	8:57	9:43	10:29	11:15	12:01	12:46	1:32	2:18	3:04	3:49
42	7:32	8:17	9:02	9:46	10:31	11:16	12:01	12:45	1:30	2:15	2:59	3:44
44	7:39	8:23	9:06	9:50	10:33	11:17	12:01	12:44	1:28	2:11	2:55	3:38
46	7:47	8:29	9:12	9:54	10:36	11:18	12:01	12:43	1:25	2:07	2:49	3:32
48	7:56	8:36	9:17	9:58	10:39	11:20	12:01	12:41	1:22	2:03	2:44	3:25
50	8:05	8:44	9:23	10:03	10:42	11:21	12:01	12:40	1:19	1:58	2:38	3:17
52	8:15	8:53	9:30	10:08	10:45	11:23	12:01	12:38	1:16	1:53	2:31	3:08
54	8:27	9:03	9:38	10:14	10:49	11:25	12:01	12:36	1:12	1:47	2:23	2:58
56	8:40	9:14	9:47	10:20	10:54	11:27	12:01	12:34	1:07	1:41	2:14	2:47
58	8:56	9:27	9:58	10:28	10:59	11:30	12:01	12:31	1:02	1:33	2:03	2:34
S	1	2	3	4	5	6	7	8	9	10	11	12

June 23rd to 30th

DAYLIGHT HOURS - DAWN TO DUSK

LAT. N	1	2	3	4	5	6	7	8	9	10	11	12
0	6:02	7:02	8:02	9:02	10:02	11:02	12:02	1:02	2:02	3:02	4:02	5:02
5	5:53	6:54	7:56	8:57	9:59	11:00	12:02	1:03	2:04	3:06	4:07	5:09
10	5:44	6:47	7:50	8:53	9:56	10:59	12:02	1:04	2:07	3:10	4:13	5:16
15	5:35	6:39	7:44	8:48	9:53	10:57	12:02	1:06	2:10	3:15	4:19	5:24
20	5:25	6:31	7:37	8:43	9:49	10:55	12:02	1:08	2:14	3:20	4:26	5:32
25	5:15	6:23	7:31	8:38	9:46	10:54	12:02	1:09	2:17	3:25	4:32	5:40
28	5:08	6:17	7:26	8:35	9:44	10:53	12:02	1:10	2:19	3:28	4:37	5:46
31	5:01	6:11	7:21	8:31	9:41	10:51	12:02	1:12	2:22	3:32	4:42	5:52
34	4:54	6:05	7:16	8:28	9:39	10:50	12:02	1:13	2:24	3:35	4:47	5:58
37	4:46	5:58	7:11	8:24	9:36	10:49	12:02	1:14	2:27	3:39	4:52	6:05
40	4:37	5:51	7:05	8:19	9:33	10:47	12:02	1:16	2:30	3:44	4:58	6:12
42	4:30	5:45	7:01	8:16	9:31	10:46	12:02	1:17	2:32	3:47	5:03	6:18
44	4:23	5:39	6:56	8:12	9:29	10:45	12:02	1:18	2:34	3:51	5:07	6:24
46	4:15	5:33	6:51	8:08	9:26	10:44	12:02	1:19	2:37	3:55	5:12	6:30
48	4:07	5:26	6:45	8:04	9:23	10:42	12:02	1:21	2:40	3:59	5:18	6:37
50	3:58	5:18	6:39	8:00	9:20	10:41	12:02	1:22	2:43	4:03	5:24	6:45
52	3:47	5:10	6:32	7:54	9:17	10:39	12:02	1:24	2:46	4:09	5:31	6:53
54	3:36	5:00	6:24	7:49	9:13	10:37	12:02	1:26	2:50	4:14	5:39	7:03
56	3:22	4:49	6:15	7:42	9:08	10:35	12:02	1:28	2:55	4:21	5:48	7:14
58	3:07	4:36	6:05	7:34	9:03	10:32	12:02	1:31	3:00	4:29	5:58	7:27
S	13	14	15	16	17	18	19	20	21	22	23	24

NIGHT HOURS - DUSK TO DAWN

LAT. N	13	14	15	16	17	18	19	20	21	22	23	24
0	6:02	7:02	8:02	9:02	10:02	11:02	12:02	1:02	2:02	3:02	4:02	5:02
5	6:10	7:09	8:07	9:06	10:04	11:03	12:02	1:00	1:59	2:57	3:56	4:54
10	6:19	7:16	8:13	9:10	10:07	11:04	12:02	12:59	1:56	2:53	3:50	4:47
15	6:28	7:24	8:19	9:15	10:10	11:06	12:02	12:57	1:53	2:48	3:44	4:39
20	6:38	7:32	8:26	9:20	10:14	11:08	12:02	12:55	1:49	2:43	3:37	4:31
25	6:48	7:40	8:32	9:25	10:17	11:09	12:02	12:54	1:46	2:38	3:31	4:23
28	6:55	7:46	8:37	9:28	10:19	11:10	12:02	12:53	1:44	2:35	3:26	4:17
31	7:02	7:52	8:42	9:32	10:22	11:12	12:02	12:51	1:41	2:31	3:21	4:11
34	7:09	7:58	8:47	9:35	10:24	11:13	12:02	12:50	1:39	2:28	3:16	4:05
37	7:17	8:05	8:52	9:39	10:27	11:14	12:02	12:49	1:36	2:24	3:11	3:58
40	7:26	8:12	8:58	9:44	10:30	11:16	12:02	12:47	1:33	2:19	3:05	3:51
42	7:33	8:18	9:03	9:47	10:32	11:17	12:02	12:46	1:31	2:16	3:01	3:45
44	7:40	8:24	9:07	9:51	10:34	11:18	12:02	12:45	1:29	2:12	2:56	3:39
46	7:48	8:30	9:12	9:55	10:37	11:19	12:02	12:44	1:26	2:08	2:51	3:33
48	7:56	8:37	9:18	9:59	10:40	11:21	12:02	12:42	1:23	2:04	2:45	3:26
50	8:05	8:45	9:24	10:03	10:43	11:22	12:02	12:41	1:20	2:00	2:39	3:18
52	8:16	8:53	9:31	10:09	10:46	11:24	12:02	12:39	1:17	1:54	2:32	3:10
54	8:27	9:03	9:39	10:14	10:50	11:26	12:02	12:37	1:13	1:49	2:24	3:00
56	8:41	9:14	9:48	10:21	10:55	11:28	12:02	12:35	1:08	1:42	2:15	2:49
58	8:56	9:27	9:58	10:29	11:00	11:31	12:02	12:32	1:03	1:34	2:05	2:36
S	1	2	3	4	5	6	7	8	9	10	11	12

July 1st to 7th

DAYLIGHT HOURS - DAWN TO DUSK

LAT. N	1	2	3	4	5	6	7	8	9	10	11	12
0	6:04	7:04	8:04	9:04	10:04	11:04	12:04	1:04	2:04	3:04	4:04	5:04
5	5:55	6:56	7:58	8:59	10:01	11:02	12:04	1:05	2:06	3:08	4:09	5:11
10	5:46	6:49	7:52	8:55	9:58	11:01	12:04	1:06	2:09	3:12	4:15	5:18
15	5:37	6:42	7:46	8:51	9:55	10:59	12:04	1:08	2:12	3:17	4:21	5:25
20	5:28	6:34	7:40	8:46	9:52	10:58	12:04	1:09	2:15	3:21	4:27	5:33
25	5:18	6:26	7:33	8:41	9:48	10:56	12:04	1:11	2:19	3:26	4:34	5:41
28	5:12	6:20	7:29	8:38	9:46	10:55	12:04	1:12	2:21	3:29	4:38	5:47
31	5:05	6:14	7:24	8:34	9:44	10:54	12:04	1:13	2:23	3:33	4:43	5:53
34	4:57	6:08	7:19	8:30	9:41	10:52	12:04	1:15	2:26	3:37	4:48	5:59
37	4:49	6:02	7:14	8:26	9:39	10:51	12:04	1:16	2:28	3:41	4:53	6:05
40	4:40	5:54	7:08	8:22	9:36	10:50	12:04	1:17	2:31	3:45	4:59	6:13
42	4:34	5:49	7:04	8:19	9:34	10:49	12:04	1:18	2:33	3:48	5:03	6:18
44	4:27	5:43	6:59	8:15	9:31	10:47	12:04	1:20	2:36	3:52	5:08	6:24
46	4:20	5:37	6:54	8:12	9:29	10:46	12:04	1:21	2:38	3:55	5:13	6:30
48	4:11	5:30	6:49	8:08	9:26	10:45	12:04	1:22	2:41	4:00	5:18	6:37
50	4:02	5:23	6:43	8:03	9:23	10:43	12:04	1:24	2:44	4:04	5:24	6:44
52	3:52	5:14	6:36	7:58	9:20	10:42	12:04	1:25	2:47	4:09	5:31	6:53
54	3:41	5:05	6:29	7:52	9:16	10:40	12:04	1:27	2:51	4:15	5:38	7:02
56	3:28	4:54	6:20	7:46	9:12	10:38	12:04	1:29	2:55	4:21	5:47	7:13
58	3:13	4:42	6:10	7:38	9:07	10:35	12:04	1:32	3:00	4:29	5:57	7:25
S	13	14	15	16	17	18	19	20	21	22	23	24

NIGHT HOURS - DUSK TO DAWN

LAT. N	13	14	15	16	17	18	19	20	21	22	23	24
0	6:04	7:04	8:04	9:04	10:04	11:04	12:04	1:04	2:04	3:04	4:04	5:04
5	6:12	7:11	8:09	9:08	10:06	11:05	12:04	1:02	2:01	2:59	3:58	4:56
10	6:21	7:18	8:15	9:12	10:09	11:06	12:04	1:01	1:58	2:55	3:52	4:49
15	6:30	7:25	8:21	9:17	10:12	11:08	12:04	12:59	1:55	2:50	3:46	4:42
20	6:39	7:33	8:27	9:21	10:15	11:09	12:04	12:58	1:52	2:46	3:40	4:34
25	6:49	7:41	8:34	9:26	10:19	11:11	12:04	12:56	1:48	2:41	3:33	4:26
28	6:55	7:47	8:38	9:29	10:21	11:12	12:04	12:55	1:46	2:38	3:29	4:20
31	7:02	7:53	8:43	9:33	10:23	11:13	12:04	12:54	1:44	2:34	3:24	4:14
34	7:10	7:59	8:48	9:37	10:26	11:15	12:04	12:52	1:41	2:30	3:19	4:08
37	7:18	8:05	8:53	9:41	10:28	11:16	12:04	12:51	1:39	2:26	3:14	4:02
40	7:27	8:13	8:59	9:45	10:31	11:17	12:04	12:50	1:36	2:22	3:08	3:54
42	7:33	8:18	9:03	9:48	10:33	11:18	12:04	12:49	1:34	2:19	3:04	3:49
44	7:40	8:24	9:08	9:52	10:36	11:20	12:04	12:47	1:31	2:15	2:59	3:43
46	7:47	8:30	9:13	9:55	10:38	11:21	12:04	12:46	1:29	2:12	2:54	3:37
48	7:56	8:37	9:18	10:00	10:41	11:22	12:04	12:45	1:26	2:08	2:49	3:30
50	8:05	8:44	9:24	10:04	10:44	11:24	12:04	12:43	1:23	2:03	2:43	3:23
52	8:15	8:53	9:31	10:09	10:47	11:25	12:04	12:42	1:20	1:58	2:36	3:14
54	8:26	9:02	9:38	10:15	10:51	11:27	12:04	12:40	1:16	1:52	2:29	3:05
56	8:39	9:13	9:47	10:21	10:55	11:29	12:04	12:38	1:12	1:46	2:20	2:54
58	8:54	9:25	9:57	10:29	11:00	11:32	12:04	12:35	1:07	1:38	2:10	2:42
S	1	2	3	4	5	6	7	8	9	10	11	12

July 8th to 15th

DAYLIGHT HOURS - DAWN TO DUSK

LAT. N	1	2	3	4	5	6	7	8	9	10	11	12
0	6:05	7:05	8:05	9:05	10:05	11:05	12:05	1:05	2:05	3:05	4:05	5:05
5	5:56	6:58	7:59	9:00	10:02	11:03	12:05	1:06	2:07	3:09	4:10	5:11
10	5:48	6:51	7:54	8:56	9:59	11:02	12:05	1:07	2:10	3:13	4:15	5:18
15	5:40	6:44	7:48	8:52	9:56	11:00	12:05	1:09	2:13	3:17	4:21	5:25
20	5:31	6:36	7:42	8:48	9:53	10:59	12:05	1:10	2:16	3:21	4:27	5:33
25	5:21	6:28	7:35	8:43	9:50	10:57	12:05	1:12	2:19	3:26	4:34	5:41
28	5:15	6:23	7:31	8:40	9:48	10:56	12:05	1:13	2:21	3:29	4:38	5:46
31	5:08	6:18	7:27	8:36	9:46	10:55	12:05	1:14	2:23	3:33	4:42	5:51
34	5:01	6:12	7:22	8:33	9:43	10:54	12:05	1:15	2:26	3:36	4:47	5:57
37	4:53	6:05	7:17	8:29	9:41	10:53	12:05	1:16	2:28	3:40	4:52	6:04
40	4:45	5:58	7:12	8:25	9:38	10:51	12:05	1:18	2:31	3:44	4:57	6:11
42	4:39	5:53	7:07	8:22	9:36	10:50	12:05	1:19	2:33	3:47	5:02	6:16
44	4:32	5:48	7:03	8:18	9:34	10:49	12:05	1:20	2:35	3:51	5:06	6:21
46	4:25	5:42	6:58	8:15	9:31	10:48	12:05	1:21	2:38	3:54	5:11	6:27
48	4:18	5:35	6:53	8:11	9:29	10:47	12:05	1:22	2:40	3:58	5:16	6:34
50	4:09	5:28	6:48	8:07	9:26	10:45	12:05	1:24	2:43	4:02	5:21	6:41
52	4:00	5:20	6:41	8:02	9:23	10:44	12:05	1:25	2:46	4:07	5:28	6:49
54	3:49	5:12	6:34	7:57	9:19	10:42	12:05	1:27	2:50	4:12	5:35	6:57
56	3:37	5:01	6:26	7:51	9:15	10:40	12:05	1:29	2:54	4:18	5:43	7:08
58	3:23	4:50	6:17	7:44	9:11	10:38	12:05	1:31	2:58	4:25	5:52	7:19
S	13	14	15	16	17	18	19	20	21	22	23	24

NIGHT HOURS - DUSK TO DAWN

LAT. N	13	14	15	16	17	18	19	20	21	22	23	24
0	6:05	7:05	8:05	9:05	10:05	11:05	12:05	1:05	2:05	3:05	4:05	5:05
5	6:13	7:11	8:10	9:09	10:07	11:06	12:05	1:03	2:02	3:00	3:59	4:58
10	6:21	7:18	8:15	9:13	10:10	11:07	12:05	1:02	1:59	2:56	3:54	4:51
15	6:29	7:25	8:21	9:17	10:13	11:09	12:05	1:00	1:56	2:52	3:48	4:44
20	6:38	7:33	8:27	9:21	10:16	11:10	12:05	12:59	1:53	2:48	3:42	4:36
25	6:48	7:41	8:34	9:26	10:19	11:12	12:05	12:57	1:50	2:43	3:35	4:28
28	6:54	7:46	8:38	9:29	10:21	11:13	12:05	12:56	1:48	2:40	3:31	4:23
31	7:01	7:51	8:42	9:33	10:23	11:14	12:05	12:55	1:46	2:36	3:27	4:18
34	7:08	7:57	8:47	9:36	10:26	11:15	12:05	12:54	1:43	2:33	3:22	4:12
37	7:16	8:04	8:52	9:40	10:28	11:16	12:05	12:53	1:41	2:29	3:17	4:05
40	7:24	8:11	8:57	9:44	10:31	11:18	12:05	12:51	1:38	2:25	3:12	3:58
42	7:30	8:16	9:02	9:47	10:33	11:19	12:05	12:50	1:36	2:22	3:07	3:53
44	7:37	8:21	9:06	9:51	10:35	11:20	12:05	12:49	1:34	2:18	3:03	3:48
46	7:44	8:27	9:11	9:54	10:38	11:21	12:05	12:48	1:31	2:15	2:58	3:42
48	7:51	8:34	9:16	9:58	10:40	11:22	12:05	12:47	1:29	2:11	2:53	3:35
50	8:00	8:41	9:21	10:02	10:43	11:24	12:05	12:45	1:26	2:07	2:48	3:28
52	8:09	8:49	9:28	10:07	10:46	11:25	12:05	12:44	1:23	2:02	2:41	3:20
54	8:20	8:57	9:35	10:12	10:50	11:27	12:05	12:42	1:19	1:57	2:34	3:12
56	8:32	9:08	9:43	10:18	10:54	11:29	12:05	12:40	1:15	1:51	2:26	3:01
58	8:46	9:19	9:52	10:25	10:58	11:31	12:05	12:38	1:11	1:44	2:17	2:50
S	1	2	3	4	5	6	7	8	9	10	11	12

July 16th to 23rd

DAYLIGHT HOURS - DAWN TO DUSK

LAT. N	1	2	3	4	5	6	7	8	9	10	11	12
0	6:06	7:06	8:06	9:06	10:06	11:06	12:06	1:06	2:06	3:06	4:06	5:06
5	5:58	6:59	8:00	9:02	10:03	11:04	12:06	1:07	2:08	3:09	4:11	5:12
10	5:50	6:53	7:55	8:58	10:00	11:03	12:06	1:08	2:11	3:13	4:16	5:18
15	5:42	6:46	7:50	8:54	9:58	11:02	12:06	1:09	2:13	3:17	4:21	5:25
20	5:34	6:39	7:44	8:50	9:55	11:00	12:06	1:11	2:16	3:21	4:27	5:32
25	5:25	6:32	7:38	8:45	9:52	10:59	12:06	1:12	2:19	3:26	4:33	5:39
28	5:19	6:27	7:34	8:42	9:50	10:58	12:06	1:13	2:21	3:29	4:37	5:44
31	5:13	6:22	7:30	8:39	9:48	10:57	12:06	1:14	2:23	3:32	4:41	5:49
34	5:06	6:16	7:26	8:36	9:46	10:56	12:06	1:15	2:25	3:35	4:45	5:55
37	4:59	6:10	7:21	8:32	9:43	10:54	12:06	1:17	2:28	3:39	4:50	6:01
40	4:51	6:04	7:16	8:28	9:41	10:53	12:06	1:18	2:30	3:43	4:55	6:07
42	4:46	5:59	7:12	8:26	9:39	10:52	12:06	1:19	2:32	3:45	4:59	6:12
44	4:40	5:54	7:08	8:23	9:37	10:51	12:06	1:20	2:34	3:48	5:03	6:17
46	4:33	5:48	7:04	8:19	9:35	10:50	12:06	1:21	2:36	3:52	5:07	6:23
48	4:26	5:42	6:59	8:16	9:32	10:49	12:06	1:22	2:39	3:55	5:12	6:29
50	4:18	5:36	6:54	8:12	9:30	10:48	12:06	1:23	2:41	3:59	5:17	6:35
52	4:09	5:29	6:48	8:07	9:27	10:46	12:06	1:25	2:44	4:04	5:23	6:42
54	4:00	5:21	6:42	8:03	9:24	10:45	12:06	1:26	2:47	4:08	5:29	6:50
56	3:49	5:11	6:34	7:57	9:20	10:43	12:06	1:28	2:51	4:14	5:37	7:00
58	3:36	5:01	6:26	7:51	9:16	10:41	12:06	1:30	2:55	4:20	5:45	7:10
S	13	14	15	16	17	18	19	20	21	22	23	24

NIGHT HOURS - DUSK TO DAWN

LAT. N	13	14	15	16	17	18	19	20	21	22	23	24
0	6:06	7:06	8:06	9:06	10:06	11:06	12:06	1:06	2:06	3:06	4:06	5:06
5	6:13	7:12	8:11	9:09	10:08	11:07	12:06	1:04	2:03	3:02	4:00	4:59
10	6:21	7:18	8:16	9:13	10:11	11:08	12:06	1:03	2:00	2:58	3:55	4:53
15	6:29	7:25	8:21	9:17	10:13	11:09	12:06	1:02	1:58	2:54	3:50	4:46
20	6:37	7:32	8:27	9:21	10:16	11:11	12:06	1:00	1:55	2:50	3:44	4:39
25	6:46	7:39	8:33	9:26	10:19	11:12	12:06	12:59	1:52	2:45	3:38	4:32
28	6:52	7:44	8:37	9:29	10:21	11:13	12:06	12:58	1:50	2:42	3:34	4:27
31	6:58	7:49	8:41	9:32	10:23	11:14	12:06	12:57	1:48	2:39	3:30	4:22
34	7:05	7:55	8:45	9:35	10:25	11:15	12:06	12:56	1:46	2:36	3:26	4:16
37	7:12	8:01	8:50	9:39	10:28	11:17	12:06	12:54	1:43	2:32	3:21	4:10
40	7:20	8:07	8:55	9:43	10:30	11:18	12:06	12:53	1:41	2:28	3:16	4:04
42	7:25	8:12	8:59	9:45	10:32	11:19	12:06	12:52	1:39	2:26	3:12	3:59
44	7:31	8:17	9:03	9:48	10:34	11:20	12:06	12:51	1:37	2:23	3:08	3:54
46	7:38	8:23	9:07	9:52	10:36	11:21	12:06	12:50	1:35	2:19	3:04	3:48
48	7:45	8:29	9:12	9:55	10:39	11:22	12:06	12:49	1:32	2:16	2:59	3:42
50	7:53	8:35	9:17	9:59	10:41	11:23	12:06	12:48	1:30	2:12	2:54	3:36
52	8:02	8:42	9:23	10:04	10:44	11:25	12:06	12:46	1:27	2:07	2:48	3:29
54	8:11	8:50	9:29	10:08	10:47	11:26	12:06	12:45	1:24	2:03	2:42	3:21
56	8:22	9:00	9:37	10:14	10:51	11:28	12:06	12:43	1:20	1:57	2:34	3:11
58	8:35	9:10	9:45	10:20	10:55	11:30	12:06	12:41	1:16	1:51	2:26	3:01
S	1	2	3	4	5	6	7	8	9	10	11	12

July 24th to 31st

DAYLIGHT HOURS - DAWN TO DUSK

LAT. N	1	2	3	4	5	6	7	8	9	10	11	12
0	6:06	7:06	8:06	9:06	10:06	11:06	12:06	1:06	2:06	3:06	4:06	5:06
5	5:59	7:00	8:01	9:02	10:03	11:04	12:06	1:07	2:08	3:09	4:10	5:11
10	5:52	6:54	7:56	8:59	10:01	11:03	12:06	1:08	2:10	3:13	4:15	5:17
15	5:44	6:48	7:51	8:55	9:58	11:02	12:06	1:09	2:13	3:16	4:20	5:23
20	5:37	6:41	7:46	8:51	9:56	11:01	12:06	1:10	2:15	3:20	4:25	5:30
25	5:28	6:35	7:41	8:47	9:53	10:59	12:06	1:12	2:18	3:24	4:30	5:36
28	5:23	6:30	7:37	8:44	9:51	10:58	12:06	1:13	2:20	3:27	4:34	5:41
31	5:17	6:25	7:33	8:41	9:49	10:58	12:06	1:14	2:22	3:30	4:38	5:46
34	5:11	6:20	7:29	8:38	9:47	10:57	12:06	1:15	2:24	3:33	4:42	5:51
37	5:05	6:15	7:25	8:35	9:45	10:55	12:06	1:16	2:26	3:36	4:46	5:56
40	4:58	6:09	7:20	8:32	9:43	10:54	12:06	1:17	2:28	3:39	4:51	6:02
42	4:53	6:05	7:17	8:29	9:41	10:53	12:06	1:18	2:30	3:42	4:54	6:06
44	4:47	6:00	7:13	8:26	9:39	10:52	12:06	1:19	2:32	3:45	4:58	6:11
46	4:41	5:55	7:09	8:23	9:37	10:51	12:06	1:20	2:34	3:48	5:02	6:16
48	4:35	5:50	7:05	8:20	9:35	10:50	12:06	1:21	2:36	3:51	5:06	6:21
50	4:28	5:44	7:01	8:17	9:33	10:49	12:06	1:22	2:38	3:54	5:11	6:27
52	4:20	5:38	6:55	8:13	9:30	10:48	12:06	1:23	2:41	3:58	5:16	6:33
54	4:12	5:31	6:50	8:09	9:28	10:47	12:06	1:24	2:43	4:02	5:21	6:40
56	4:02	5:23	6:43	8:04	9:24	10:45	12:06	1:26	2:47	4:07	5:28	6:48
58	3:51	5:13	6:36	7:58	9:21	10:43	12:06	1:28	2:50	4:13	5:35	6:58
S	13	14	15	16	17	18	19	20	21	22	23	24

NIGHT HOURS - DUSK TO DAWN

LAT. N	13	14	15	16	17	18	19	20	21	22	23	24
0	6:06	7:06	8:06	9:06	10:06	11:06	12:06	1:06	2:06	3:06	4:06	5:06
5	6:12	7:11	8:10	9:09	10:08	11:07	12:06	1:04	2:03	3:02	4:01	5:00
10	6:20	7:17	8:15	9:13	10:10	11:08	12:06	1:03	2:01	2:59	3:56	4:54
15	6:27	7:23	8:20	9:16	10:13	11:09	12:06	1:02	1:58	2:55	3:51	4:48
20	6:34	7:30	8:25	9:20	10:15	11:10	12:06	1:01	1:56	2:51	3:46	4:41
25	6:43	7:36	8:30	9:24	10:18	11:12	12:06	12:59	1:53	2:47	3:41	4:35
28	6:48	7:41	8:34	9:27	10:20	11:13	12:06	12:58	1:51	2:44	3:37	4:30
31	6:54	7:46	8:38	9:30	10:22	11:14	12:06	12:58	1:49	2:41	3:33	4:25
34	7:00	7:51	8:42	9:33	10:24	11:15	12:06	12:57	1:47	2:38	3:29	4:20
37	7:06	7:56	8:46	9:36	10:26	11:16	12:06	12:55	1:45	2:35	3:25	4:15
40	7:13	8:02	8:51	9:39	10:28	11:17	12:06	12:54	1:43	2:32	3:20	4:09
42	7:18	8:06	8:54	9:42	10:30	11:18	12:06	12:53	1:41	2:29	3:17	4:05
44	7:24	8:11	8:58	9:45	10:32	11:19	12:06	12:52	1:39	2:26	3:13	4:00
46	7:30	8:16	9:02	9:48	10:34	11:20	12:06	12:51	1:37	2:23	3:09	3:55
48	7:36	8:21	9:06	9:51	10:36	11:21	12:06	12:50	1:35	2:20	3:05	3:50
50	7:43	8:27	9:11	9:54	10:38	11:22	12:06	12:49	1:33	2:17	3:01	3:44
52	7:51	8:33	9:16	9:58	10:41	11:23	12:06	12:48	1:30	2:13	2:55	3:38
54	7:59	8:40	9:21	10:02	10:43	11:24	12:06	12:47	1:28	2:09	2:50	3:31
56	8:09	8:48	9:28	10:07	10:47	11:26	12:06	12:45	1:24	2:04	2:43	3:23
58	8:20	8:58	9:35	10:13	10:50	11:28	12:06	12:43	1:21	1:58	2:36	3:13
S	1	2	3	4	5	6	7	8	9	10	11	12

August 1st to 7th

DAYLIGHT HOURS - DAWN TO DUSK

LAT. N	1	2	3	4	5	6	7	8	9	10	11	12
0	6:06	7:06	8:06	9:06	10:06	11:06	12:06	1:06	2:06	3:06	4:06	5:06
5	5:59	7:00	8:01	9:02	10:03	11:04	12:06	1:07	2:08	3:09	4:10	5:11
10	5:53	6:55	7:57	8:59	10:01	11:03	12:06	1:08	2:10	3:12	4:14	5:16
15	5:46	6:49	7:53	8:56	9:59	11:02	12:06	1:09	2:12	3:15	4:18	5:22
20	5:39	6:44	7:48	8:52	9:57	11:01	12:06	1:10	2:14	3:19	4:23	5:27
25	5:32	6:38	7:43	8:49	9:54	11:00	12:06	1:11	2:17	3:22	4:28	5:33
28	5:27	6:34	7:40	8:46	9:53	10:59	12:06	1:12	2:18	3:25	4:31	5:37
31	5:22	6:29	7:37	8:44	9:51	10:58	12:06	1:13	2:20	3:27	4:34	5:42
34	5:17	6:25	7:33	8:41	9:49	10:57	12:06	1:14	2:22	3:30	4:38	5:46
37	5:11	6:20	7:29	8:38	9:47	10:56	12:06	1:15	2:24	3:33	4:42	5:51
40	5:05	6:15	7:25	8:35	9:45	10:55	12:06	1:16	2:26	3:36	4:46	5:56
42	5:00	6:11	7:22	8:33	9:44	10:55	12:06	1:16	2:27	3:38	4:49	6:00
44	4:55	6:07	7:19	8:30	9:42	10:54	12:06	1:17	2:29	3:41	4:52	6:04
46	4:50	6:02	7:15	8:28	9:40	10:53	12:06	1:18	2:31	3:43	4:56	6:09
48	4:44	5:58	7:11	8:25	9:38	10:52	12:06	1:19	2:33	3:46	5:00	6:13
50	4:38	5:52	7:07	8:22	9:36	10:51	12:06	1:20	2:35	3:49	5:04	6:19
52	4:31	5:47	7:03	8:18	9:34	10:50	12:06	1:21	2:37	3:53	5:08	6:24
54	4:23	5:40	6:57	8:14	9:31	10:48	12:06	1:23	2:40	3:57	5:14	6:31
56	4:15	5:33	6:52	8:10	9:29	10:47	12:06	1:24	2:42	4:01	5:19	6:38
58	4:05	5:25	6:45	8:05	9:25	10:45	12:06	1:26	2:46	4:06	5:26	6:46
S	13	14	15	16	17	18	19	20	21	22	23	24

NIGHT HOURS - DUSK TO DAWN

LAT. N	13	14	15	16	17	18	19	20	21	22	23	24
0	6:06	7:06	8:06	9:06	10:06	11:06	12:06	1:06	2:06	3:06	4:06	5:06
5	6:12	7:11	8:10	9:09	10:08	11:07	12:06	1:04	2:03	3:02	4:01	5:00
10	6:18	7:16	8:14	9:12	10:10	11:08	12:06	1:03	2:01	2:59	3:57	4:55
15	6:25	7:22	8:18	9:15	10:12	11:09	12:06	1:02	1:59	2:56	3:53	4:49
20	6:32	7:27	8:23	9:19	10:14	11:10	12:06	1:01	1:57	2:52	3:48	4:44
25	6:39	7:33	8:28	9:22	10:17	11:11	12:06	1:00	1:54	2:49	3:43	4:38
28	6:44	7:37	8:31	9:25	10:18	11:12	12:06	12:59	1:53	2:46	3:40	4:34
31	6:49	7:42	8:34	9:27	10:20	11:13	12:06	12:58	1:51	2:44	3:37	4:29
34	6:54	7:46	8:38	9:30	10:22	11:14	12:06	12:57	1:49	2:41	3:33	4:25
37	7:00	7:51	8:42	9:33	10:24	11:15	12:06	12:56	1:47	2:38	3:29	4:20
40	7:06	7:56	8:46	9:36	10:26	11:16	12:06	12:55	1:45	2:35	3:25	4:15
42	7:11	8:00	8:49	9:38	10:27	11:16	12:06	12:55	1:44	2:33	3:22	4:11
44	7:16	8:04	8:52	9:41	10:29	11:17	12:06	12:54	1:42	2:30	3:19	4:07
46	7:21	8:09	8:56	9:43	10:31	11:18	12:06	12:53	1:40	2:28	3:15	4:02
48	7:27	8:13	9:00	9:46	10:33	11:19	12:06	12:52	1:38	2:25	3:11	3:58
50	7:33	8:19	9:04	9:49	10:35	11:20	12:06	12:51	1:36	2:22	3:07	3:52
52	7:40	8:24	9:09	9:53	10:37	11:21	12:06	12:50	1:34	2:18	3:03	3:47
54	7:48	8:31	9:14	9:57	10:40	11:23	12:06	12:48	1:31	2:14	2:57	3:40
56	7:56	8:38	9:19	10:01	10:42	11:24	12:06	12:47	1:29	2:10	2:52	3:33
58	8:06	8:46	9:26	10:06	10:46	11:26	12:06	12:45	1:25	2:05	2:45	3:25
S	1	2	3	4	5	6	7	8	9	10	11	12

August 8th to 15th

DAYLIGHT HOURS - DAWN TO DUSK

LAT. N	1	2	3	4	5	6	7	8	9	10	11	12
0	6:05	7:05	8:05	9:05	10:05	11:05	12:05	1:05	2:05	3:05	4:05	5:05
5	5:59	7:00	8:01	9:02	10:03	11:04	12:05	1:05	2:06	3:07	4:08	5:09
10	5:54	6:55	7:57	8:59	10:01	11:03	12:05	1:06	2:08	3:10	4:12	5:14
15	5:48	6:51	7:53	8:56	9:59	11:02	12:05	1:07	2:10	3:13	4:16	5:18
20	5:42	6:46	7:49	8:53	9:57	11:01	12:05	1:08	2:12	3:16	4:20	5:23
25	5:36	6:40	7:45	8:50	9:55	11:00	12:05	1:09	2:14	3:19	4:24	5:29
28	5:31	6:37	7:42	8:48	9:53	10:59	12:05	1:10	2:16	3:21	4:27	5:32
31	5:27	6:33	7:40	8:46	9:52	10:58	12:05	1:11	2:17	3:23	4:29	5:36
34	5:22	6:29	7:36	8:43	9:50	10:58	12:05	1:12	2:19	3:26	4:33	5:40
37	5:17	6:25	7:33	8:41	9:49	10:57	12:05	1:12	2:20	3:28	4:36	5:44
40	5:12	6:21	7:30	8:38	9:47	10:56	12:05	1:13	2:22	3:31	4:39	5:48
42	5:08	6:18	7:27	8:36	9:46	10:55	12:05	1:14	2:23	3:33	4:42	5:51
44	5:04	6:14	7:24	8:34	9:44	10:54	12:05	1:15	2:25	3:35	4:45	5:55
46	4:59	6:10	7:21	8:32	9:43	10:54	12:05	1:15	2:26	3:37	4:48	5:59
48	4:55	6:06	7:18	8:30	9:41	10:53	12:05	1:16	2:28	3:39	4:51	6:03
50	4:49	6:02	7:14	8:27	9:39	10:52	12:05	1:17	2:30	3:42	4:55	6:07
52	4:44	5:57	7:11	8:24	9:38	10:51	12:05	1:18	2:32	3:45	4:59	6:12
54	4:37	5:52	7:06	8:21	9:35	10:50	12:05	1:19	2:34	3:48	5:03	6:17
56	4:30	5:46	7:01	8:17	9:33	10:49	12:05	1:20	2:36	3:52	5:08	6:23
58	4:22	5:39	6:56	8:13	9:30	10:47	12:05	1:22	2:39	3:56	5:13	6:30
S	13	14	15	16	17	18	19	20	21	22	23	24

NIGHT HOURS - DUSK TO DAWN

LAT. N	13	14	15	16	17	18	19	20	21	22	23	24
0	6:05	7:05	8:05	9:05	10:05	11:05	12:05	1:05	2:05	3:05	4:05	5:05
5	6:10	7:09	8:08	9:07	10:06	11:05	12:05	1:04	2:03	3:02	4:01	5:00
10	6:15	7:14	8:12	9:10	10:08	11:06	12:05	1:03	2:01	2:59	3:57	4:55
15	6:21	7:18	8:16	9:13	10:10	11:07	12:05	1:02	1:59	2:56	3:53	4:51
20	6:27	7:23	8:20	9:16	10:12	11:08	12:05	1:01	1:57	2:53	3:49	4:46
25	6:33	7:29	8:24	9:19	10:14	11:09	12:05	1:00	1:55	2:50	3:45	4:40
28	6:38	7:32	8:27	9:21	10:16	11:10	12:05	12:59	1:53	2:48	3:42	4:37
31	6:42	7:36	8:29	9:23	10:17	11:11	12:05	12:58	1:52	2:46	3:40	4:33
34	6:47	7:40	8:33	9:26	10:19	11:12	12:05	12:58	1:50	2:43	3:36	4:29
37	6:52	7:44	8:36	9:28	10:20	11:12	12:05	12:57	1:49	2:41	3:33	4:25
40	6:57	7:48	8:39	9:31	10:22	11:13	12:05	12:56	1:47	2:38	3:30	4:21
42	7:01	7:51	8:42	9:33	10:23	11:14	12:05	12:55	1:46	2:36	3:27	4:18
44	7:05	7:55	8:45	9:35	10:25	11:15	12:05	12:54	1:44	2:34	3:24	4:14
46	7:10	7:59	8:48	9:37	10:26	11:15	12:05	12:54	1:43	2:32	3:21	4:10
48	7:14	8:03	8:51	9:39	10:28	11:16	12:05	12:53	1:41	2:30	3:18	4:06
50	7:20	8:07	8:55	9:42	10:30	11:17	12:05	12:52	1:39	2:27	3:14	4:02
52	7:26	8:12	8:59	9:45	10:32	11:18	12:05	12:51	1:38	2:24	3:11	3:57
54	7:32	8:17	9:03	9:48	10:34	11:19	12:05	12:50	1:35	2:21	3:06	3:52
56	7:39	8:23	9:08	9:52	10:36	11:20	12:05	12:49	1:33	2:17	3:01	3:46
58	7:47	8:30	9:13	9:56	10:39	11:22	12:05	12:47	1:30	2:13	2:56	3:39
S	1	2	3	4	5	6	7	8	9	10	11	12

August 16th to 23rd

DAYLIGHT HOURS - DAWN TO DUSK

LAT. N	1	2	3	4	5	6	7	8	9	10	11	12
0	6:06	7:06	8:06	9:06	10:06	11:06	12:06	1:06	2:06	3:06	4:06	5:06
5	6:01	7:02	8:03	9:03	10:04	11:05	12:06	1:06	2:07	3:08	4:09	5:09
10	5:56	6:58	7:59	9:01	10:02	11:04	12:06	1:07	2:09	3:10	4:12	5:13
15	5:52	6:54	7:56	8:59	10:01	11:03	12:06	1:08	2:10	3:12	4:15	5:17
20	5:47	6:50	7:53	8:56	9:59	11:02	12:06	1:09	2:12	3:15	4:18	5:21
25	5:42	6:46	7:50	8:54	9:58	11:02	12:06	1:10	2:13	3:17	4:21	5:25
28	5:38	6:43	7:47	8:52	9:56	11:01	12:06	1:10	2:15	3:19	4:24	5:28
31	5:35	6:40	7:45	8:50	9:55	11:00	12:06	1:11	2:16	3:21	4:26	5:31
34	5:31	6:37	7:42	8:48	9:54	11:00	12:06	1:11	2:17	3:23	4:29	5:34
37	5:27	6:33	7:40	8:46	9:53	10:59	12:06	1:12	2:18	3:25	4:31	5:38
40	5:22	6:29	7:37	8:44	9:51	10:58	12:06	1:13	2:20	3:27	4:34	5:42
42	5:19	6:27	7:35	8:42	9:50	10:58	12:06	1:13	2:21	3:29	4:37	5:44
44	5:16	6:24	7:32	8:41	9:49	10:57	12:06	1:14	2:22	3:30	4:39	5:47
46	5:12	6:21	7:30	8:39	9:48	10:57	12:06	1:14	2:23	3:32	4:41	5:50
48	5:08	6:18	7:27	8:37	9:46	10:56	12:06	1:15	2:25	3:34	4:44	5:53
50	5:04	6:14	7:24	8:35	9:45	10:55	12:06	1:16	2:26	3:36	4:47	5:57
52	4:59	6:10	7:21	8:32	9:43	10:54	12:06	1:17	2:28	3:39	4:50	6:01
54	4:54	6:06	7:18	8:30	9:42	10:54	12:06	1:17	2:29	3:41	4:53	6:05
56	4:48	6:01	7:14	8:27	9:40	10:53	12:06	1:18	2:31	3:44	4:57	6:10
58	4:42	5:56	7:10	8:24	9:38	10:52	12:06	1:20	2:33	3:47	5:01	6:15
S	13	14	15	16	17	18	19	20	21	22	23	24

NIGHT HOURS - DUSK TO DAWN

LAT. N	13	14	15	16	17	18	19	20	21	22	23	24
0	6:06	7:06	8:06	9:06	10:06	11:06	12:06	1:06	2:06	3:06	4:06	5:06
5	6:10	7:09	8:09	9:08	10:07	11:06	12:06	1:05	2:04	3:03	4:03	5:02
10	6:15	7:13	8:12	9:10	10:09	11:07	12:06	1:04	2:02	3:01	3:59	4:58
15	6:19	7:17	8:15	9:12	10:10	11:08	12:06	1:03	2:01	2:59	3:56	4:54
20	6:24	7:21	8:18	9:15	10:12	11:09	12:06	1:02	1:59	2:56	3:53	4:50
25	6:29	7:25	8:21	9:17	10:13	11:10	12:06	1:02	1:58	2:54	3:50	4:46
28	6:33	7:28	8:24	9:19	10:15	11:10	12:06	1:01	1:56	2:52	3:47	4:43
31	6:36	7:31	8:26	9:21	10:16	11:11	12:06	1:00	1:55	2:50	3:45	4:40
34	6:40	7:34	8:29	9:23	10:17	11:11	12:06	1:00	1:54	2:48	3:42	4:37
37	6:44	7:38	8:31	9:25	10:18	11:12	12:06	12:59	1:53	2:46	3:40	4:33
40	6:49	7:42	8:34	9:27	10:20	11:13	12:06	12:58	1:51	2:44	3:37	4:29
42	6:52	7:44	8:37	9:29	10:21	11:13	12:06	12:58	1:50	2:42	3:35	4:27
44	6:55	7:47	8:39	9:30	10:22	11:14	12:06	12:57	1:49	2:41	3:32	4:24
46	6:59	7:50	8:41	9:32	10:23	11:14	12:06	12:57	1:48	2:39	3:30	4:21
48	7:03	7:53	8:44	9:34	10:25	11:15	12:06	12:56	1:46	2:37	3:27	4:18
50	7:07	7:57	8:47	9:36	10:26	11:16	12:06	12:55	1:45	2:35	3:24	4:14
52	7:12	8:01	8:50	9:39	10:28	11:17	12:06	12:54	1:43	2:32	3:21	4:10
54	7:17	8:05	8:53	9:41	10:29	11:17	12:06	12:54	1:42	2:30	3:18	4:06
56	7:23	8:10	8:57	9:44	10:31	11:18	12:06	12:53	1:40	2:27	3:14	4:01
58	7:29	8:15	9:01	9:47	10:33	11:20	12:06	12:52	1:38	2:24	3:10	3:56
S	1	2	3	4	5	6	7	8	9	10	11	12

August 24th to 31st

DAYLIGHT HOURS - DAWN TO DUSK

LAT. N	1	2	3	4	5	6	7	8	9	10	11	12
0	6:01	7:01	8:01	9:01	10:01	11:01	12:01	1:01	2:01	3:01	4:01	5:01
5	5:57	6:58	7:58	8:59	9:59	11:00	12:01	1:01	2:02	3:02	4:03	5:03
10	5:53	6:55	7:56	8:57	9:58	10:59	12:01	1:02	2:03	3:04	4:05	5:06
15	5:50	6:52	7:53	8:55	9:57	10:59	12:01	1:02	2:04	3:06	4:08	5:09
20	5:46	6:48	7:51	8:53	9:56	10:58	12:01	1:03	2:05	3:08	4:10	5:13
25	5:42	6:45	7:48	8:51	9:54	10:57	12:01	1:04	2:07	3:10	4:13	5:16
28	5:39	6:43	7:46	8:50	9:53	10:57	12:01	1:04	2:08	3:11	4:15	5:18
31	5:36	6:40	7:44	8:48	9:52	10:56	12:01	1:05	2:09	3:13	4:17	5:21
34	5:33	6:38	7:42	8:47	9:51	10:56	12:01	1:05	2:10	3:14	4:19	5:23
37	5:30	6:35	7:40	8:45	9:50	10:55	12:01	1:06	2:11	3:16	4:21	5:26
40	5:27	6:32	7:38	8:44	9:49	10:55	12:01	1:06	2:12	3:17	4:23	5:29
42	5:24	6:30	7:36	8:42	9:48	10:54	12:01	1:07	2:13	3:19	4:25	5:31
44	5:22	6:28	7:35	8:41	9:48	10:54	12:01	1:07	2:13	3:20	4:26	5:33
46	5:19	6:26	7:33	8:40	9:47	10:54	12:01	1:07	2:14	3:21	4:28	5:35
48	5:16	6:23	7:31	8:38	9:46	10:53	12:01	1:08	2:15	3:23	4:30	5:38
50	5:12	6:20	7:28	8:36	9:45	10:53	12:01	1:09	2:17	3:25	4:33	5:41
52	5:09	6:17	7:26	8:35	9:43	10:52	12:01	1:09	2:18	3:26	4:35	5:44
54	5:05	6:14	7:23	8:33	9:42	10:51	12:01	1:10	2:19	3:28	4:38	5:47
56	5:01	6:11	7:21	8:31	9:41	10:51	12:01	1:11	2:21	3:30	4:40	5:50
58	4:56	6:06	7:17	8:28	9:39	10:50	12:01	1:11	2:22	3:33	4:44	5:55
S	13	14	15	16	17	18	19	20	21	22	23	24

NIGHT HOURS - DUSK TO DAWN

LAT. N	13	14	15	16	17	18	19	20	21	22	23	24
0	6:01	7:01	8:01	9:01	10:01	11:01	12:01	1:01	2:01	3:01	4:01	5:01
5	6:04	7:03	8:03	9:02	10:02	11:01	12:01	1:00	1:59	2:59	3:58	4:58
10	6:08	7:06	8:05	9:04	10:03	11:02	12:01	12:59	1:58	2:57	3:56	4:55
15	6:11	7:09	8:08	9:06	10:04	11:02	12:01	12:59	1:57	2:55	3:53	4:52
20	6:15	7:13	8:10	9:08	10:05	11:03	12:01	12:58	1:56	2:53	3:51	4:48
25	6:19	7:16	8:13	9:10	10:07	11:04	12:01	12:57	1:54	2:51	3:48	4:45
28	6:22	7:18	8:15	9:11	10:08	11:04	12:01	12:57	1:53	2:50	3:46	4:43
31	6:25	7:21	8:17	9:13	10:09	11:05	12:01	12:56	1:52	2:48	3:44	4:40
34	6:28	7:23	8:19	9:14	10:10	11:05	12:01	12:56	1:51	2:47	3:42	4:38
37	6:31	7:26	8:21	9:16	10:11	11:06	12:01	12:55	1:50	2:45	3:40	4:35
40	6:34	7:29	8:23	9:17	10:12	11:06	12:01	12:55	1:49	2:44	3:38	4:32
42	6:37	7:31	8:25	9:19	10:13	11:07	12:01	12:54	1:48	2:42	3:36	4:30
44	6:39	7:33	8:26	9:20	10:13	11:07	12:01	12:54	1:48	2:41	3:35	4:28
46	6:42	7:35	8:28	9:21	10:14	11:07	12:01	12:54	1:47	2:40	3:33	4:26
48	6:45	7:38	8:30	9:23	10:15	11:08	12:01	12:53	1:46	2:38	3:31	4:23
50	6:49	7:41	8:33	9:25	10:17	11:09	12:01	12:53	1:45	2:36	3:28	4:20
52	6:52	7:44	8:35	9:26	10:18	11:09	12:01	12:52	1:43	2:35	3:26	4:17
54	6:56	7:47	8:38	9:28	10:19	11:10	12:01	12:51	1:42	2:33	3:23	4:14
56	7:00	7:50	8:40	9:31	10:21	11:11	12:01	12:51	1:41	2:31	3:21	4:11
58	7:05	7:55	8:44	9:33	10:22	11:11	12:01	12:50	1:39	2:28	3:17	4:06
S	1	2	3	4	5	6	7	8	9	10	11	12

September 1st to 7th

DAYLIGHT HOURS - DAWN TO DUSK

LAT. N	1	2	3	4	5	6	7	8	9	10	11	12
0	5:59	6:59	7:59	8:59	9:59	10:59	11:59	12:59	1:59	2:59	3:59	4:59
5	5:56	6:56	7:57	8:57	9:58	10:58	11:59	12:59	1:59	3:00	4:00	5:01
10	5:53	6:54	7:55	8:56	9:57	10:58	11:59	12:59	2:00	3:01	4:02	5:03
15	5:51	6:52	7:53	8:55	9:56	10:57	11:59	1:00	2:01	3:02	4:04	5:05
20	5:48	6:50	7:51	8:53	9:55	10:57	11:59	1:00	2:02	3:04	4:06	5:07
25	5:45	6:47	7:49	8:52	9:54	10:56	11:59	1:01	2:03	3:05	4:08	5:10
28	5:43	6:45	7:48	8:51	9:53	10:56	11:59	1:01	2:04	3:06	4:09	5:12
31	5:41	6:44	7:47	8:50	9:53	10:56	11:59	1:01	2:04	3:07	4:10	5:13
34	5:38	6:42	7:45	8:49	9:52	10:55	11:59	1:02	2:05	3:09	4:12	5:15
37	5:36	6:40	7:44	8:47	9:51	10:55	11:59	1:02	2:06	3:10	4:13	5:17
40	5:34	6:38	7:42	8:46	9:50	10:54	11:59	1:03	2:07	3:11	4:15	5:19
42	5:32	6:36	7:41	8:45	9:50	10:54	11:59	1:03	2:07	3:12	4:16	5:21
44	5:30	6:35	7:39	8:44	9:49	10:54	11:59	1:03	2:08	3:13	4:18	5:22
46	5:28	6:33	7:38	8:43	9:48	10:53	11:59	1:04	2:09	3:14	4:19	5:24
48	5:25	6:31	7:36	8:42	9:48	10:53	11:59	1:04	2:10	3:15	4:21	5:26
50	5:23	6:29	7:35	8:41	9:47	10:53	11:59	1:04	2:10	3:16	4:22	5:28
52	5:20	6:27	7:33	8:39	9:46	10:52	11:59	1:05	2:11	3:18	4:24	5:30
54	5:18	6:24	7:31	8:38	9:45	10:52	11:59	1:05	2:12	3:19	4:26	5:33
56	5:14	6:22	7:29	8:36	9:44	10:51	11:59	1:06	2:13	3:21	4:28	5:35
58	5:11	6:19	7:27	8:35	9:43	10:51	11:59	1:06	2:14	3:22	4:30	5:38
S	13	14	15	16	17	18	19	20	21	22	23	24

NIGHT HOURS - DUSK TO DAWN

LAT. N	13	14	15	16	17	18	19	20	21	22	23	24
0	5:59	6:59	7:59	8:59	9:59	10:59	11:59	12:59	1:59	2:59	3:59	4:59
5	6:01	7:01	8:00	9:00	9:59	10:59	11:59	12:58	1:58	2:57	3:57	4:56
10	6:04	7:03	8:02	9:01	10:00	10:59	11:59	12:58	1:57	2:56	3:55	4:54
15	6:06	7:05	8:04	9:02	10:01	11:00	11:59	12:57	1:56	2:55	3:53	4:52
20	6:09	7:07	8:06	9:04	10:02	11:00	11:59	12:57	1:55	2:53	3:51	4:50
25	6:12	7:10	8:08	9:05	10:03	11:01	11:59	12:56	1:54	2:52	3:49	4:47
28	6:14	7:12	8:09	9:06	10:04	11:01	11:59	12:56	1:53	2:51	3:48	4:45
31	6:16	7:13	8:10	9:07	10:04	11:01	11:59	12:56	1:53	2:50	3:47	4:44
34	6:19	7:15	8:12	9:09	10:05	11:02	11:59	12:55	1:52	2:49	3:45	4:42
37	6:21	7:17	8:13	9:10	10:06	11:02	11:59	12:55	1:51	2:47	3:44	4:40
40	6:23	7:19	8:15	9:11	10:07	11:03	11:59	12:54	1:50	2:46	3:42	4:38
42	6:25	7:21	8:16	9:12	10:07	11:03	11:59	12:54	1:50	2:45	3:41	4:36
44	6:27	7:22	8:18	9:13	10:08	11:03	11:59	12:54	1:49	2:44	3:39	4:35
46	6:29	7:24	8:19	9:14	10:09	11:04	11:59	12:53	1:48	2:43	3:38	4:33
48	6:32	7:26	8:21	9:15	10:10	11:04	11:59	12:53	1:48	2:42	3:36	4:31
50	6:34	7:28	8:22	9:16	10:10	11:04	11:59	12:53	1:47	2:41	3:35	4:29
52	6:37	7:30	8:24	9:18	10:11	11:05	11:59	12:52	1:46	2:39	3:33	4:27
54	6:40	7:33	8:26	9:19	10:12	11:05	11:59	12:52	1:45	2:38	3:31	4:24
56	6:43	7:35	8:28	9:21	10:13	11:06	11:59	12:51	1:44	2:36	3:29	4:22
58	6:46	7:38	8:30	9:22	10:14	11:06	11:59	12:51	1:43	2:35	3:27	4:19
S	1	2	3	4	5	6	7	8	9	10	11	12

September 8th to 14th

DAYLIGHT HOURS - DAWN TO DUSK

LAT. N	1	2	3	4	5	6	7	8	9	10	11	12
0	5:56	6:56	7:56	8:56	9:56	10:56	11:56	12:56	1:56	2:56	3:56	4:56
5	5:54	6:54	7:54	8:55	9:55	10:55	11:56	12:56	1:56	2:56	3:57	4:57
10	5:52	6:53	7:53	8:54	9:54	10:55	11:56	12:56	1:57	2:57	3:58	4:58
15	5:51	6:52	7:52	8:53	9:54	10:55	11:56	12:56	1:57	2:58	3:59	4:59
20	5:49	6:50	7:51	8:52	9:53	10:54	11:56	12:57	1:58	2:59	4:00	5:01
25	5:47	6:49	7:50	8:51	9:53	10:54	11:56	12:57	1:58	3:00	4:01	5:02
28	5:46	6:48	7:49	8:51	9:52	10:54	11:56	12:57	1:59	3:00	4:02	5:03
31	5:45	6:47	7:48	8:50	9:52	10:54	11:56	12:57	1:59	3:01	4:03	5:04
34	5:44	6:46	7:48	8:50	9:52	10:54	11:56	12:57	1:59	3:01	4:03	5:05
37	5:42	6:45	7:47	8:49	9:51	10:53	11:56	12:58	2:00	3:02	4:04	5:07
40	5:41	6:43	7:46	8:48	9:51	10:53	11:56	12:58	2:00	3:03	4:05	5:08
42	5:40	6:42	7:45	8:48	9:50	10:53	11:56	12:58	2:01	3:03	4:06	5:09
44	5:39	6:41	7:44	8:47	9:50	10:53	11:56	12:58	2:01	3:04	4:07	5:10
46	5:37	6:40	7:43	8:46	9:49	10:52	11:56	12:59	2:02	3:05	4:08	5:11
48	5:36	6:39	7:43	8:46	9:49	10:52	11:56	12:59	2:02	3:05	4:08	5:12
50	5:35	6:38	7:42	8:45	9:49	10:52	11:56	12:59	2:02	3:06	4:09	5:13
52	5:33	6:37	7:41	8:44	9:48	10:52	11:56	12:59	2:03	3:07	4:10	5:14
54	5:31	6:35	7:39	8:43	9:47	10:51	11:56	1:00	2:04	3:08	4:12	5:16
56	5:30	6:34	7:38	8:43	9:47	10:51	11:56	1:00	2:04	3:09	4:13	5:17
58	5:27	6:32	7:37	8:41	9:46	10:51	11:56	1:00	2:05	3:10	4:14	5:19
S	13	14	15	16	17	18	19	20	21	22	23	24

NIGHT HOURS - DUSK TO DAWN

LAT. N	13	14	15	16	17	18	19	20	21	22	23	24
0	5:56	6:56	7:56	8:56	9:56	10:56	11:56	12:56	1:56	2:56	3:56	4:56
5	5:57	6:57	7:57	8:56	9:56	10:56	11:56	12:55	1:55	2:55	3:54	4:54
10	5:59	6:58	7:58	8:57	9:57	10:56	11:56	12:55	1:54	2:54	3:53	4:53
15	6:00	6:59	7:59	8:58	9:57	10:56	11:56	12:55	1:54	2:53	3:52	4:52
20	6:02	7:01	8:00	8:59	9:58	10:57	11:56	12:54	1:53	2:52	3:51	4:50
25	6:04	7:02	8:01	9:00	9:58	10:57	11:56	12:54	1:53	2:51	3:50	4:49
28	6:05	7:03	8:02	9:00	9:59	10:57	11:56	12:54	1:52	2:51	3:49	4:48
31	6:06	7:04	8:03	9:01	9:59	10:57	11:56	12:54	1:52	2:50	3:48	4:47
34	6:07	7:05	8:03	9:01	9:59	10:57	11:56	12:54	1:52	2:50	3:48	4:46
37	6:09	7:07	8:04	9:02	10:00	10:58	11:56	12:53	1:51	2:49	3:47	4:45
40	6:10	7:08	8:05	9:03	10:00	10:58	11:56	12:53	1:51	2:48	3:46	4:43
42	6:11	7:09	8:06	9:03	10:01	10:58	11:56	12:53	1:50	2:48	3:45	4:42
44	6:12	7:10	8:07	9:04	10:01	10:58	11:56	12:53	1:50	2:47	3:44	4:41
46	6:14	7:11	8:08	9:05	10:02	10:59	11:56	12:52	1:49	2:46	3:43	4:40
48	6:15	7:12	8:08	9:05	10:02	10:59	11:56	12:52	1:49	2:46	3:43	4:39
50	6:16	7:13	8:09	9:06	10:02	10:59	11:56	12:52	1:49	2:45	3:42	4:38
52	6:18	7:14	8:10	9:07	10:03	10:59	11:56	12:52	1:48	2:44	3:41	4:37
54	6:20	7:16	8:12	9:08	10:04	11:00	11:56	12:51	1:47	2:43	3:39	4:35
56	6:22	7:17	8:13	9:09	10:04	11:00	11:56	12:51	1:47	2:43	3:38	4:34
58	6:24	7:19	8:14	9:10	10:05	11:00	11:56	12:51	1:46	2:41	3:37	4:32
S	1	2	3	4	5	6	7	8	9	10	11	12

September 15th to 22nd

DAYLIGHT HOURS - DAWN TO DUSK

LAT. N	1	2	3	4	5	6	7	8	9	10	11	12
0	5:53	6:53	7:53	8:53	9:53	10:53	11:53	12:53	1:53	2:53	3:53	4:53
5	5:52	6:52	7:52	8:52	9:52	10:52	11:53	12:53	1:53	2:53	3:53	4:53
10	5:52	6:52	7:52	8:52	9:52	10:52	11:53	12:53	1:53	2:53	3:53	4:53
15	5:51	6:51	7:52	8:52	9:52	10:52	11:53	12:53	1:53	2:53	3:53	4:54
20	5:51	6:51	7:51	8:52	9:52	10:52	11:53	12:53	1:53	2:53	3:54	4:54
25	5:50	6:50	7:51	8:51	9:52	10:52	11:53	12:53	1:53	2:54	3:54	4:55
28	5:50	6:50	7:51	8:51	9:52	10:52	11:53	12:53	1:53	2:54	3:54	4:55
31	5:49	6:50	7:50	8:51	9:51	10:52	11:53	12:53	1:54	2:54	3:55	4:55
34	5:49	6:50	7:50	8:51	9:51	10:52	11:53	12:53	1:54	2:54	3:55	4:55
37	5:49	6:49	7:50	8:51	9:51	10:52	11:53	12:53	1:54	2:54	3:55	4:56
40	5:48	6:49	7:50	8:50	9:51	10:52	11:53	12:53	1:54	2:55	3:55	4:56
42	5:48	6:49	7:49	8:50	9:51	10:52	11:53	12:53	1:54	2:55	3:56	4:56
44	5:47	6:48	7:49	8:50	9:51	10:52	11:53	12:53	1:54	2:55	3:56	4:57
46	5:47	6:48	7:49	8:50	9:51	10:52	11:53	12:53	1:54	2:55	3:56	4:57
48	5:47	6:48	7:49	8:50	9:51	10:52	11:53	12:53	1:54	2:55	3:56	4:57
50	5:46	6:47	7:48	8:49	9:50	10:51	11:53	12:54	1:55	2:56	3:57	4:58
52	5:46	6:47	7:48	8:49	9:50	10:51	11:53	12:54	1:55	2:56	3:57	4:58
54	5:45	6:47	7:48	8:49	9:50	10:51	11:53	12:54	1:55	2:56	3:57	4:58
56	5:45	6:46	7:47	8:49	9:50	10:51	11:53	12:54	1:55	2:56	3:58	4:59
58	5:44	6:46	7:47	8:48	9:50	10:51	11:53	12:54	1:55	2:57	3:58	4:59
S	13	14	15	16	17	18	19	20	21	22	23	24

NIGHT HOURS - DUSK TO DAWN

LAT. N	13	14	15	16	17	18	19	20	21	22	23	24
0	5:53	6:53	7:53	8:53	9:53	10:53	11:53	12:53	1:53	2:53	3:53	4:53
5	5:53	6:53	7:53	8:53	9:53	10:53	11:53	12:52	1:52	2:52	3:52	4:52
10	5:53	6:53	7:53	8:53	9:53	10:53	11:53	12:52	1:52	2:52	3:52	4:52
15	5:54	6:54	7:53	8:53	9:53	10:53	11:53	12:52	1:52	2:52	3:52	4:51
20	5:54	6:54	7:54	8:53	9:53	10:53	11:53	12:52	1:52	2:52	3:51	4:51
25	5:55	6:55	7:54	8:54	9:53	10:53	11:53	12:52	1:52	2:51	3:51	4:50
28	5:55	6:55	7:54	8:54	9:53	10:53	11:53	12:52	1:52	2:51	3:51	4:50
31	5:56	6:55	7:55	8:54	9:54	10:53	11:53	12:52	1:51	2:51	3:50	4:50
34	5:56	6:55	7:55	8:54	9:54	10:53	11:53	12:52	1:51	2:51	3:50	4:50
37	5:56	6:56	7:55	8:54	9:54	10:53	11:53	12:52	1:51	2:51	3:50	4:49
40	5:57	6:56	7:55	8:55	9:54	10:53	11:53	12:52	1:51	2:50	3:50	4:49
42	5:57	6:56	7:56	8:55	9:54	10:53	11:53	12:52	1:51	2:50	3:49	4:49
44	5:58	6:57	7:56	8:55	9:54	10:53	11:53	12:52	1:51	2:50	3:49	4:48
46	5:58	6:57	7:56	8:55	9:54	10:53	11:53	12:52	1:51	2:50	3:49	4:48
48	5:58	6:57	7:56	8:55	9:54	10:53	11:53	12:52	1:51	2:50	3:49	4:48
50	5:59	6:58	7:57	8:56	9:55	10:54	11:53	12:51	1:50	2:49	3:48	4:47
52	5:59	6:58	7:57	8:56	9:55	10:54	11:53	12:51	1:50	2:49	3:48	4:47
54	6:00	6:58	7:57	8:56	9:55	10:54	11:53	12:51	1:50	2:49	3:48	4:47
56	6:00	6:59	7:58	8:56	9:55	10:54	11:53	12:51	1:50	2:49	3:47	4:46
58	6:01	6:59	7:58	8:57	9:55	10:54	11:53	12:51	1:50	2:48	3:47	4:46
S	1	2	3	4	5	6	7	8	9	10	11	12

September 23rd to 30th

DAYLIGHT HOURS - DAWN TO DUSK

LAT. N	1	2	3	4	5	6	7	8	9	10	11	12
0	5:51	6:51	7:51	8:51	9:51	10:51	11:51	12:51	1:51	2:51	3:51	4:51
5	5:51	6:51	7:51	8:51	9:51	10:51	11:51	12:50	1:50	2:50	3:50	4:50
10	5:52	6:51	7:51	8:51	9:51	10:51	11:51	12:50	1:50	2:50	3:50	4:50
15	5:52	6:52	7:52	8:51	9:51	10:51	11:51	12:50	1:50	2:50	3:49	4:49
20	5:53	6:52	7:52	8:52	9:51	10:51	11:51	12:50	1:50	2:49	3:49	4:49
25	5:53	6:53	7:52	8:52	9:51	10:51	11:51	12:50	1:50	2:49	3:49	4:48
28	5:54	6:53	7:53	8:52	9:52	10:51	11:51	12:50	1:49	2:49	3:48	4:48
31	5:54	6:53	7:53	8:52	9:52	10:51	11:51	12:50	1:49	2:49	3:48	4:48
34	5:54	6:54	7:53	8:52	9:52	10:51	11:51	12:50	1:49	2:49	3:48	4:47
37	5:55	6:54	7:53	8:53	9:52	10:51	11:51	12:50	1:49	2:48	3:48	4:47
40	5:55	6:55	7:54	8:53	9:52	10:51	11:51	12:50	1:49	2:48	3:47	4:46
42	5:56	6:55	7:54	8:53	9:52	10:51	11:51	12:50	1:49	2:48	3:47	4:46
44	5:56	6:55	7:54	8:53	9:52	10:51	11:51	12:50	1:49	2:48	3:47	4:46
46	5:56	6:55	7:54	8:53	9:52	10:51	11:51	12:50	1:49	2:48	3:47	4:46
48	5:57	6:56	7:55	8:54	9:53	10:52	11:51	12:49	1:48	2:47	3:46	4:45
50	5:57	6:56	7:55	8:54	9:53	10:52	11:51	12:49	1:48	2:47	3:46	4:45
52	5:58	6:57	7:55	8:54	9:53	10:52	11:51	12:49	1:48	2:47	3:46	4:44
54	5:58	6:57	7:56	8:54	9:53	10:52	11:51	12:49	1:48	2:47	3:45	4:44
56	5:59	6:58	7:56	8:55	9:53	10:52	11:51	12:49	1:48	2:46	3:45	4:43
58	6:00	6:58	7:57	8:55	9:54	10:52	11:51	12:49	1:47	2:46	3:44	4:43
S	13	14	15	16	17	18	19	20	21	22	23	24

NIGHT HOURS - DUSK TO DAWN

LAT. N	13	14	15	16	17	18	19	20	21	22	23	24
0	5:51	6:51	7:51	8:51	9:51	10:51	11:51	12:51	1:51	2:51	3:51	4:51
5	5:50	6:50	7:50	8:50	9:50	10:50	11:51	12:51	1:51	2:51	3:51	4:51
10	5:49	6:50	7:50	8:50	9:50	10:50	11:51	12:51	1:51	2:51	3:51	4:51
15	5:49	6:49	7:49	8:50	9:50	10:50	11:51	12:51	1:51	2:51	3:52	4:52
20	5:48	6:49	7:49	8:49	9:50	10:50	11:51	12:51	1:51	2:52	3:52	4:52
25	5:48	6:48	7:49	8:49	9:50	10:50	11:51	12:51	1:51	2:52	3:52	4:53
28	5:47	6:48	7:48	8:49	9:49	10:50	11:51	12:51	1:52	2:52	3:53	4:53
31	5:47	6:48	7:48	8:49	9:49	10:50	11:51	12:51	1:52	2:52	3:53	4:53
34	5:47	6:47	7:48	8:49	9:49	10:50	11:51	12:51	1:52	2:52	3:53	4:54
37	5:46	6:47	7:48	8:48	9:49	10:50	11:51	12:51	1:52	2:53	3:53	4:54
40	5:46	6:46	7:47	8:48	9:49	10:50	11:51	12:51	1:52	2:53	3:54	4:55
42	5:45	6:46	7:47	8:48	9:49	10:50	11:51	12:51	1:52	2:53	3:54	4:55
44	5:45	6:46	7:47	8:48	9:49	10:50	11:51	12:51	1:52	2:53	3:54	4:55
46	5:45	6:46	7:47	8:48	9:49	10:50	11:51	12:51	1:52	2:53	3:54	4:55
48	5:44	6:45	7:46	8:47	9:48	10:49	11:51	12:52	1:53	2:54	3:55	4:56
50	5:44	6:45	7:46	8:47	9:48	10:49	11:51	12:52	1:53	2:54	3:55	4:56
52	5:43	6:44	7:46	8:47	9:48	10:49	11:51	12:52	1:53	2:54	3:55	4:57
54	5:43	6:44	7:45	8:47	9:48	10:49	11:51	12:52	1:53	2:54	3:56	4:57
56	5:42	6:43	7:45	8:46	9:48	10:49	11:51	12:52	1:53	2:55	3:56	4:58
58	5:41	6:43	7:44	8:46	9:47	10:49	11:51	12:52	1:54	2:55	3:57	4:58
S	1	2	3	4	5	6	7	8	9	10	11	12

October 1st to 7th

DAYLIGHT HOURS - DAWN TO DUSK

LAT. N	1	2	3	4	5	6	7	8	9	10	11	12
0	5:48	6:48	7:48	8:48	9:48	10:48	11:48	12:48	1:48	2:48	3:48	4:48
5	5:49	6:49	7:48	8:48	9:48	10:48	11:48	12:47	1:47	2:47	3:47	4:46
10	5:50	6:50	7:49	8:49	9:48	10:48	11:48	12:47	1:47	2:46	3:46	4:45
15	5:52	6:51	7:50	8:50	9:49	10:48	11:48	12:47	1:46	2:45	3:45	4:44
20	5:54	6:53	7:52	8:51	9:50	10:49	11:48	12:46	1:45	2:44	3:43	4:42
25	5:55	6:54	7:53	8:51	9:50	10:49	11:48	12:46	1:45	2:44	3:42	4:41
28	5:56	6:55	7:53	8:52	9:50	10:49	11:48	12:46	1:45	2:43	3:42	4:40
31	5:58	6:56	7:54	8:53	9:51	10:49	11:48	12:46	1:44	2:43	3:41	4:39
34	5:59	6:57	7:55	8:53	9:51	10:49	11:48	12:46	1:44	2:42	3:40	4:38
37	6:00	6:58	7:56	8:54	9:52	10:50	11:48	12:45	1:43	2:41	3:39	4:37
40	6:01	6:59	7:57	8:54	9:52	10:50	11:48	12:45	1:43	2:41	3:38	4:36
42	6:02	7:00	7:57	8:55	9:53	10:50	11:48	12:45	1:43	2:40	3:38	4:35
44	6:04	7:01	7:58	8:56	9:53	10:50	11:48	12:45	1:42	2:39	3:37	4:34
46	6:05	7:02	7:59	8:56	9:53	10:50	11:48	12:45	1:42	2:39	3:36	4:33
48	6:06	7:03	8:00	8:57	9:54	10:51	11:48	12:44	1:41	2:38	3:35	4:32
50	6:07	7:04	8:01	8:57	9:54	10:51	11:48	12:44	1:41	2:38	3:34	4:31
52	6:09	7:05	8:02	8:58	9:55	10:51	11:48	12:44	1:40	2:37	3:33	4:30
54	6:10	7:07	8:03	8:59	9:55	10:51	11:48	12:44	1:40	2:36	3:32	4:28
56	6:12	7:08	8:04	9:00	9:56	10:52	11:48	12:43	1:39	2:35	3:31	4:27
58	6:14	7:10	8:05	9:01	9:56	10:52	11:48	12:43	1:39	2:34	3:30	4:25
S	13	14	15	16	17	18	19	20	21	22	23	24

NIGHT HOURS - DUSK TO DAWN

LAT. N	13	14	15	16	17	18	19	20	21	22	23	24
0	5:48	6:48	7:48	8:48	9:48	10:48	11:48	12:48	1:48	2:48	3:48	4:48
5	5:46	6:46	7:47	8:47	9:47	10:47	11:48	12:48	1:48	2:48	3:48	4:49
10	5:45	6:45	7:46	8:46	9:47	10:47	11:48	12:48	1:48	2:49	3:49	4:50
15	5:43	6:44	7:45	8:45	9:46	10:47	11:48	12:48	1:49	2:50	3:50	4:51
20	5:41	6:42	7:43	8:44	9:45	10:46	11:48	12:49	1:50	2:51	3:52	4:53
25	5:40	6:41	7:42	8:44	9:45	10:46	11:48	12:49	1:50	2:51	3:53	4:54
28	5:39	6:40	7:42	8:43	9:45	10:46	11:48	12:49	1:50	2:52	3:53	4:55
31	5:38	6:39	7:41	8:43	9:44	10:46	11:48	12:49	1:51	2:53	3:54	4:56
34	5:36	6:38	7:40	8:42	9:44	10:46	11:48	12:49	1:51	2:53	3:55	4:57
37	5:35	6:37	7:39	8:41	9:43	10:45	11:48	12:50	1:52	2:54	3:56	4:58
40	5:34	6:36	7:38	8:41	9:43	10:45	11:48	12:50	1:52	2:54	3:57	4:59
42	5:33	6:35	7:38	8:40	9:43	10:45	11:48	12:50	1:53	2:55	3:57	5:00
44	5:31	6:34	7:37	8:39	9:42	10:45	11:48	12:50	1:53	2:56	3:58	5:01
46	5:30	6:33	7:36	8:39	9:42	10:45	11:48	12:50	1:53	2:56	3:59	5:02
48	5:29	6:32	7:35	8:38	9:41	10:44	11:48	12:51	1:54	2:57	4:00	5:03
50	5:28	6:31	7:34	8:38	9:41	10:44	11:48	12:51	1:54	2:57	4:01	5:04
52	5:26	6:30	7:33	8:37	9:40	10:44	11:48	12:51	1:55	2:58	4:02	5:05
54	5:25	6:28	7:32	8:36	9:40	10:44	11:48	12:51	1:55	2:59	4:03	5:07
56	5:23	6:27	7:31	8:35	9:39	10:43	11:48	12:52	1:56	3:00	4:04	5:08
58	5:21	6:25	7:30	8:34	9:39	10:43	11:48	12:52	1:56	3:01	4:05	5:10
S	1	2	3	4	5	6	7	8	9	10	11	12

October 8th to 15th

DAYLIGHT HOURS - DAWN TO DUSK

LAT. N	1	2	3	4	5	6	7	8	9	10	11	12
0	5:46	6:46	7:46	8:46	9:46	10:46	11:46	12:46	1:46	2:46	3:46	4:46
5	5:48	6:48	7:47	8:47	9:46	10:46	11:46	12:45	1:45	2:44	3:44	4:43
10	5:51	6:50	7:49	8:48	9:47	10:46	11:46	12:45	1:44	2:43	3:42	4:41
15	5:53	6:52	7:51	8:49	9:48	10:47	11:46	12:44	1:43	2:42	3:40	4:39
20	5:56	6:54	7:53	8:51	9:49	10:47	11:46	12:44	1:42	2:40	3:38	4:37
25	5:59	6:57	7:55	8:52	9:50	10:48	11:46	12:43	1:41	2:39	3:37	4:34
28	6:01	6:58	7:56	8:53	9:51	10:48	11:46	12:43	1:40	2:38	3:35	4:33
31	6:03	7:00	7:57	8:54	9:51	10:48	11:46	12:43	1:40	2:37	3:34	4:31
34	6:05	7:02	7:59	8:55	9:52	10:49	11:46	12:42	1:39	2:36	3:32	4:29
37	6:07	7:04	8:00	8:56	9:53	10:49	11:46	12:42	1:38	2:35	3:31	4:27
40	6:10	7:06	8:02	8:58	9:54	10:50	11:46	12:41	1:37	2:33	3:29	4:25
42	6:12	7:07	8:03	8:59	9:54	10:50	11:46	12:41	1:37	2:32	3:28	4:24
44	6:14	7:09	8:04	9:00	9:55	10:50	11:46	12:41	1:36	2:31	3:27	4:22
46	6:16	7:11	8:06	9:01	9:56	10:51	11:46	12:40	1:35	2:30	3:25	4:20
48	6:18	7:12	8:07	9:02	9:56	10:51	11:46	12:40	1:35	2:29	3:24	4:19
50	6:20	7:14	8:09	9:03	9:57	10:51	11:46	12:40	1:34	2:28	3:22	4:17
52	6:23	7:17	8:10	9:04	9:58	10:52	11:46	12:39	1:33	2:27	3:21	4:14
54	6:26	7:19	8:12	9:06	9:59	10:52	11:46	12:39	1:32	2:25	3:19	4:12
56	6:29	7:21	8:14	9:07	10:00	10:53	11:46	12:38	1:31	2:24	3:17	4:10
58	6:32	7:24	8:17	9:09	10:01	10:53	11:46	12:38	1:30	2:22	3:14	4:07
S	13	14	15	16	17	18	19	20	21	22	23	24

NIGHT HOURS - DUSK TO DAWN

LAT. N	13	14	15	16	17	18	19	20	21	22	23	24
0	5:46	6:46	7:46	8:46	9:46	10:46	11:46	12:46	1:46	2:46	3:46	4:46
5	5:43	6:43	7:44	8:44	9:45	10:45	11:46	12:46	1:46	2:47	3:47	4:48
10	5:40	6:41	7:42	8:43	9:44	10:45	11:46	12:46	1:47	2:48	3:49	4:50
15	5:38	6:39	7:40	8:42	9:43	10:44	11:46	12:47	1:48	2:49	3:51	4:52
20	5:35	6:37	7:38	8:40	9:42	10:44	11:46	12:47	1:49	2:51	3:53	4:54
25	5:32	6:34	7:37	8:39	9:41	10:43	11:46	12:48	1:50	2:52	3:55	4:57
28	5:30	6:33	7:35	8:38	9:40	10:43	11:46	12:48	1:51	2:53	3:56	4:58
31	5:28	6:31	7:34	8:37	9:40	10:43	11:46	12:48	1:51	2:54	3:57	5:00
34	5:26	6:29	7:32	8:36	9:39	10:42	11:46	12:49	1:52	2:55	3:59	5:02
37	5:24	6:27	7:31	8:35	9:38	10:42	11:46	12:49	1:53	2:56	4:00	5:04
40	5:21	6:25	7:29	8:33	9:37	10:41	11:46	12:50	1:54	2:58	4:02	5:06
42	5:19	6:24	7:28	8:32	9:37	10:41	11:46	12:50	1:54	2:59	4:03	5:07
44	5:17	6:22	7:27	8:31	9:36	10:41	11:46	12:50	1:55	3:00	4:04	5:09
46	5:15	6:20	7:25	8:30	9:35	10:40	11:46	12:51	1:56	3:01	4:06	5:11
48	5:13	6:19	7:24	8:29	9:35	10:40	11:46	12:51	1:56	3:02	4:07	5:12
50	5:11	6:17	7:22	8:28	9:34	10:40	11:46	12:51	1:57	3:03	4:09	5:14
52	5:08	6:14	7:21	8:27	9:33	10:39	11:46	12:52	1:58	3:04	4:10	5:17
54	5:05	6:12	7:19	8:25	9:32	10:39	11:46	12:52	1:59	3:06	4:12	5:19
56	5:02	6:10	7:17	8:24	9:31	10:38	11:46	12:53	2:00	3:07	4:14	5:21
58	4:59	6:07	7:14	8:22	9:30	10:38	11:46	12:53	2:01	3:09	4:17	5:24
S	1	2	3	4	5	6	7	8	9	10	11	12

October 16th to 23rd

DAYLIGHT HOURS - DAWN TO DUSK

LAT. N	1	2	3	4	5	6	7	8	9	10	11	12
0	5:44	6:44	7:44	8:44	9:44	10:44	11:44	12:44	1:44	2:44	3:44	4:44
5	5:47	6:47	7:46	8:45	9:45	10:44	11:44	12:43	1:42	2:42	3:41	4:41
10	5:51	6:50	7:48	8:47	9:46	10:45	11:44	12:42	1:41	2:40	3:39	4:37
15	5:55	6:53	7:51	8:49	9:47	10:45	11:44	12:42	1:40	2:38	3:36	4:34
20	5:58	6:56	7:53	8:51	9:48	10:46	11:44	12:41	1:39	2:36	3:34	4:31
25	6:03	6:59	7:56	8:53	9:50	10:47	11:44	12:40	1:37	2:34	3:31	4:28
28	6:05	7:02	7:58	8:54	9:51	10:47	11:44	12:40	1:36	2:33	3:29	4:25
31	6:08	7:04	8:00	8:56	9:52	10:48	11:44	12:39	1:35	2:31	3:27	4:23
34	6:11	7:07	8:02	8:57	9:53	10:48	11:44	12:39	1:34	2:30	3:25	4:20
37	6:15	7:09	8:04	8:59	9:54	10:49	11:44	12:38	1:33	2:28	3:23	4:18
40	6:18	7:12	8:07	9:01	9:55	10:49	11:44	12:38	1:32	2:26	3:20	4:15
42	6:21	7:14	8:08	9:02	9:56	10:50	11:44	12:37	1:31	2:25	3:19	4:13
44	6:23	7:17	8:10	9:03	9:57	10:50	11:44	12:37	1:30	2:24	3:17	4:10
46	6:26	7:19	8:12	9:05	9:58	10:51	11:44	12:36	1:29	2:22	3:15	4:08
48	6:29	7:22	8:14	9:06	9:59	10:51	11:44	12:36	1:28	2:21	3:13	4:05
50	6:33	7:25	8:16	9:08	10:00	10:52	11:44	12:35	1:27	2:19	3:11	4:02
52	6:36	7:28	8:19	9:10	10:01	10:52	11:44	12:35	1:26	2:17	3:08	3:59
54	6:41	7:31	8:22	9:12	10:03	10:53	11:44	12:34	1:24	2:15	3:05	3:56
56	6:45	7:35	8:25	9:14	10:04	10:54	11:44	12:33	1:23	2:13	3:02	3:52
58	6:50	7:39	8:28	9:17	10:06	10:55	11:44	12:32	1:21	2:10	2:59	3:48
S	13	14	15	16	17	18	19	20	21	22	23	24

NIGHT HOURS - DUSK TO DAWN

LAT. N	13	14	15	16	17	18	19	20	21	22	23	24
0	5:44	6:44	7:44	8:44	9:44	10:44	11:44	12:44	1:44	2:44	3:44	4:44
5	5:40	6:41	7:41	8:42	9:42	10:43	11:44	12:44	1:45	2:45	3:46	4:46
10	5:36	6:37	7:39	8:40	9:41	10:42	11:44	12:45	1:46	2:47	3:48	4:50
15	5:33	6:34	7:36	8:38	9:40	10:42	11:44	12:45	1:47	2:49	3:51	4:53
20	5:29	6:31	7:34	8:36	9:39	10:41	11:44	12:46	1:48	2:51	3:53	4:56
25	5:24	6:28	7:31	8:34	9:37	10:40	11:44	12:47	1:50	2:53	3:56	4:59
28	5:22	6:25	7:29	8:33	9:36	10:40	11:44	12:47	1:51	2:54	3:58	5:02
31	5:19	6:23	7:27	8:31	9:35	10:39	11:44	12:48	1:52	2:56	4:00	5:04
34	5:16	6:20	7:25	8:30	9:34	10:39	11:44	12:48	1:53	2:57	4:02	5:07
37	5:12	6:18	7:23	8:28	9:33	10:38	11:44	12:49	1:54	2:59	4:04	5:09
40	5:09	6:15	7:20	8:26	9:32	10:38	11:44	12:49	1:55	3:01	4:07	5:12
42	5:06	6:13	7:19	8:25	9:31	10:37	11:44	12:50	1:56	3:02	4:08	5:14
44	5:04	6:10	7:17	8:24	9:30	10:37	11:44	12:50	1:57	3:03	4:10	5:17
46	5:01	6:08	7:15	8:22	9:29	10:36	11:44	12:51	1:58	3:05	4:12	5:19
48	4:58	6:05	7:13	8:21	9:28	10:36	11:44	12:51	1:59	3:06	4:14	5:22
50	4:54	6:02	7:11	8:19	9:27	10:35	11:44	12:52	2:00	3:08	4:16	5:25
52	4:51	5:59	7:08	8:17	9:26	10:35	11:44	12:52	2:01	3:10	4:19	5:28
54	4:46	5:56	7:05	8:15	9:24	10:34	11:44	12:53	2:03	3:12	4:22	5:31
56	4:42	5:52	7:02	8:13	9:23	10:33	11:44	12:54	2:04	3:14	4:25	5:35
58	4:37	5:48	6:59	8:10	9:21	10:32	11:44	12:55	2:06	3:17	4:28	5:39
S	1	2	3	4	5	6	7	8	9	10	11	12

October 24th to 31st

DAYLIGHT HOURS - DAWN TO DUSK

LAT. N	1	2	3	4	5	6	7	8	9	10	11	12
0	5:43	6:43	7:43	8:43	9:43	10:43	11:43	12:43	1:43	2:43	3:43	4:43
5	5:47	6:46	7:46	8:45	9:44	10:43	11:43	12:42	1:41	2:40	3:39	4:39
10	5:52	6:50	7:49	8:47	9:46	10:44	11:43	12:41	1:39	2:38	3:36	4:35
15	5:57	6:54	7:52	8:50	9:47	10:45	11:43	12:40	1:38	2:35	3:33	4:31
20	6:02	6:59	7:55	8:52	9:49	10:46	11:43	12:39	1:36	2:33	3:30	4:27
25	6:07	7:03	7:59	8:55	9:51	10:47	11:43	12:38	1:34	2:30	3:26	4:22
28	6:11	7:06	8:01	8:57	9:52	10:47	11:43	12:38	1:33	2:28	3:24	4:19
31	6:14	7:09	8:04	8:58	9:53	10:48	11:43	12:37	1:32	2:27	3:21	4:16
34	6:18	7:12	8:06	9:00	9:54	10:48	11:43	12:37	1:31	2:25	3:19	4:13
37	6:22	7:16	8:09	9:02	9:56	10:49	11:43	12:36	1:29	2:23	3:16	4:09
40	6:27	7:20	8:12	9:05	9:57	10:50	11:43	12:35	1:28	2:20	3:13	4:05
42	6:30	7:22	8:14	9:06	9:58	10:50	11:43	12:35	1:27	2:19	3:11	4:03
44	6:34	7:25	8:17	9:08	10:00	10:51	11:43	12:34	1:25	2:17	3:08	4:00
46	6:38	7:28	8:19	9:10	10:01	10:52	11:43	12:33	1:24	2:15	3:06	3:57
48	6:42	7:32	8:22	9:12	10:02	10:52	11:43	12:33	1:23	2:13	3:03	3:53
50	6:46	7:36	8:25	9:14	10:04	10:53	11:43	12:32	1:21	2:11	3:00	3:49
52	6:51	7:40	8:28	9:17	10:05	10:54	11:43	12:31	1:20	2:08	2:57	3:45
54	6:56	7:44	8:32	9:19	10:07	10:55	11:43	12:30	1:18	2:06	2:53	3:41
56	7:02	7:49	8:36	9:22	10:09	10:56	11:43	12:29	1:16	2:03	2:49	3:36
58	7:09	7:54	8:40	9:26	10:11	10:57	11:43	12:28	1:14	1:59	2:45	3:31
S	13	14	15	16	17	18	19	20	21	22	23	24

NIGHT HOURS - DUSK TO DAWN

LAT. N	13	14	15	16	17	18	19	20	21	22	23	24
0	5:43	6:43	7:43	8:43	9:43	10:43	11:43	12:43	1:43	2:43	3:43	4:43
5	5:38	6:39	7:39	8:40	9:41	10:42	11:43	12:43	1:44	2:45	3:46	4:46
10	5:33	6:35	7:36	8:38	9:39	10:41	11:43	12:44	1:46	2:47	3:49	4:50
15	5:28	6:31	7:33	8:35	9:38	10:40	11:43	12:45	1:47	2:50	3:52	4:54
20	5:23	6:27	7:30	8:33	9:36	10:39	11:43	12:46	1:49	2:52	3:55	4:59
25	5:18	6:22	7:26	8:30	9:34	10:38	11:43	12:47	1:51	2:55	3:59	5:03
28	5:14	6:19	7:24	8:28	9:33	10:38	11:43	12:47	1:52	2:57	4:01	5:06
31	5:11	6:16	7:21	8:27	9:32	10:37	11:43	12:48	1:53	2:58	4:04	5:09
34	5:07	6:13	7:19	8:25	9:31	10:37	11:43	12:48	1:54	3:00	4:06	5:12
37	5:03	6:09	7:16	8:23	9:29	10:36	11:43	12:49	1:56	3:02	4:09	5:16
40	4:58	6:05	7:13	8:20	9:28	10:35	11:43	12:50	1:57	3:05	4:12	5:20
42	4:55	6:03	7:11	8:19	9:27	10:35	11:43	12:50	1:58	3:06	4:14	5:22
44	4:51	6:00	7:08	8:17	9:25	10:34	11:43	12:51	2:00	3:08	4:17	5:25
46	4:47	5:57	7:06	8:15	9:24	10:33	11:43	12:52	2:01	3:10	4:19	5:28
48	4:43	5:53	7:03	8:13	9:23	10:33	11:43	12:52	2:02	3:12	4:22	5:32
50	4:39	5:49	7:00	8:11	9:21	10:32	11:43	12:53	2:04	3:14	4:25	5:36
52	4:34	5:45	6:57	8:08	9:20	10:31	11:43	12:54	2:05	3:17	4:28	5:40
54	4:29	5:41	6:53	8:06	9:18	10:30	11:43	12:55	2:07	3:19	4:32	5:44
56	4:23	5:36	6:49	8:03	9:16	10:29	11:43	12:56	2:09	3:22	4:36	5:49
58	4:16	5:31	6:45	7:59	9:14	10:28	11:43	12:57	2:11	3:26	4:40	5:54
S	1	2	3	4	5	6	7	8	9	10	11	12

November 1st to 7th

DAYLIGHT HOURS - DAWN TO DUSK

LAT. N	1	2	3	4	5	6	7	8	9	10	11	12
0	5:43	6:43	7:43	8:43	9:43	10:43	11:43	12:43	1:43	2:43	3:43	4:43
5	5:48	6:47	7:46	8:45	9:44	10:43	11:43	12:42	1:41	2:40	3:39	4:38
10	5:54	6:52	7:50	8:48	9:46	10:44	11:43	12:41	1:39	2:37	3:35	4:33
15	5:59	6:56	7:54	8:51	9:48	10:45	11:43	12:40	1:37	2:34	3:31	4:29
20	6:05	7:01	7:58	8:54	9:50	10:46	11:43	12:39	1:35	2:31	3:27	4:24
25	6:12	7:07	8:02	8:57	9:52	10:47	11:43	12:38	1:33	2:28	3:23	4:18
28	6:16	7:10	8:05	8:59	9:54	10:48	11:43	12:37	1:31	2:26	3:20	4:15
31	6:20	7:14	8:08	9:01	9:55	10:49	11:43	12:36	1:30	2:24	3:17	4:11
34	6:25	7:18	8:11	9:04	9:57	10:50	11:43	12:35	1:28	2:21	3:14	4:07
37	6:30	7:22	8:14	9:06	9:58	10:50	11:43	12:35	1:27	2:19	3:11	4:03
40	6:35	7:26	8:18	9:09	10:00	10:51	11:43	12:34	1:25	2:16	3:07	3:59
42	6:39	7:30	8:20	9:11	10:01	10:52	11:43	12:33	1:24	2:14	3:05	3:55
44	6:43	7:33	8:23	9:13	10:03	10:53	11:43	12:32	1:22	2:12	3:02	3:52
46	6:48	7:37	8:26	9:15	10:04	10:53	11:43	12:32	1:21	2:10	2:59	3:48
48	6:53	7:41	8:29	9:18	10:06	10:54	11:43	12:31	1:19	2:07	2:56	3:44
50	6:58	7:46	8:33	9:20	10:08	10:55	11:43	12:30	1:17	2:05	2:52	3:39
52	7:04	7:50	8:37	9:23	10:10	10:56	11:43	12:29	1:15	2:02	2:48	3:35
54	7:10	7:56	8:41	9:26	10:12	10:57	11:43	12:28	1:13	1:59	2:44	3:29
56	7:18	8:02	8:46	9:30	10:14	10:58	11:43	12:27	1:11	1:55	2:39	3:23
58	7:26	8:09	8:51	9:34	10:17	11:00	11:43	12:25	1:08	1:51	2:34	3:16
S	13	14	15	16	17	18	19	20	21	22	23	24

NIGHT HOURS - DUSK TO DAWN

LAT. N	13	14	15	16	17	18	19	20	21	22	23	24
0	5:43	6:43	7:43	8:43	9:43	10:43	11:43	12:43	1:43	2:43	3:43	4:43
5	5:37	6:38	7:39	8:40	9:41	10:42	11:43	12:43	1:44	2:45	3:46	4:47
10	5:32	6:33	7:35	8:37	9:39	10:41	11:43	12:44	1:46	2:48	3:50	4:52
15	5:26	6:29	7:31	8:34	9:37	10:40	11:43	12:45	1:48	2:51	3:54	4:56
20	5:20	6:24	7:27	8:31	9:35	10:39	11:43	12:46	1:50	2:54	3:58	5:01
25	5:13	6:18	7:23	8:28	9:33	10:38	11:43	12:47	1:52	2:57	4:02	5:07
28	5:09	6:15	7:20	8:26	9:31	10:37	11:43	12:48	1:54	2:59	4:05	5:10
31	5:05	6:11	7:17	8:24	9:30	10:36	11:43	12:49	1:55	3:01	4:08	5:14
34	5:00	6:07	7:14	8:21	9:28	10:35	11:43	12:50	1:57	3:04	4:11	5:18
37	4:55	6:03	7:11	8:19	9:27	10:35	11:43	12:50	1:58	3:06	4:14	5:22
40	4:50	5:59	7:07	8:16	9:25	10:34	11:43	12:51	2:00	3:09	4:18	5:26
42	4:46	5:55	7:05	8:14	9:24	10:33	11:43	12:52	2:01	3:11	4:20	5:30
44	4:42	5:52	7:02	8:12	9:22	10:32	11:43	12:53	2:03	3:13	4:23	5:33
46	4:37	5:48	6:59	8:10	9:21	10:32	11:43	12:53	2:04	3:15	4:26	5:37
48	4:32	5:44	6:56	8:07	9:19	10:31	11:43	12:54	2:06	3:18	4:29	5:41
50	4:27	5:39	6:52	8:05	9:17	10:30	11:43	12:55	2:08	3:20	4:33	5:46
52	4:21	5:35	6:48	8:02	9:15	10:29	11:43	12:56	2:10	3:23	4:37	5:50
54	4:15	5:29	6:44	7:59	9:13	10:28	11:43	12:57	2:12	3:26	4:41	5:56
56	4:07	5:23	6:39	7:55	9:11	10:27	11:43	12:58	2:14	3:30	4:46	6:02
58	3:59	5:16	6:34	7:51	9:08	10:25	11:43	1:00	2:17	3:34	4:51	6:09
S	1	2	3	4	5	6	7	8	9	10	11	12

November 8th to 14th

DAYLIGHT HOURS - DAWN TO DUSK

LAT. N	1	2	3	4	5	6	7	8	9	10	11	12
0	5:44	6:44	7:44	8:44	9:44	10:44	11:44	12:44	1:44	2:44	3:44	4:44
5	5:50	6:49	7:48	8:47	9:46	10:45	11:44	12:42	1:41	2:40	3:39	4:38
10	5:56	6:54	7:52	8:50	9:48	10:46	11:44	12:41	1:39	2:37	3:35	4:33
15	6:03	7:00	7:56	8:53	9:50	10:47	11:44	12:40	1:37	2:34	3:31	4:27
20	6:10	7:06	8:01	8:57	9:52	10:48	11:44	12:39	1:35	2:30	3:26	4:21
25	6:17	7:12	8:06	9:00	9:55	10:49	11:44	12:38	1:32	2:27	3:21	4:15
28	6:22	7:16	8:09	9:03	9:56	10:50	11:44	12:37	1:31	2:24	3:18	4:11
31	6:27	7:20	8:13	9:05	9:58	10:51	11:44	12:36	1:29	2:22	3:14	4:07
34	6:33	7:25	8:16	9:08	10:00	10:52	11:44	12:35	1:27	2:19	3:11	4:02
37	6:39	7:29	8:20	9:11	10:02	10:53	11:44	12:34	1:25	2:16	3:07	3:58
40	6:45	7:35	8:25	9:14	10:04	10:54	11:44	12:33	1:23	2:13	3:02	3:52
42	6:50	7:39	8:28	9:17	10:06	10:55	11:44	12:32	1:21	2:10	2:59	3:48
44	6:55	7:43	8:31	9:19	10:07	10:55	11:44	12:32	1:20	2:08	2:56	3:44
46	7:00	7:47	8:34	9:22	10:09	10:56	11:44	12:31	1:18	2:05	2:53	3:40
48	7:06	7:52	8:38	9:25	10:11	10:57	11:44	12:30	1:16	2:02	2:49	3:35
50	7:12	7:57	8:43	9:28	10:13	10:58	11:44	12:29	1:14	1:59	2:44	3:30
52	7:19	8:03	8:47	9:31	10:15	10:59	11:44	12:28	1:12	1:56	2:40	3:24
54	7:27	8:10	8:52	9:35	10:18	11:01	11:44	12:26	1:09	1:52	2:35	3:17
56	7:35	8:17	8:58	9:39	10:21	11:02	11:44	12:25	1:06	1:48	2:29	3:10
58	7:45	8:25	9:05	9:44	10:24	11:04	11:44	12:23	1:03	1:43	2:22	3:02
S	13	14	15	16	17	18	19	20	21	22	23	24

NIGHT HOURS - DUSK TO DAWN

LAT. N	13	14	15	16	17	18	19	20	21	22	23	24
0	5:44	6:44	7:44	8:44	9:44	10:44	11:44	12:44	1:44	2:44	3:44	4:44
5	5:37	6:38	7:39	8:40	9:41	10:42	11:44	12:45	1:46	2:47	3:48	4:49
10	5:31	6:33	7:35	8:37	9:39	10:41	11:44	12:46	1:48	2:50	3:52	4:54
15	5:24	6:27	7:31	8:34	9:37	10:40	11:44	12:47	1:50	2:53	3:56	5:00
20	5:17	6:21	7:26	8:30	9:35	10:39	11:44	12:48	1:52	2:57	4:01	5:06
25	5:10	6:15	7:21	8:27	9:32	10:38	11:44	12:49	1:55	3:00	4:06	5:12
28	5:05	6:11	7:18	8:24	9:31	10:37	11:44	12:50	1:56	3:03	4:09	5:16
31	5:00	6:07	7:14	8:22	9:29	10:36	11:44	12:51	1:58	3:05	4:13	5:20
34	4:54	6:02	7:11	8:19	9:27	10:35	11:44	12:52	2:00	3:08	4:16	5:25
37	4:48	5:58	7:07	8:16	9:25	10:34	11:44	12:53	2:02	3:11	4:20	5:29
40	4:42	5:52	7:02	8:13	9:23	10:33	11:44	12:54	2:04	3:14	4:25	5:35
42	4:37	5:48	6:59	8:10	9:21	10:32	11:44	12:55	2:06	3:17	4:28	5:39
44	4:32	5:44	6:56	8:08	9:20	10:32	11:44	12:55	2:07	3:19	4:31	5:43
46	4:27	5:40	6:53	8:05	9:18	10:31	11:44	12:56	2:09	3:22	4:34	5:47
48	4:21	5:35	6:49	8:02	9:16	10:30	11:44	12:57	2:11	3:25	4:38	5:52
50	4:15	5:30	6:44	7:59	9:14	10:29	11:44	12:58	2:13	3:28	4:43	5:57
52	4:08	5:24	6:40	7:56	9:12	10:28	11:44	12:59	2:15	3:31	4:47	6:03
54	4:00	5:17	6:35	7:52	9:09	10:26	11:44	1:01	2:18	3:35	4:52	6:10
56	3:52	5:10	6:29	7:48	9:06	10:25	11:44	1:02	2:21	3:39	4:58	6:17
58	3:42	5:02	6:22	7:43	9:03	10:23	11:44	1:04	2:24	3:44	5:05	6:25
S	1	2	3	4	5	6	7	8	9	10	11	12

November 15th to 22nd

DAYLIGHT HOURS - DAWN TO DUSK

LAT. N	1	2	3	4	5	6	7	8	9	10	11	12
0	5:45	6:45	7:45	8:45	9:45	10:45	11:45	12:45	1:45	2:45	3:45	4:45
5	5:52	6:50	7:49	8:48	9:47	10:46	11:45	12:43	1:42	2:41	3:40	4:39
10	5:59	6:56	7:54	8:52	9:49	10:47	11:45	12:42	1:40	2:37	3:35	4:33
15	6:06	7:03	7:59	8:55	9:52	10:48	11:45	12:41	1:37	2:34	3:30	4:26
20	6:14	7:09	8:04	8:59	9:54	10:49	11:45	12:40	1:35	2:30	3:25	4:20
25	6:23	7:16	8:10	9:04	9:57	10:51	11:45	12:38	1:32	2:25	3:19	4:13
28	6:28	7:21	8:14	9:06	9:59	10:52	11:45	12:37	1:30	2:23	3:15	4:08
31	6:34	7:26	8:17	9:09	10:01	10:53	11:45	12:36	1:28	2:20	3:12	4:03
34	6:40	7:31	8:21	9:12	10:03	10:54	11:45	12:35	1:26	2:17	3:08	3:58
37	6:47	7:36	8:26	9:16	10:05	10:55	11:45	12:34	1:24	2:13	3:03	3:53
40	6:54	7:42	8:31	9:19	10:08	10:56	11:45	12:33	1:21	2:10	2:58	3:47
42	6:59	7:47	8:34	9:22	10:09	10:57	11:45	12:32	1:20	2:07	2:55	3:42
44	7:05	7:51	8:38	9:25	10:11	10:58	11:45	12:31	1:18	2:04	2:51	3:38
46	7:11	7:56	8:42	9:28	10:13	10:59	11:45	12:30	1:16	2:01	2:47	3:33
48	7:18	8:02	8:47	9:31	10:16	11:00	11:45	12:29	1:14	1:58	2:43	3:27
50	7:25	8:08	8:51	9:35	10:18	11:01	11:45	12:28	1:11	1:54	2:38	3:21
52	7:33	8:15	8:57	9:39	10:21	11:03	11:45	12:26	1:08	1:50	2:32	3:14
54	7:42	8:22	9:03	9:43	10:24	11:04	11:45	12:25	1:05	1:46	2:26	3:07
56	7:52	8:31	9:09	9:48	10:27	11:06	11:45	12:23	1:02	1:41	2:20	2:59
58	8:03	8:40	9:17	9:54	10:31	11:08	11:45	12:21	12:58	1:35	2:12	2:49
S	13	14	15	16	17	18	19	20	21	22	23	24

NIGHT HOURS - DUSK TO DAWN

LAT. N	13	14	15	16	17	18	19	20	21	22	23	24
0	5:45	6:45	7:45	8:45	9:45	10:45	11:45	12:45	1:45	2:45	3:45	4:45
5	5:37	6:39	7:40	8:41	9:42	10:43	11:45	12:46	1:47	2:48	3:49	4:50
10	5:30	6:33	7:35	8:37	9:40	10:42	11:45	12:47	1:49	2:52	3:54	4:56
15	5:23	6:26	7:30	8:34	9:37	10:41	11:45	12:48	1:52	2:55	3:59	5:03
20	5:15	6:20	7:25	8:30	9:35	10:40	11:45	12:49	1:54	2:59	4:04	5:09
25	5:06	6:13	7:19	8:25	9:32	10:38	11:45	12:51	1:57	3:04	4:10	5:16
28	5:01	6:08	7:15	8:23	9:30	10:37	11:45	12:52	1:59	3:06	4:14	5:21
31	4:55	6:03	7:12	8:20	9:28	10:36	11:45	12:53	2:01	3:09	4:17	5:26
34	4:49	5:58	7:08	8:17	9:26	10:35	11:45	12:54	2:03	3:12	4:21	5:31
37	4:42	5:53	7:03	8:13	9:24	10:34	11:45	12:55	2:05	3:16	4:26	5:36
40	4:35	5:47	6:58	8:10	9:21	10:33	11:45	12:56	2:08	3:19	4:31	5:42
42	4:30	5:42	6:55	8:07	9:20	10:32	11:45	12:57	2:09	3:22	4:34	5:47
44	4:24	5:38	6:51	8:04	9:18	10:31	11:45	12:58	2:11	3:25	4:38	5:51
46	4:18	5:33	6:47	8:01	9:16	10:30	11:45	12:59	2:13	3:28	4:42	5:56
48	4:12	5:27	6:43	7:58	9:14	10:29	11:45	1:00	2:16	3:31	4:47	6:02
50	4:04	5:21	6:38	7:54	9:11	10:28	11:45	1:01	2:18	3:35	4:51	6:08
52	3:56	5:14	6:32	7:50	9:08	10:26	11:45	1:03	2:21	3:39	4:57	6:15
54	3:47	5:07	6:26	7:46	9:05	10:25	11:45	1:04	2:24	3:43	5:03	6:22
56	3:37	4:59	6:20	7:41	9:02	10:23	11:45	1:06	2:27	3:48	5:09	6:31
58	3:26	4:49	6:12	7:35	8:58	10:21	11:45	1:08	2:31	3:54	5:17	6:40
S	1	2	3	4	5	6	7	8	9	10	11	12

November 23rd to 30th

DAYLIGHT HOURS - DAWN TO DUSK

LAT. N	1	2	3	4	5	6	7	8	9	10	11	12
0	5:47	6:47	7:47	8:47	9:47	10:47	11:47	12:47	1:47	2:47	3:47	4:47
5	5:54	6:53	7:52	8:50	9:49	10:48	11:47	12:45	1:44	2:43	3:41	4:40
10	6:02	6:59	7:57	8:54	9:52	10:49	11:47	12:44	1:41	2:39	3:36	4:34
15	6:10	7:06	8:02	8:58	9:54	10:50	11:47	12:43	1:39	2:35	3:31	4:27
20	6:19	7:13	8:08	9:03	9:57	10:52	11:47	12:41	1:36	2:30	3:25	4:20
25	6:28	7:21	8:14	9:07	10:00	10:53	11:47	12:40	1:33	2:26	3:19	4:12
28	6:34	7:26	8:18	9:10	10:02	10:54	11:47	12:39	1:31	2:23	3:15	4:07
31	6:40	7:31	8:22	9:13	10:04	10:55	11:47	12:38	1:29	2:20	3:11	4:02
34	6:47	7:37	8:27	9:17	10:07	10:57	11:47	12:36	1:26	2:16	3:06	3:56
37	6:54	7:43	8:31	9:20	10:09	10:58	11:47	12:35	1:24	2:13	3:02	3:50
40	7:02	7:49	8:37	9:24	10:12	10:59	11:47	12:34	1:21	2:09	2:56	3:44
42	7:08	7:54	8:41	9:27	10:14	11:00	11:47	12:33	1:19	2:06	2:52	3:39
44	7:14	7:59	8:45	9:30	10:16	11:01	11:47	12:32	1:17	2:03	2:48	3:34
46	7:20	8:05	8:49	9:33	10:18	11:02	11:47	12:31	1:15	2:00	2:44	3:28
48	7:28	8:11	8:54	9:37	10:20	11:03	11:47	12:30	1:13	1:56	2:39	3:22
50	7:36	8:17	8:59	9:41	10:23	11:05	11:47	12:28	1:10	1:52	2:34	3:16
52	7:44	8:25	9:05	9:45	10:26	11:06	11:47	12:27	1:07	1:48	2:28	3:08
54	7:54	8:33	9:12	9:50	10:29	11:08	11:47	12:25	1:04	1:43	2:21	3:00
56	8:06	8:42	9:19	9:56	10:33	11:10	11:47	12:23	1:00	1:37	2:14	2:51
58	8:18	8:53	9:28	10:02	10:37	11:12	11:47	12:21	12:56	1:31	2:05	2:40
S	13	14	15	16	17	18	19	20	21	22	23	24

NIGHT HOURS - DUSK TO DAWN

LAT. N	13	14	15	16	17	18	19	20	21	22	23	24
0	5:47	6:47	7:47	8:47	9:47	10:47	11:47	12:47	1:47	2:47	3:47	4:47
5	5:39	6:40	7:41	8:43	9:44	10:45	11:47	12:48	1:49	2:50	3:52	4:53
10	5:31	6:34	7:36	8:39	9:41	10:44	11:47	12:49	1:52	2:54	3:57	4:59
15	5:23	6:27	7:31	8:35	9:39	10:43	11:47	12:50	1:54	2:58	4:02	5:06
20	5:14	6:20	7:25	8:30	9:36	10:41	11:47	12:52	1:57	3:03	4:08	5:13
25	5:05	6:12	7:19	8:26	9:33	10:40	11:47	12:53	2:00	3:07	4:14	5:21
28	4:59	6:07	7:15	8:23	9:31	10:39	11:47	12:54	2:02	3:10	4:18	5:26
31	4:53	6:02	7:11	8:20	9:29	10:38	11:47	12:55	2:04	3:13	4:22	5:31
34	4:46	5:56	7:06	8:16	9:26	10:36	11:47	12:57	2:07	3:17	4:27	5:37
37	4:39	5:50	7:02	8:13	9:24	10:35	11:47	12:58	2:09	3:20	4:31	5:43
40	4:31	5:44	6:56	8:09	9:21	10:34	11:47	12:59	2:12	3:24	4:37	5:49
42	4:25	5:39	6:52	8:06	9:19	10:33	11:47	1:00	2:14	3:27	4:41	5:54
44	4:19	5:34	6:48	8:03	9:17	10:32	11:47	1:01	2:16	3:30	4:45	5:59
46	4:13	5:28	6:44	8:00	9:15	10:31	11:47	1:02	2:18	3:33	4:49	6:05
48	4:05	5:22	6:39	7:56	9:13	10:30	11:47	1:03	2:20	3:37	4:54	6:11
50	3:57	5:16	6:34	7:52	9:10	10:28	11:47	1:05	2:23	3:41	4:59	6:17
52	3:49	5:08	6:28	7:48	9:07	10:27	11:47	1:06	2:26	3:45	5:05	6:25
54	3:39	5:00	6:21	7:43	9:04	10:25	11:47	1:08	2:29	3:50	5:12	6:33
56	3:27	4:51	6:14	7:37	9:00	10:23	11:47	1:10	2:33	3:56	5:19	6:42
58	3:15	4:40	6:05	7:31	8:56	10:21	11:47	1:12	2:37	4:02	5:28	6:53
S	1	2	3	4	5	6	7	8	9	10	11	12

December 1st to 7th

DAYLIGHT HOURS - DAWN TO DUSK

LAT. N	1	2	3	4	5	6	7	8	9	10	11	12
0	5:50	6:50	7:50	8:50	9:50	10:50	11:50	12:50	1:50	2:50	3:50	4:50
5	5:58	6:56	7:55	8:54	9:52	10:51	11:50	12:48	1:47	2:45	3:44	4:43
10	6:06	7:03	8:00	8:58	9:55	10:52	11:50	12:47	1:44	2:41	3:39	4:36
15	6:15	7:10	8:06	9:02	9:58	10:54	11:50	12:45	1:41	2:37	3:33	4:29
20	6:24	7:18	8:12	9:07	10:01	10:55	11:50	12:44	1:38	2:32	3:27	4:21
25	6:33	7:26	8:19	9:11	10:04	10:57	11:50	12:42	1:35	2:28	3:20	4:13
28	6:40	7:31	8:23	9:15	10:06	10:58	11:50	12:41	1:33	2:24	3:16	4:08
31	6:46	7:37	8:27	9:18	10:08	10:59	11:50	12:40	1:31	2:21	3:12	4:02
34	6:53	7:43	8:32	9:21	10:11	11:00	11:50	12:39	1:28	2:18	3:07	3:56
37	7:01	7:49	8:37	9:25	10:13	11:01	11:50	12:38	1:26	2:14	3:02	3:50
40	7:09	7:56	8:43	9:29	10:16	11:03	11:50	12:36	1:23	2:10	2:56	3:43
42	7:16	8:01	8:47	9:33	10:18	11:04	11:50	12:35	1:21	2:06	2:52	3:38
44	7:22	8:07	8:51	9:36	10:20	11:05	11:50	12:34	1:19	2:03	2:48	3:32
46	7:29	8:13	8:56	9:39	10:23	11:06	11:50	12:33	1:16	2:00	2:43	3:26
48	7:37	8:19	9:01	9:43	10:25	11:07	11:50	12:32	1:14	1:56	2:38	3:20
50	7:46	8:26	9:07	9:48	10:28	11:09	11:50	12:30	1:11	1:51	2:32	3:13
52	7:55	8:34	9:13	9:52	10:31	11:10	11:50	12:29	1:08	1:47	2:26	3:05
54	8:06	8:43	9:20	9:58	10:35	11:12	11:50	12:27	1:04	1:41	2:19	2:56
56	8:18	8:53	9:29	10:04	10:39	11:14	11:50	12:25	1:00	1:35	2:10	2:46
58	8:32	9:05	9:38	10:11	10:44	11:17	11:50	12:22	12:55	1:28	2:01	2:34
S	13	14	15	16	17	18	19	20	21	22	23	24

NIGHT HOURS - DUSK TO DAWN

LAT. N	13	14	15	16	17	18	19	20	21	22	23	24
0	5:50	6:50	7:50	8:50	9:50	10:50	11:50	12:50	1:50	2:50	3:50	4:50
5	5:41	6:43	7:44	8:45	9:47	10:48	11:50	12:51	1:52	2:54	3:55	4:56
10	5:33	6:36	7:39	8:41	9:44	10:47	11:50	12:52	1:55	2:58	4:00	5:03
15	5:24	6:29	7:33	8:37	9:41	10:45	11:50	12:54	1:58	3:02	4:06	5:10
20	5:15	6:21	7:27	8:32	9:38	10:44	11:50	12:55	2:01	3:07	4:12	5:18
25	5:06	6:13	7:20	8:28	9:35	10:42	11:50	12:57	2:04	3:11	4:19	5:26
28	4:59	6:08	7:16	8:24	9:33	10:41	11:50	12:58	2:06	3:15	4:23	5:31
31	4:53	6:02	7:12	8:21	9:31	10:40	11:50	12:59	2:08	3:18	4:27	5:37
34	4:46	5:56	7:07	8:18	9:28	10:39	11:50	1:00	2:11	3:21	4:32	5:43
37	4:38	5:50	7:02	8:14	9:26	10:38	11:50	1:01	2:13	3:25	4:37	5:49
40	4:30	5:43	6:56	8:10	9:23	10:36	11:50	1:03	2:16	3:29	4:43	5:56
42	4:23	5:38	6:52	8:06	9:21	10:35	11:50	1:04	2:18	3:33	4:47	6:01
44	4:17	5:32	6:48	8:03	9:19	10:34	11:50	1:05	2:20	3:36	4:51	6:07
46	4:10	5:26	6:43	8:00	9:16	10:33	11:50	1:06	2:23	3:39	4:56	6:13
48	4:02	5:20	6:38	7:56	9:14	10:32	11:50	1:07	2:25	3:43	5:01	6:19
50	3:53	5:13	6:32	7:51	9:11	10:30	11:50	1:09	2:28	3:48	5:07	6:26
52	3:44	5:05	6:26	7:47	9:08	10:29	11:50	1:10	2:31	3:52	5:13	6:34
54	3:33	4:56	6:19	7:41	9:04	10:27	11:50	1:12	2:35	3:58	5:20	6:43
56	3:21	4:46	6:10	7:35	9:00	10:25	11:50	1:14	2:39	4:04	5:29	6:53
58	3:07	4:34	6:01	7:28	8:55	10:22	11:50	1:17	2:44	4:11	5:38	7:05
S	1	2	3	4	5	6	7	8	9	10	11	12

December 8th to 15th

DAYLIGHT HOURS - DAWN TO DUSK

LAT. N	1	2	3	4	5	6	7	8	9	10	11	12
0	5:53	6:53	7:53	8:53	9:53	10:53	11:53	12:53	1:53	2:53	3:53	4:53
5	6:01	7:00	7:58	8:57	9:55	10:54	11:53	12:51	1:50	2:48	3:47	4:45
10	6:10	7:07	8:04	9:01	9:58	10:55	11:53	12:50	1:47	2:44	3:41	4:38
15	6:19	7:14	8:10	9:06	10:01	10:57	11:53	12:48	1:44	2:39	3:35	4:31
20	6:28	7:22	8:16	9:10	10:04	10:58	11:53	12:47	1:41	2:35	3:29	4:23
25	6:38	7:31	8:23	9:15	10:08	11:00	11:53	12:45	1:37	2:30	3:22	4:14
28	6:45	7:36	8:27	9:19	10:10	11:01	11:53	12:44	1:35	2:26	3:18	4:09
31	6:52	7:42	8:32	9:22	10:12	11:02	11:53	12:43	1:33	2:23	3:13	4:03
34	6:59	7:48	8:37	9:26	10:15	11:04	11:53	12:41	1:30	2:19	3:08	3:57
37	7:07	7:55	8:42	9:30	10:17	11:05	11:53	12:40	1:28	2:15	3:03	3:50
40	7:16	8:02	8:48	9:34	10:20	11:06	11:53	12:39	1:25	2:11	2:57	3:43
42	7:23	8:08	8:53	9:38	10:23	11:08	11:53	12:38	1:22	2:07	2:52	3:37
44	7:29	8:13	8:57	9:41	10:25	11:09	11:53	12:36	1:20	2:04	2:48	3:32
46	7:37	8:20	9:02	9:45	10:27	11:10	11:53	12:35	1:18	2:00	2:43	3:25
48	7:45	8:26	9:08	9:49	10:30	11:11	11:53	12:34	1:15	1:56	2:37	3:19
50	7:54	8:34	9:14	9:53	10:33	11:13	11:53	12:32	1:12	1:52	2:31	3:11
52	8:04	8:42	9:20	9:58	10:36	11:14	11:53	12:31	1:09	1:47	2:25	3:03
54	8:16	8:52	9:28	10:04	10:40	11:16	11:53	12:29	1:05	1:41	2:17	2:53
56	8:29	9:03	9:37	10:11	10:45	11:19	11:53	12:26	1:00	1:34	2:08	2:42
58	8:44	9:15	9:47	10:18	10:50	11:21	11:53	12:24	12:55	1:27	1:58	2:30
S	13	14	15	16	17	18	19	20	21	22	23	24

NIGHT HOURS - DUSK TO DAWN

LAT. N	13	14	15	16	17	18	19	20	21	22	23	24
0	5:53	6:53	7:53	8:53	9:53	10:53	11:53	12:53	1:53	2:53	3:53	4:53
5	5:44	6:45	7:47	8:48	9:50	10:51	11:53	12:54	1:55	2:57	3:58	5:00
10	5:35	6:38	7:41	8:44	9:47	10:50	11:53	12:55	1:58	3:01	4:04	5:07
15	5:26	6:31	7:35	8:39	9:44	10:48	11:53	12:57	2:01	3:06	4:10	5:14
20	5:17	6:23	7:29	8:35	9:41	10:47	11:53	12:58	2:04	3:10	4:16	5:22
25	5:07	6:14	7:22	8:30	9:37	10:45	11:53	1:00	2:08	3:15	4:23	5:31
28	5:00	6:09	7:18	8:26	9:35	10:44	11:53	1:01	2:10	3:19	4:27	5:36
31	4:53	6:03	7:13	8:23	9:33	10:43	11:53	1:02	2:12	3:22	4:32	5:42
34	4:46	5:57	7:08	8:19	9:30	10:41	11:53	1:04	2:15	3:26	4:37	5:48
37	4:38	5:50	7:03	8:15	9:28	10:40	11:53	1:05	2:17	3:30	4:42	5:55
40	4:29	5:43	6:57	8:11	9:25	10:39	11:53	1:06	2:20	3:34	4:48	6:02
42	4:22	5:37	6:52	8:07	9:22	10:38	11:53	1:08	2:23	3:38	4:53	6:08
44	4:16	5:32	6:48	8:04	9:20	10:36	11:53	1:09	2:25	3:41	4:57	6:13
46	4:08	5:25	6:43	8:00	9:18	10:35	11:53	1:10	2:27	3:45	5:02	6:20
48	4:00	5:19	6:37	7:56	9:15	10:34	11:53	1:11	2:30	3:49	5:08	6:26
50	3:51	5:11	6:31	7:52	9:12	10:32	11:53	1:13	2:33	3:53	5:14	6:34
52	3:41	5:03	6:25	7:47	9:09	10:31	11:53	1:14	2:36	3:58	5:20	6:42
54	3:29	4:53	6:17	7:41	9:05	10:29	11:53	1:16	2:40	4:04	5:28	6:52
56	3:16	4:42	6:08	7:34	9:00	10:26	11:53	1:19	2:45	4:11	5:37	7:03
58	3:01	4:30	5:58	7:27	8:55	10:24	11:53	1:21	2:50	4:18	5:47	7:15
S	1	2	3	4	5	6	7	8	9	10	11	12

December 16th to 23rd

DAYLIGHT HOURS - DAWN TO DUSK

LAT. N	1	2	3	4	5	6	7	8	9	10	11	12
0	5:57	6:57	7:57	8:57	9:57	10:57	11:57	12:57	1:57	2:57	3:57	4:57
5	6:05	7:04	8:02	9:01	9:59	10:58	11:57	12:55	1:54	2:52	3:51	4:49
10	6:14	7:11	8:08	9:05	10:02	10:59	11:57	12:54	1:51	2:48	3:45	4:42
15	6:23	7:19	8:14	9:10	10:05	11:01	11:57	12:52	1:48	2:43	3:39	4:34
20	6:33	7:27	8:21	9:15	10:09	11:03	11:57	12:50	1:44	2:38	3:32	4:26
25	6:43	7:35	8:28	9:20	10:12	11:04	11:57	12:49	1:41	2:33	3:25	4:18
28	6:50	7:41	8:32	9:23	10:14	11:05	11:57	12:48	1:39	2:30	3:21	4:12
31	6:57	7:47	8:37	9:27	10:17	11:07	11:57	12:46	1:36	2:26	3:16	4:06
34	7:04	7:53	8:42	9:30	10:19	11:08	11:57	12:45	1:34	2:23	3:11	4:00
37	7:13	8:00	8:47	9:35	10:22	11:09	11:57	12:44	1:31	2:18	3:06	3:53
40	7:22	8:08	8:53	9:39	10:25	11:11	11:57	12:42	1:28	2:14	3:00	3:45
42	7:28	8:13	8:58	9:42	10:27	11:12	11:57	12:41	1:26	2:11	2:55	3:40
44	7:35	8:19	9:02	9:46	10:29	11:13	11:57	12:40	1:24	2:07	2:51	3:34
46	7:43	8:25	9:08	9:50	10:32	11:14	11:57	12:39	1:21	2:03	2:45	3:28
48	7:52	8:32	9:13	9:54	10:35	11:16	11:57	12:37	1:18	1:59	2:40	3:21
50	8:01	8:40	9:19	9:59	10:38	11:17	11:57	12:36	1:15	1:54	2:34	3:13
52	8:11	8:49	9:26	10:04	10:41	11:19	11:57	12:34	1:12	1:49	2:27	3:04
54	8:23	8:58	9:34	10:10	10:45	11:21	11:57	12:32	1:08	1:43	2:19	2:55
56	8:36	9:10	9:43	10:16	10:50	11:23	11:57	12:30	1:03	1:37	2:10	2:43
58	8:52	9:23	9:54	10:24	10:55	11:26	11:57	12:27	12:58	1:29	2:00	2:30
S	13	14	15	16	17	18	19	20	21	22	23	24

NIGHT HOURS - DUSK TO DAWN

LAT. N	13	14	15	16	17	18	19	20	21	22	23	24
0	5:57	6:57	7:57	8:57	9:57	10:57	11:57	12:57	1:57	2:57	3:57	4:57
5	5:48	6:49	7:51	8:52	9:54	10:55	11:57	12:58	1:59	3:01	4:02	5:04
10	5:39	6:42	7:45	8:48	9:51	10:54	11:57	12:59	2:02	3:05	4:08	5:11
15	5:30	6:34	7:39	8:43	9:48	10:52	11:57	1:01	2:05	3:10	4:14	5:19
20	5:20	6:26	7:32	8:38	9:44	10:50	11:57	1:03	2:09	3:15	4:21	5:27
25	5:10	6:18	7:25	8:33	9:41	10:49	11:57	1:04	2:12	3:20	4:28	5:35
28	5:03	6:12	7:21	8:30	9:39	10:48	11:57	1:05	2:14	3:23	4:32	5:41
31	4:56	6:06	7:16	8:26	9:36	10:46	11:57	1:07	2:17	3:27	4:37	5:47
34	4:49	6:00	7:11	8:23	9:34	10:45	11:57	1:08	2:19	3:30	4:42	5:53
37	4:40	5:53	7:06	8:18	9:31	10:44	11:57	1:09	2:22	3:35	4:47	6:00
40	4:31	5:45	7:00	8:14	9:28	10:42	11:57	1:11	2:25	3:39	4:53	6:08
42	4:25	5:40	6:55	8:11	9:26	10:41	11:57	1:12	2:27	3:42	4:58	6:13
44	4:18	5:34	6:51	8:07	9:24	10:40	11:57	1:13	2:29	3:46	5:02	6:19
46	4:10	5:28	6:45	8:03	9:21	10:39	11:57	1:14	2:32	3:50	5:08	6:25
48	4:02	5:21	6:40	7:59	9:18	10:37	11:57	1:16	2:35	3:54	5:13	6:32
50	3:52	5:13	6:34	7:54	9:15	10:36	11:57	1:17	2:38	3:59	5:19	6:40
52	3:42	5:04	6:27	7:49	9:12	10:34	11:57	1:19	2:41	4:04	5:26	6:49
54	3:30	4:55	6:19	7:43	9:08	10:32	11:57	1:21	2:45	4:10	5:34	6:58
56	3:17	4:43	6:10	7:37	9:03	10:30	11:57	1:23	2:50	4:16	5:43	7:10
58	3:01	4:30	6:00	7:29	8:58	10:27	11:57	1:26	2:55	4:24	5:54	7:23
S	1	2	3	4	5	6	7	8	9	10	11	12

December 24th to 31st

DAYLIGHT HOURS - DAWN TO DUSK

LAT. N	1	2	3	4	5	6	7	8	9	10	11	12
0	6:01	7:01	8:01	9:01	10:01	11:01	12:01	1:01	2:01	3:01	4:01	5:01
5	6:09	7:08	8:06	9:05	10:03	11:02	12:01	12:59	1:58	2:56	3:55	4:53
10	6:18	7:15	8:12	9:09	10:06	11:03	12:01	12:58	1:55	2:52	3:49	4:46
15	6:27	7:23	8:18	9:14	10:09	11:05	12:01	12:56	1:52	2:47	3:43	4:38
20	6:37	7:31	8:25	9:19	10:13	11:07	12:01	12:54	1:48	2:42	3:36	4:30
25	6:47	7:39	8:31	9:24	10:16	11:08	12:01	12:53	1:45	2:37	3:30	4:22
28	6:53	7:45	8:36	9:27	10:18	11:09	12:01	12:52	1:43	2:34	3:25	4:16
31	7:00	7:50	8:41	9:31	10:21	11:11	12:01	12:51	1:41	2:31	3:21	4:11
34	7:08	7:57	8:46	9:34	10:23	11:12	12:01	12:49	1:38	2:27	3:15	4:04
37	7:16	8:04	8:51	9:38	10:26	11:13	12:01	12:48	1:35	2:23	3:10	3:57
40	7:25	8:11	8:57	9:43	10:29	11:15	12:01	12:46	1:32	2:18	3:04	3:50
42	7:32	8:17	9:01	9:46	10:31	11:16	12:01	12:45	1:30	2:15	3:00	3:44
44	7:39	8:22	9:06	9:50	10:33	11:17	12:01	12:44	1:28	2:11	2:55	3:39
46	7:46	8:29	9:11	9:53	10:36	11:18	12:01	12:43	1:25	2:08	2:50	3:32
48	7:55	8:36	9:17	9:58	10:39	11:20	12:01	12:41	1:22	2:03	2:44	3:25
50	8:04	8:43	9:23	10:02	10:42	11:21	12:01	12:40	1:19	1:59	2:38	3:18
52	8:14	8:52	9:30	10:07	10:45	11:23	12:01	12:38	1:16	1:54	2:31	3:09
54	8:26	9:02	9:37	10:13	10:49	11:25	12:01	12:36	1:12	1:48	2:24	2:59
56	8:39	9:13	9:46	10:20	10:53	11:27	12:01	12:34	1:08	1:41	2:15	2:48
58	8:55	9:26	9:57	10:28	10:59	11:30	12:01	12:31	1:02	1:33	2:04	2:35
S	13	14	15	16	17	18	19	20	21	22	23	24

NIGHT HOURS - DUSK TO DAWN

LAT. N	13	14	15	16	17	18	19	20	21	22	23	24
0	6:01	7:01	8:01	9:01	10:01	11:01	12:01	1:01	2:01	3:01	4:01	5:01
5	5:52	6:53	7:55	8:56	9:58	10:59	12:01	1:02	2:03	3:05	4:06	5:08
10	5:43	6:46	7:49	8:52	9:55	10:58	12:01	1:03	2:06	3:09	4:12	5:15
15	5:34	6:38	7:43	8:47	9:52	10:56	12:01	1:05	2:09	3:14	4:18	5:23
20	5:24	6:30	7:36	8:42	9:48	10:54	12:01	1:07	2:13	3:19	4:25	5:31
25	5:14	6:22	7:30	8:37	9:45	10:53	12:01	1:08	2:16	3:24	4:31	5:39
28	5:08	6:16	7:25	8:34	9:43	10:52	12:01	1:09	2:18	3:27	4:36	5:45
31	5:01	6:11	7:21	8:31	9:41	10:51	12:01	1:11	2:21	3:31	4:41	5:50
34	4:53	6:04	7:15	8:27	9:38	10:49	12:01	1:12	2:23	3:34	4:46	5:57
37	4:45	5:57	7:10	8:23	9:35	10:48	12:01	1:13	2:26	3:38	4:51	6:04
40	4:36	5:50	7:04	8:18	9:32	10:46	12:01	1:15	2:29	3:43	4:57	6:11
42	4:29	5:44	7:00	8:15	9:30	10:45	12:01	1:16	2:31	3:46	5:01	6:17
44	4:22	5:39	6:55	8:11	9:28	10:44	12:01	1:17	2:33	3:50	5:06	6:22
46	4:15	5:32	6:50	8:08	9:25	10:43	12:01	1:18	2:36	3:53	5:11	6:29
48	4:06	5:25	6:44	8:03	9:22	10:41	12:01	1:20	2:39	3:58	5:17	6:36
50	3:57	5:18	6:38	7:59	9:19	10:40	12:01	1:21	2:42	4:02	5:23	6:43
52	3:47	5:09	6:31	7:54	9:16	10:38	12:01	1:23	2:45	4:07	5:30	6:52
54	3:35	4:59	6:24	7:48	9:12	10:36	12:01	1:25	2:49	4:13	5:37	7:02
56	3:22	4:48	6:15	7:41	9:08	10:34	12:01	1:27	2:53	4:20	5:46	7:13
58	3:06	4:35	6:04	7:33	9:02	10:31	12:01	1:30	2:59	4:28	5:57	7:26
S	1	2	3	4	5	6	7	8	9	10	11	12

Other books by Bob Makransky

Planetary Strength – A Commentary on Morinus

An intermediate-level textbook on horoscope interpretation

An essential contribution to natal horoscope interpretation. Taking as its point of departure *Astrologia Gallica* by Jean Baptiste Morin de Villefranche (1583–1656), *Planetary Strength* compares and contrasts the differences between the strengths conferred upon planets by virtue of their sign placements (celestial state), house placements (terrestrial state), and aspects (aspectual state). The strength factors of retrogradation/station, synodic phase, and conjunction with fixed stars are also explained and interpreted. A detailed system of keywords is augmented by insightful "cookbook" interpretations for each and every planetary combination. The depth and quality of the analysis – as well as the hundreds of practical examples and tips – make *Planetary Strength* an indispensable reference work which both neophyte and experienced practitioners will consult every time they read a horoscope.

"The book is beautifully written. With Makransky, whether you agree or disagree is not the issue - you will always get a good read. It is clear. He has done his homework. He makes the genius of Morinus accessable to English speakers. He shows us how to 'think astrologically'."

Joseph Polansky, *Diamond Fire Magazine*

"What's fascinating about Planetary Strength is that the author is using his own prose to describe the planets' conditions. In the introduction, he advises readers to study Morinus, but clearly Makransky's efforts are the better source. ... Try them in practice and compare these interpretations to what you might otherwise think about a planet. It may just sharpen your ability to make accurate statements about character, a person's history, and even to make predictions. And what more do you ask of astrology?"

Chris Lorenz, Dell Horoscope magazine

"This is certainly an interesting addition to reading and interpreting the translations of Morinus' original work. It is detailed and considered, and the author's knowledge and experience are evident throughout."

Helen Stokes, AA *Journal*

"Presenting a mixture of discussion, detailed cookbook offerings and chart examples as well as keywords and tables, this fascinating book also addresses the fixed stars. ... This fascinating book assumes a fair knowledge of astrology as well as some experience in preparing charts."

Margaret Gray, ISAR

"This is a book that every beginner as well as advanced student of astrology would do well to possess. The author is extremely perceptive in his descriptions of the planets in their various strength and weaknesses ... this book would be a helpful aid to the researcher, as it would point him in the right direction."

Wanda Sellar, *Correlation*

Paperback ISBN 9781902405506 The Wessex Astrologer

Listen to Bob discuss *Planetary Strength* at:
http://www.myspiritradio.com/show-profiles?programme_id=46

Planetary Combination

Planetary Combination picks up where *Planetary Strength* left off, explaining how the planetary influences combine in aspects and configurations to paint a picture of a person and his or her life.

Descriptions of planetary configurations such as grand trines, grand squares, T-squares, wedges, fans, rectangles, kites, and trapezoids provide overall schematics of people's psychological dynamics.

Then, detailed interpretations for the conjunctions, sextiles/trines, squares, oppositions, parallels/contraparallels, and mutual receptions between the individual planets enable the practitioner to see clearly how these dynamics work out in a particular horoscope.

An illuminating chapter on planetary conjunctions with the Moon's nodes reveals the underlying karmic influences at work. An indispensable reference you'll consult every time you read a chart.

"Planetary Combination is an excellent and comprehensive summary of all the relevant chart factors... One has to search hard to find such material! But this is all presented, as is all of Makransky's work, with vigour, wisdom and accessibility... Much of the book is taken up – as we might expect – with a very generous coverage of the astrological aspects. I looked up a few of my own and they were spot on... Planetary Combination *fills a gap in the current state of astrological literature. It manages to retain both a sense of firm tradition whilst feeling utterly new and fresh."*

James Lynn Page, author of *Everyday Tarot*, *Celtic Magic*,
The Christ Enigma and *The New Positive Thinking*.

Paperback ISBN 9781910531105 The Wessex Astrologer

Coming Soon from Dear Brutus Press

Topics in Astrology

A delightful cornucopia of over three dozen essays on a wide variety of astrological topics ranging from practical, hands-on advice to technical issues to humor and satire. *Topics in Astrology* is chock-full of original tips and guidelines for experienced practitioners (it may be a bit advanced for beginners, but even they will find parts of the book fascinating).

Partial Contents:
The natal horoscopes of Philadelphia hippie guru-cum-murderer Ira Einhorn and polygamist Mormon guru-cum-murderer Ervil LeBaron are thoroughly analyzed, as is the abortive romance between Nobel laureate William Butler Yeats and the unattainable beauty Maud Gonne.

Exhaustive, in-depth discussions of how transits, primary directions, and secondary progressions work are illustrated with scores of examples taken from the horoscopes of notables.

How to use astrolocality (employing astrology to find favorable and avoid unfavorable places to live or visit) is described in detail.

The traditional rules of horary astrology are examined and evaluated in the cases of the Titanic disaster, the Nixon resignation, and the onsets of wars.

The rules of electional astrology are illustrated in a chapter on how to pick winning lottery tickets.

The validity of eclipses and comets is examined; and technical issues such as how house systems are constructed are discussed in depth.

Oh yes – Bob pokes fun at astrology too, with convincing analyses of the natal horoscopes (including predictions which came true!) for a couple of fictional characters.

Bob Makransky's *Introduction to Magic Series* from Dear Brutus Press

"*In this series, not only do we get an author who knows his subject inside out, but also a directness of approach often not seen in works of this kind. Not for Makransky the wishy-washy approach that attempts to soothe and reassure the reader with false promises of magical success – something about which many customer complaints arise on the Amazon website – but, rather, an honest and uncompromising study of what Magic really entails.*

James Lynn Page (author of *Celtic Magic*, *Everyday Tarot* and *The Christ Enigma*)

Volume I of Bob's *Introduction to Magic* series

What is Magic?

Magic is a spiritual path which is not very well understood in our society. This is because the theory and practice of magic have never before been explained clearly and convincingly, in a way that makes sense to intelligent and thoughtful people. Written in a sassy, irreverent style, *What is Magic?* discusses how such otherworldly concepts as demons, casting spells, and bewitching are just the hidden underside of everyday society – the skeletons in everybody's closet. *What is Magic?* answers the questions which all serious spiritual seekers, no matter what their spiritual path, ask at one time or another, but can never find satisfactorily answered:

What is the difference between faith and fooling yourself?

What is the relationship between altered states and normal, everyday life?

If you lose your desires, as many spiritual paths advocate, what zest or spice does life have left?

If the world is an illusion or dream, as it's said to be, then why does it seem so real?

Where does the world of magic – the shaman's world – take off from the world of everyday life? What and where is the interface?

Why is it so difficult to achieve real, permanent spiritual growth?

"Bob is daring, willing to be offensive with his truths, and wise in the ways of words and magic... Bob Makransky, I feel, has written a great treatise on magic. I urge you to enjoy it as much as I have."

from the foreword by Michael Peter Langevin,
publisher of *Magical Blend* magazine.

Contents:

Spirits, Intent, The Nature of Reality, Spells, Charms & Rituals, Science Debunked, Demons, The Nature of the Self, Bewitching, Magic & Money, Death, Black Magicians & Vampires, Power Places, The Magician's God, Magical Time, Magic and Morality, Dreaming & Stalking, Magic and Sex.

Volume II of Bob's *Introduction to Magic* series

Magical Living

Winner of the Sacramento Publishers' Association awards for Best Nonfiction and Best Spiritual book of 2001, *Magical Living* is a collection of essays which give detailed, how-to instructions on channeling spirit guides, communicating with plants and nature spirits, developing your psychic vision, together with inspirational essays on managing love relationships, handling oppressive people, and dealing with hurt.

"I love this little book! ... Carry this book with you, read and reread the essays, and connect with joy."

Kathryn Lanier, *InnerChange* magazine

"He writes beautifully, clearly, elegantly... he is incapable of an unoriginal thought."

Joseph Polansky, *Diamond Fire* magazine

"I could not get enough! I actually read some of the essays 2 to 3 times and discovered new insights each time... A great book to revisit more than once!"

Susan Violante, *Reader Views*

Magical Living – ISBN-13: 978-1499279337 – 173 pages
paperback $14.95 at: http://www.createspace.com/4780358
ebook $9.95: https://www.smashwords.com/books/view/22860

Volume III of Bob's *Introduction to Magic* series

Thought Forms

Astronomical and astrological explanations of Mercury's synodic cycle – its cycle of phases as it circles the sun, with tables 1900-2050.

Complete delineations for superior and inferior conjunction, greatest Eastern and Western elongation, stationary retrograde and direct, and their intervening phases in the natal, progressed, and transiting horoscopes.

Explanation of the astrological/magical view of mind (the theory of Thought Forms): what consciousness is, how it arose, and whither it is going.

Basic course in white magic with detailed instructions on:

How to Channel and Banish Thought Forms;
Creative Visualization;
How to banish the Black Magicians in everyday life; How to Cast out Demons;
How to use Tree Spirits.

"Bob Makransky is a knowledgeable, purposeful and entertaining writer."

Paul F. Newman, *The International Astrologer*

"*Steady* Diamond Fire *readers are well acquainted with the genius of Bob Makransky. Highly recommendable.*"

Joseph Polansky, *Diamond Fire*

"*Readers have become familiar with [Makransky's] fresh insights into different facets of astrology. In this book* Thought Forms *he is especially provocative and I strongly recommend its purchase and study.*"

Ken Gillman, *Considerations*

"*I will fully agree with the statement that 'You've never read a book like this before!' The material is fresh and woven very skillfully to conclusion. I look forward to his next installment of the trilogy.*"

Marion MacMillan, SHAPE

Thought Forms – ISBN-13: 978-1499267440 – 323 pages
paperback - $19.95 at: https://www.createspace.com/4770114
ebook $9.95 at https://www.smashwords.com/books/view/22859

Volume IV of Bob's *Introduction to Magic* series

The Great Wheel

The Great Wheel is the wheel of karma;
of reincarnation – of death and rebirth.
It is the wheel of the law;
the wheel of retribution.
It is number and it is measure.
It consists of wheels upon wheels,
and wheels within wheels;
and it is symbolized by
the phases of the moon.

"*On the afternoon of October 24th, 1917, four days after my marriage, my wife surprised me by attempting automatic writing. What came in disjointed sentences, in almost illegible writing, was so exciting, sometimes so profound, that I... offered to spend what remained of life explaining and piecing together those scattered sentences.*"

William Butler Yeats

It is often said in spiritual literature that time and space are an illusion, *maya, samsara*. But what exactly does this mean? And what implications does it have for how you should live your everyday life? *The Great Wheel* is an explanation of the system of birth, death, and rebirth which Nobel laureate William Butler Yeats' described in his masterpiece, *A Vision*.

Starting out with a discussion of how you can connect with your true purpose in this life – the reason why you incarnated on the earth at this time – *The Great Wheel* describes simple techniques you can use (such as past life regressions, probable reality progressions, and recapitulation of present life memories) to glimpse different facets of your *daimon* (your oversoul; the totality of who you are), in order to understand clearly how you got to where you are at right now. To live your true life's purpose rather than drift along helplessly, it is necessary to see how your present life situation is the end result of decisions which you, yourself, made in other lifetimes and realities.

An in-depth discussion of twenty-eight personality types (depending upon where you were born in the Moon's monthly cycle of phases) illuminates your individual true purpose in incarnating in this life, and helps you to understand where you belong and where you are going.

The Great Wheel concludes with a fascinating explanation of what reality is all about: Mind and Memory, Waking and Dreaming, Change, Familiarity, and the Akashic Records.

"This new work in Bob Makransky's excellent and thought provoking 'Introduction to Magic' *series … is a fascinating and illuminating take on the meaning of the Moon and I learned a great deal, but there is much more, particularly a discussion of the daimon, the part of you that encompasses all your human memories past present and future. It's truly a Moon book unlike any other and is guaranteed to alter your perception of yourself and the world."*

Paul F. Newman, author of *Luna: The Astrological Moon*

The Great Wheel ebook $9.95: http://www.smashwords.com/books/view/306020

Magical Almanac
http://groups.yahoo.com/group/MagicalAlmanac

is Bob Makransky's ezine of astrology and magic for thoughtful, intelligent people who are seeking something deeper than the usual New Age – astrological fare. To subscribe send an e-mail to: MagicalAlmanac-subscribe@yahoogroups.com.

www.DearBrutus.com

is Bob Makransky's personal website offering insightful articles on astrology and magic, as well as books and astrology services. Also: complete instructions on how to channel spirit guides and how to run past life regressions; free downloadable Mayan Horoscope software; information on the natural treatment of cancer and AIDS; articles on Mayan folklore; humorous short stories, cartoons, and lots, lots more!

Other Titles from The Wessex Astrologer

www.wessexastrologer.com

Martin Davis	Astrolocality Astrology From Here to There
Wanda Sellar	The Consultation Chart An Introduction to Medical Astrology Decumbiture
Geoffrey Cornelius	The Moment of Astrology
Darrelyn Gunzburg	Life After Grief AstroGraphology: The Hidden Link between your Horoscope and your Handwriting
Paul F. Newman	Declination: The Steps of the Sun Luna: The Book of the Moon
Jamie Macphail	Astrology and the Causes of War
Deborah Houlding	The Houses: Temples of the Sky
Dorian Geiseler Greenbaum	Temperament: Astrology's Forgotten Key
Howard Sasportas	The Gods of Change
Patricia L. Walsh	Understanding Karmic Complexes
M. Kelly Hunter	Living Lilith
Barbara Dunn	Horary Astrology Re-Examined
Deva Green	Evolutionary Astrology
Jeff Green	Pluto 1 Pluto 2 Essays on Evolutionary Astrology (edited by Deva Green)
Dolores Ashcroft-Nowicki and Stephanie V. Norris	The Door Unlocked: An Astrological Insight into Initiation
Martha Betz	The Betz Placidus Table of Houses
Greg Bogart	Astrology and Meditation
Kim Farnell	Flirting with the Zodiac
Henry Seltzer	The Tenth Planet
Ray Grasse	Under a Sacred Sky
Joseph Crane	Astrological Roots: The Hellenistic Legacy Between Fortune and Providence
Komilla Sutton	The Essentials of Vedic Astrology The Lunar Nodes Personal Panchanga The Nakshatras
Anthony Louis	The Art of Forecasting using Solar Returns
Lorna Green	Your Horoscope in Your Hands
Martin Gansten	Primary Directions
Reina James	All the Sun Goes Round
Oscar Hofman	Classical Medical Astrology
Bernadette Brady	Astrology, A Place in Chaos Star and Planet Combinations
Richard Idemon	The Magic Thread Through the Looking Glass
Nick Campion	The Book of World Horoscopes
Judy Hall	Patterns of the Past Karmic Connections Good Vibrations The Soulmate Myth The Book of Why Book of Psychic Development
John Gadbury	The Nativity of the Late King Charles
Neil D. Paris	Surfing your Solar Cycles
Michele Finey	The Sacred Dance of Venus and Mars
David Hamblin	The Spirit of Numbers
Dennis Elwell	Cosmic Loom
Gillian Helfgott	The Insightful Turtle
Christina Rose	The Tapestry of Planetary Phases

CPSIA information can be obtained
at www.ICGtesting.com
Printed in the USA
LVOW13s1621020617
536736LV00003B/139/P